Computer Composer's Toolbox

Computer Composer's Toolbox

Phil Winsor

Windcrest books are published by Windcrest Books, a division of TAB BOOKS Inc. The
name "Windcrest" is a registered trademark of TAB BOOKS Inc.

A Petrocelli book

Published by **Windcrest Books**
FIRST EDITION/FIRST PRINTING

Library of Congress Cataloging-in-Publication Data

Winsor, Phil, 1938-
    Computer composer's toolbox.

    1. Computer composition. 2. BASIC (Computer program
language) I. Title.
MT56.W54 1989   781.3'45369   89-20384
ISBN 0-8306-3384-7

TAB BOOKS Inc. offers software for sale. For information and a catalog, please contact
TAB Software Department, Blue Ridge Summit, PA 17294-0850.

Questions regarding the content of this book should be addressed to:

Windcrest Books
Division of TAB BOOKS Inc.
Blue Ridge Summit, PA 17294-0850

Technical Editor: Roman H. Gorski
Production: Katherine Brown
Series Design: Jaclyn B. Saunders

Contents

2   *Series and Motive Operations*   *58*

3   *Probability Distribution Functions*   *113*

4   Sorting and Searching   *141*

5   *Sound/Text Composition*   *164*

6   General Composition   180

Preface

This book is intended to be part of an ever-growing collection of procedures and functions which serve either synthetic or analytic compositional goals. It is hoped that this volume will expand over time, reflecting contributions of compositional algorithms by composers active in the area of experimental music.

For the first edition, the author has selected 117 subroutines organized into six groups which are of importance to computer-assisted composition. Before delving into the subroutines piecemeal, the reader should become acquainted with the nature and scope of the algorithms by examining the descriptions in the Table of Contents.

As this volume is a reference work, detailed applications and musical examples have been omitted. The author's objective is to present a wide selection of useful algorithms, leaving a detailed discussion of specific musical contexts to another volume.

The software was developed on a Texas Instruments Professional Computer with 256K of RAM. The BASIC used was Microsoft's MS-BASIC, at this writing the most prevalent interpreted BASIC available for micros. It is an extended, enhanced dialect, allowing such niceties as multistatement lines, descriptive variables, nested IF-THEN-ELSE statements, and other features which encourage a structured approach to program design.

The subroutines have been kept as trim as possible to illuminate their structure. Driver programs have been included to obviate the need for input data test statements which would pad program code considerably and diminish clarity. (The reader is reminded that, in interactive use, the subroutines will require additional statements to make them user-proof.)

Introduction

BOOK ORGANIZATION

This volume contains 117 subroutines grouped into six broad categories: utilities, series and motive operations, probability distribution functions, sorting and searching, sound/text composition, and general composition. The presentation of an algorithm here in a particular category simply reflects its garb. A process contained in a string-handling subroutine, for example, may be equally useful in manipulating integers; specifics of coding, however, limit its immediate application to ASCII text characters.

Each subroutine or subroutine group is preceded by preliminary remarks that explain the purpose of an algorithm, and that point out pertinent implementation considerations which offer programming ideas. A complete driver program and subroutine listing follows, along with a program execution printout.

The book's layout mirrors its intended use: as a modular library of procedures and functions available for immediate extraction. So, while it may be desirable to read the book cover-to-cover, it is not a precondition of use. The Table of Contents offers an overview and is intended to serve those who wish to scan the library for specific procedures and functions.

PROGRAMMING STYLE

Although BASIC is perhaps the most ubiquitous computer language in current use, PASCAL and C are rapidly becoming popular in the computer-music community as alternatives to FORTRAN. For this reason, every effort was made to structure program design in a manner which would facilitate translation of the code. The features of (enhanced) Microsoft BASIC were used wherever possible. The articulative use of white space, multistatement lines, module indentation, descriptive variables, and (almost) GOTOless code have been incorporated to promote functional clarity and intelligibility. Long program lines and nested IF . . . THEN . . . ELSE statements can be typed into your computer using line feeds without carriage returns (Microsoft BASIC allows up to 255 characters per line).

The drivers and subroutines are all "hardwired" for presentation in stripped-down form. Therefore, anyone wishing to modify the programs for interactive use must add

1) INPUT statements

2) Code to test the viability of data entered from the terminal

3) Prompts to guide the program user

Arrays should also be redimensioned to accommodate variable-size output requests.

ADAPTATION TO OLDER FORMS OF BASIC

The BASIC on your mainframe or micro may not permit all the niceties offered by Microsoft BASIC. Therefore, some minor alterations must be made in the subroutines before they will execute properly. Consult your user's manual to determine whether nested IF . . . THEN . . . ELSE statements and the SWAP, MID$, and INSTR functions are allowed, and to see whether you need to convert WHILE . . . WEND loops to FOR . . . NEXT form. If multistatement lines are not permitted, then give each statement a separate line and number. Finally, some systems limit the length of variable identifiers, so you may need to substitute shorter variable names.

1
Utilities

SUBROUTINE: Tunings   CTB1.1

Purpose

Compile a table of equal-tempered, octave-repeating, microtonal scale frequencies measured in cycles per second (Hertz).

One direct application of the scale compiler is to generate microtonal scales for the pitch output of a sound synthesizer. You will discover other interesting uses for this subroutine by mapping variously tuned scales to volume, rhythm, timbre, and articulation parameters.

To map one set of values onto another parameter, interpret the first data table (array) as a set of pointers to the addresses of values stored in the second data table.

Notes

The variable OCTDIV controls the number of equal-size intervals contained within one octave, the variable FREQ1 sets the initial (tonic) scale pitch, and the variable NUMTONES builds the scale upward over the required number of tones. To illustrate, if NUMTONES = 60 and OCTDIV = 12, then a five-octave scale will be compiled.

Programming Ideas

1) Experiment with several different tunings of your microcomputer sound synthesizer chip using output of the scale compiler.

2) Read the frequency data table into a program which converts the values via the MOD function to a small set of rhythm values (CTB1.2 provides a MOD function if your BASIC lacks one).

Program Listing

```
100 REM  ==========================================================
110 REM                      DRIVER PROGRAM
115 REM                        (Tunings)
120 REM  ==========================================================
130     DIM TONE(84)
140     NUMTONES = 84
150     OCTDIV = 19            '<< specify a 19-tone per octave scale
160     FREQ1 = 61.735
170     GOSUB 1000                        '<< call tuning compiler
180       FOR J= 1 TO NUMTONES
190         PRINT TONE(J),   '<< send scale frequencies to screen
200       NEXT J
210 END
1000 REM  ======================================================== CTB1.1
1010 REM  *******************>> TUNINGS <<***********************
1020 REM  ==========================================================
1030 REM     This subroutine compiles a data table containing
1040 REM     equal-tempered, octave-repeating pitch scales.
1050 REM  ==========================================================
1060 REM                   Variable Descriptions
1070 REM
1080 REM     Entering -
1090 REM        FREQ1: frequency in hertz (cps) of scale tonic
1100 REM        NUMTONES: number of pitches to compute
1110 REM        OCTDIV: number of equalsize steps within octave
1120 REM     Exiting -
1130 REM        TONE(): array of computed scale frequencies
1140 REM     Local -
1150 REM        COEFF: coefficient for specified octave division
1160 REM        K9: loop index, pointer to array TONE()
1170 REM
1180 REM  ==========================================================
1190     COEFF = 2^(1 / OCTDIV)
1200     TONE(1) = INT(FREQ1 + .5)
1210       FOR K9 = 2 TO NUMTONES
1220         TONE(K9) = INT(TONE(K9-1) * COEFF + .5)
1230       NEXT K9
1240 RETURN
```

RUN (Tunings)

62	64	66	68	71
74	77	80	83	86
89	92	95	99	103
107	111	115	119	123
128	133	138	143	148

RUN (Tunings)

153	159	165	171	177
184	191	198	205	213
221	229	238	247	256
266	276	286	297	308
319	331	343	356	369
383	397	412	427	443
459	476	494	512	531
551	571	592	614	637
661	686	711	737	764
792	821	852	884	917
951	986	1023	1061	1100
1141	1183	1227	1273	

Purpose

Provide a modulus function for use in BASIC dialects that lack an intrinsic MOD function.

Many situations require the conversion of wide-range data to scalar values within a modulus. For example, a synthesizer keyboard encompassing 61 notes (C1 to C7) is represented by the scalar range 0 to 60; any number within range can be converted to one of the 12 chromatic scale pitch/numbers using the MOD function, which is simply a way of wrapping-around expansive data on a smaller set of values. In the case of our equal-tempered, 12-tone scale, the modulus is 12. In the case of a seven-tone diatonic scale, the modulus is 7, and so on.

You will discover many other applications of this function, such as formatting program output directed to a file.

Notes

A more practical alternative to coding the modulus operation as a subroutine is to write a defined function—

```
125 DEF FNM (J,M) = J - INT (J / M) * M
```

and change Line 150 to

```
150 R = FNM(J,M)
```

Programming Idea

Couple CTB1.2 with CTB1.1 to map randomly-generated integers, range 0 to 87, onto the pitches of a synthesizer keyboard tuned to 36 tones per octave.

Program Listing

```
100 REM ==============================================================
110 REM                      DRIVER PROGRAM
115 REM                        (Modulo)
120 REM ==============================================================
125        M = 12                              '<< set modulus to 12
130        FOR J = 0 TO 83        '<< values to be converted mod M
140          M = 12                            '<< set modulus to 12
150          GOSUB 1000                        '<< call mod function
160          PRINT R;                   '<< send remainder to screen
170          IF R = 11 THEN PRINT              '<< start newline
180        NEXT J
190 END
1000 REM =========================================== CTB1.2
1010 REM *******************>> MODULO <<************************
1020 REM ==============================================================
1030 REM     This subroutine is actually a function which
1040 REM     receives an integer and returns the value of the
```

```
1050 REM      integer modulo n. A more practical alternative
1060 REM      is to code it as a user-defined function:
1070 REM          DEF FNM(J,M) = J - INT(J / M) * M
1080 REM ============================================================
1090 REM
1100 REM                    Variable Descriptions
1110 REM      Entering -
1120 REM        M: the modulus to be applied
1130 REM        J: the integer to be returned mod M
1140 REM      Exiting -
1150 REM        R: the remainder mod I to be returned
1160 REM      Local -
1170 REM        none
1180 REM
1190 REM ============================================================
1200 R = J - INT(J / M) * M
1210 RETURN
```

RUN (Modulo)

```
0  1  2  3  4  5  6  7  8  9  10  11
0  1  2  3  4  5  6  7  8  9  10  11
0  1  2  3  4  5  6  7  8  9  10  11
0  1  2  3  4  5  6  7  8  9  10  11
0  1  2  3  4  5  6  7  8  9  10  11
0  1  2  3  4  5  6  7  8  9  10  11
0  1  2  3  4  5  6  7  8  9  10  11
```

Purpose

Provide a registered pitch element table for the conversion of integers to chromatic scale pitches from low-octave to high-octave.

Notes

There are several ways to accomplish this procedure. One alternative to the method used by this subroutine is to itemize all pitches and octave registers in DATA statements (C1, C#1, D1, D#1, etc.), and then READ them into an element table array during program initialization. The primary disadvantage of the data-reading solution is that the programmer must type in each of the alphanumerically characterized pitches. However, program execution will be slightly faster due to the elimination of arithmetic computation and substring extraction.

Programming Ideas

In interactive programs, a pitch table helps the user by converting the data to familiar terms.

1) Write a program which generates random integers and offers a user-option to view them either as pitches or numbers.

2) Modify the subroutine to hold the elements of other parameters, such as rhythm or volume. Use the data-reading method if the elements are few in number.

Program Listing

```
100 REM  ===============================================================
110 REM                       DRIVER PROGRAM
115 REM                        (Pitchtab)
120 REM  ===============================================================
130      DIM P$(84)                '<< prepare array to hold 7 octaves
140      GOSUB 1000                        '<< initialize pitch table
150        FOR J = 1 TO 84
160           PRINT "NUM";J;"=";        '<< send a number to screen
170           PRINT P$(J), '<< send corresponding pitch to screen
180        NEXT J
190 END
1000 REM  =========================================== CTB1.3
1010 REM  ****************>> PITCHTAB <<**********************
1020 REM  ===============================================================
1030 REM     This subroutine initializes a pitch data table
1040 REM     corresponding to integer values 1-n.
1050 REM  ===============================================================
1060 REM                  Variable Descriptions
1070 REM
1080 REM     Entering -
```

```
1090 REM        none
1100 REM
1110 REM        Exiting -
1120 REM          P$(): hold pitch element table
1130 REM
1140 REM        Local -
1150 REM          NOTE$: char string holding pitch class names
1160 REM          OCTAVE$: char string holding octave registers
1170 REM          K9: loop index, pointer to NOTE$ substring
1180 REM          L9: loop index, pointer to OCTAVE$ substring
1190 REM
1200 REM ==========================================================
1210     NOTE$ = " CC# DD# E FF# GG# AA# B"
1220     OCTAVE$ = "1234567"
1230       FOR K9 = 1 TO 7
1240         FOR L9 = 1 TO 12
1250           P$(L9+(K9-1)*12)     =        MID$(NOTE$,(L9*2-1),2)
+ MID$(OCTAVE$,K9,1)
1260         NEXT L9
1270       NEXT K9
1280 RETURN
```

RUN (Pitchtab)

```
NUM 1 = C1     NUM 2 =C#1    NUM 3 = D1    NUM 4 =D#1    NUM 5 = E1
NUM 6 = F1     NUM 7 =F#1    NUM 8 = G1    NUM 9 =G#1    NUM 10 = A1
NUM 11 =A#1    NUM 12 = B1   NUM 13 = C2   NUM 14 =C#2   NUM 15 = D2
NUM 16 =D#2    NUM 17 = E2   NUM 18 = F2   NUM 19 =F#2   NUM 20 = G2
NUM 21 =G#2    NUM 22 = A2   NUM 23 =A#2   NUM 24 = B2   NUM 25 = C3
NUM 26 =C#3    NUM 27 = D3   NUM 28 =D#3   NUM 29 = E3   NUM 30 = F3
NUM 31 =F#3    NUM 32 = G3   NUM 33 =G#3   NUM 34 = A3   NUM 35 =A#3
NUM 36 = B3    NUM 37 = C4   NUM 38 =C#4   NUM 39 = D4   NUM 40 =D#4
NUM 41 = E4    NUM 42 = F4   NUM 43 =F#4   NUM 44 = G4   NUM 45 =G#4
NUM 46 = A4    NUM 47 =A#4   NUM 48 = B4   NUM 49 = C5   NUM 50 =C#5
NUM 51 = D5    NUM 52 =D#5   NUM 53 = E5   NUM 54 = F5   NUM 55 =F#5
NUM 56 = G5    NUM 57 =G#5   NUM 58 = A5   NUM 59 =A#5   NUM 60 = B5
NUM 61 = C6    NUM 62 =C#6   NUM 63 = D6   NUM 64 =D#6   NUM 65 = E6
NUM 66 = F6    NUM 67 =F#6   NUM 68 = G6   NUM 69 =G#6   NUM 70 = A6
NUM 71 =A#6    NUM 72 = B6   NUM 73 = C7   NUM 74 =C#7   NUM 75 = D7
NUM 76 =D#7    NUM 77 = E7   NUM 78 = F7   NUM 79 =F#7   NUM 80 = G7
NUM 81 =G#7    NUM 82 = A7   NUM 83 =A#7   NUM 84 = B7
```

SUBROUTINE GROUP: VECTORS

- Parstore   CTB1.4
- Parxtrct   CTB1.5

Purpose

To configure an event vector array by calling the composite number storage (Parstore) and extraction (Parxtrct) procedures. Each address in the array must hold pitch, rhythm, and volume parameter data for a single musical tone.

Although this program deals specifically with musical elements, there are other circumstances in which the need arises for compressing numeric data due to system memory limitations. These subroutines will "come to the rescue."

Notes

Composite number storage and extraction works by assigning each musical parameter value to a separate segment of the number—

$$\frac{000 \; 000 \; 000}{\text{V} \quad \text{R} \quad \text{P}}$$

For this reason, a double precision variable is required. The only restriction is that the parameter value range must be $< \; = 999$. Any musical dimension that you wish to control may be substituted for program variables P, R, and V.

Programming Ideas

1) Modify the program to store information about other compositional dimensions such as texture density, timbre, and articulation.

2) Shift program focus from the single sonic-event level to the macro-formal level by storing information to determine the number of melodic notes in a phrase, number of phrases in a phrase-group, and number of phrase-groups in a formal section.

Program Listing

```
100 REM  ===========================================================
110 REM                       VECTORS
120 REM  ===========================================================
130 REM     The subroutine PARSTORE creates 'event vectors'
140 REM     by storing pitch, rhythm and volume data for a
150 REM     single musical event in one double precision number.
170 REM     The subroutine PARXTRCT extracts the event attributes
180 REM     from the composite value.
200 REM  ===========================================================
210 REM  ===========================================================
220 REM                  Variable Descriptions
```

```
230 REM
240 REM       P: holds value of event vector pitch parameter
250 REM       R: holds value of event vector rhythm parameter
260 REM       V: holds value of event vector volume parameter
270 REM       COMP#(): double precision vector  (values P,R,V)
280 REM       K9: loop index, pointer to array COMP#()
290 REM
300 REM ============================================================
310 REM                    DRIVER PROGRAM
320 REM ============================================================
330     DIM COMP#(10)
340     GOSUB 1000                      '<< call event vector storage
350     PRINT
360     GOSUB 2000                      '<< call event vector extract
370 END
1000 REM ================================================= CTB1.4
1010 REM *****************>> PARSTORE <<***********************
1020 REM ====================================================
1030     PRINT "STORE EVENT PARAMETERS IN DBL PRECIS. NUMBER --
1040       FOR K9= 1 TO 10
1050         P  = K9                         '<< assign pitch value
1060         R  = K9 * 5        '<< assign rhythm duration value
1070         V  = K9 * 10        '<< assign volume level value
1080         PRINT "PITCH = ";P,"RHYTHM = ";R, "VOLUME =";V,
1090         COMP#(K9) = (P * 1000000!) + (R * 1000) + V
1100         PRINT "COMPOSITE IS ";COMP#(K9)
1110       NEXT K9
1120 RETURN
2000 REM ================================================= CTB1.5
2010 REM *****************>> PARXTRCT <<***********************
2020 REM ====================================================
2030     PRINT "EXTRACT EVENT PARAMETERS FROM COMPOSITE NUMBER--"
2040       FOR K9 = 1 TO 10
2050         COMP#(K9)  = COMP#(K9)/1000000!
2060         P  = INT(COMP#(K9))
2070         PRINT "P=";P ,
2080         R  = INT((COMP#(K9) - INT(COMP#(K9))) * 1000)
2090         PRINT "R=";R ,
2100         COMP#(K9)  = COMP#(K9) * 1000
2110         V  = INT((COMP#(K9) - INT(COMP#(K9))) * 1000+.5)
2120         PRINT "V=";V
2130       NEXT K9
2140 RETURN
```

RUN (Vectors)

```
STORE EVENT PARAMETERS IN DBL PRECIS. NUMBER --
PITCH =    1    RHYTHM =    5    VOLUME = 10    COMPOSITE IS   1005010
PITCH =    2    RHYTHM =   10    VOLUME = 20    COMPOSITE IS   2010020
PITCH =    3    RHYTHM =   15    VOLUME = 30    COMPOSITE IS   3015030
PITCH =    4    RHYTHM =   20    VOLUME = 40    COMPOSITE IS   4020040
PITCH =    5    RHYTHM =   25    VOLUME = 50    COMPOSITE IS   5025050
PITCH =    6    RHYTHM =   30    VOLUME = 60    COMPOSITE IS   6030060
PITCH =    7    RHYTHM =   35    VOLUME = 70    COMPOSITE IS   7035070
PITCH =    8    RHYTHM =   40    VOLUME = 80    COMPOSITE IS   8040080
PITCH =    9    RHYTHM =   45    VOLUME = 90    COMPOSITE IS   9045090
PITCH =   10    RHYTHM =   50    VOLUME = 100   COMPOSITE IS  10050100
```

```
EXTRACT EVENT PARAMETERS FROM COMPOSITE NUMBER--
P= 1        R= 5        V= 10
P= 2        R= 10       V= 20
P= 3        R= 15       V= 30
P= 4        R= 20       V= 40
P= 5        R= 25       V= 50
P= 6        R= 30       V= 60
P= 7        R= 35       V= 70
P= 8        R= 40       V= 80
P= 9        R= 45       V= 90
P= 10       R= 50       V= 100
```

SUBROUTINE GROUP: 1MATOP

○ Matprint	CTB1.6
○ Matmult	CTB1.7
○ Matransp	CTB1.8
○ Zeromat	CTB1.9

Purpose

Provide procedural subroutines for standard operations on one two-dimensional matrix.

Many situations entail routine, repeated transformations of musical parameter data stored in multidimensional matrices. For example, rhythm data may be subjected to augmentation or diminution processes over successive calls to various subroutines.

Notes

MATPRINT sends matrix data to the CRT screen in ordered rows and columns, MATMULT multiplies the contents of each array address by a constant value, MATRANSP exchanges matrix rows and columns, and ZEROMAT resets all matrix addresses to 0. Change the value of the variable m.

Programming Ideas

1) Matrix operations are often used in conjunction with table lookup, sorting, and searching procedures. Apply them in various ways to matrices which have undergone transformations.

2) Add subroutines to this group that expand the available processing methods. (Division, subtraction, exponentiation, and the application of defined functions are useful extensions.)

Program Listing

```
100 REM =============================================================
110 REM                          1MATOP
120 REM =============================================================
130 REM     These subroutines deal with single 2-d matrix
140 REM     operations.
190 REM =============================================================
200 REM                     Variable Descriptions
210 REM         D: full row counter
220 REM         F: flag to print transposed matrix
230 REM         M: scalar multiplication factor
240 REM         X(n,n): matrix 1 to hold primary & multiplied data
250 REM         Y(n,n): matrix 2 to hold transposed data
260 REM         J1: loop index, pointer to matrix rows
270 REM         J2: loop index, pointer to matrix columns
280 REM         K9: subroutine loop index
290 REM         L9: subroutine loop index
```

```
300 REM ================================================================
310 REM                        DRIVER PROGRAM
320 REM ================================================================
330     DIM X(8,8),Y(8,8)
340     D = 0
350     F = 0
360     M = 8
370     PRINT "A 2-DIMENSIONAL MATRIX OF SEQUENTIAL NUMBERS --"
380        FOR J1 = 1 TO 8
390           FOR J2 = 1 TO 8
400              X(J1,J2) = J2 + D
410           NEXT J2
420           D = D + 8
430        NEXT J1
440     GOSUB 1000                              '<< call matrix print
450     PRINT
460     GOSUB 2010            '<< call matrix scalar multiplication
470     PRINT
480     PRINT "MATRIX MULTIPLIED BY 8 --"
490     GOSUB 1000                              '<< call matrix print
500     PRINT
510     GOSUB 3010                         '<< call matrix transposition
520     PRINT
530     PRINT "TRANSPOSED MATRIX (ROWS & COLUMNS EXCHANGED) --"
540     GOSUB 1000                              '<< call matrix print
550     PRINT
560     GOSUB 4000                         '<< call matrix reset
570     PRINT "MATRICES RESET TO ZERO --"
580     GOSUB 1000
590 END
1000 REM ================================================== CTB1.6
1010 REM *****************>> MATPRINT <<************************
1020 REM ================================================================
1030        FOR K9 = 1 TO 8
1040           FOR L9 = 1 TO 8
1050              IF F = 0 THEN PRINT TAB(8*(L9-1))X(K9,L9); ELSE
PRINT TAB(8*(L9-1))Y(K9,L9);
1060           NEXT L9
1070           PRINT
1080        NEXT K9
1090 RETURN
2000 REM ================================================== CTB1.7
2010 REM *****************>> MATMULT <<************************
2020 REM ================================================================
2030        FOR K9 = 1 TO 8
2040           FOR L9 = 1 TO 8
2050              X(K9,L9) = X(K9,L9) * M
2060           NEXT L9
2070        NEXT K9
2080 RETURN
3000 REM ================================================== CTB1.8
3010 REM *****************>>  MATRANSP <<************************
3020 REM ================================================================
3030        FOR K9 = 1 TO 8
3040           FOR L9 = 1 TO 8
3050              Y(K9,L9) = X(L9,K9)
3060           NEXT L9
3070        NEXT K9
3080     F = 1
3090 RETURN
```

```
4000 REM ======================================================= CTB1.9
4010 REM *******************>> ZEROMAT <<***********************
4020 REM =======================================================
4030    FOR K9 = 1 TO 8
4040       FOR L9 = 1 TO 8
4050          X(K9,L9) = 0
4060          Y(K9,L9) = 0
4070       NEXT L9
4080    NEXT K9
4090 RETURN
```

RUN (1Matop)

A 2-DIMENTIONAL MATRIX OF SEQUENTIAL NUMBERS --

1	2	3	4	5	6	7	8
9	10	11	12	13	14	15	16
17	18	19	20	21	22	23	24
25	26	27	28	29	30	31	32
33	34	35	36	37	38	39	40
41	42	43	44	45	46	47	48
49	50	51	52	53	54	55	56
57	58	59	60	61	62	63	64

MATRIX MULTIPLIED BY 8 --

8	16	24	32	40	48	56	64
72	80	88	96	104	112	120	128
136	144	152	160	168	176	184	192
200	208	216	224	232	240	248	256
264	272	280	288	296	304	312	320
328	336	344	352	360	368	376	384
392	400	408	416	424	432	440	448
456	464	472	480	488	496	504	512

TRANSPOSED MATRIX (ROWS & COLUMNS EXCHANGED) --

8	72	136	200	264	328	392	456
16	80	144	208	272	336	400	464
24	88	152	216	280	344	408	472
32	96	160	224	288	352	416	480
40	104	168	232	296	360	424	488
48	112	176	240	304	368	432	496
56	120	184	248	312	376	440	504
64	128	192	256	320	384	448	512

MATRICES RESET TO ZERO --

0	0	0	0	0	0	0	0
0	0	0	0	0	0	0	0
0	0	0	0	0	0	0	0
0	0	0	0	0	0	0	0
0	0	0	0	0	0	0	0
0	0	0	0	0	0	0	0
0	0	0	0	0	0	0	0
0	0	0	0	0	0	0	0

SUBROUTINE GROUP: 2MATOP

- Print2mat   CTB1.6
- Add2mat   CTB1.10
- Mult2mat   CTB1.11

Purpose

Provide procedural subroutines for standard operations involving two two-dimensional matrices.

Notes

Print2mat separately prints out the rows and columns of two two-dimensional matrices; Add2mat adds the contents of two two-dimensional matrices and places the result in a third array; Mult2mat multiplies the contents of the first array by the contents of the second array and places the result in a third array. To reconfigure arrays, change the DRIVER PROGRAM dimension statement, loop index values, and variable D value accordingly.

Programming Ideas

Spin-up two arrays containing integers corresponding to the pitches of two long melodic sequences. Add the contents of one array to the contents of the other. Use Modulo (CTB1.2) and Pitchtab (CTB1.3) to print out the results (modulo 12) as note names (C#, F, G#, etc.). Observe the effect that intermodulation of the first sequence with the second sequence has on the third sequence.

Program Listing

```
100 REM ============================================================
110 REM                         2MATOP
120 REM ============================================================
130 REM     These subroutines deal with operations on
140 REM     two discrete matrices.
180 REM ============================================================
190 REM                   Variable Descriptions
200 REM
210 REM        D: full row counter
220 REM        X(n,n): matrix 1
230 REM        Y(n,n): matrix 2
240 REM        Z(n,n): matrix holding operation result
250 REM        J1: driver loop index, pointer to matrix rows
260 REM        J2: driver loop index, pointer to matrix columns
270 REM        K9: subroutine loop index
280 REM        L9: subroutine loop index
290 REM
300 REM ============================================================
310 REM                      DRIVER PROGRAM
320 REM ============================================================
```

```
 330     DIM X(8,8),Y(8,8),Z(8,8)
 340     D = 0
 350       FOR J1 = 1 TO 8
 360         FOR J2 = 1 TO 8
 370           X(J1,J2) = J2+D        '<< fill with numbers 1-100
 380           Y(J1,J2) = J2+D+100    '<< fill with nums 101-200
 390         NEXT J2
 400         D = D + 8
 410       NEXT J1
 420     GOSUB 1000                          '<< print original matrices
 430     PRINT
 440     GOSUB 2000              '<< add matrix x to matrix y and print
 450     PRINT
 460     GOSUB 3000       '<< multiply matrix x by matrix y and print
 470 END
1000 REM ================================================= CTB1.6
1010 REM ******************>> PRINT2MAT <<**********************
1020 REM =================================================
1030     PRINT "MATRIX X --"
1040       FOR K9 = 1 TO 8
1050         FOR L9 = 1 TO 8
1060           PRINT TAB(8*(L9-1))X(K9,L9);
1070         NEXT L9
1080         PRINT
1090       NEXT K9
1100       PRINT
1110     PRINT "MATRIX Y --"
1120     FOR K9 = 1 TO 8
1130         FOR L9 = 1 TO 8
1140           PRINT TAB(8*(L9-1))Y(K9,L9);
1150         NEXT L9
1160         PRINT
1170       NEXT K9
1180 RETURN
2000 REM ================================================= CTB1.10
2010 REM ******************>> ADD2MAT <<************************
2020 REM =================================================
2030     PRINT "THE SUM OF MATRICES X & Y --"
2040       FOR K9 = 1 TO 8
2050         FOR L9 = 1 TO 8
2060           Z(K9,L9) = X(K9,L9) + Y(K9,L9)
2070           PRINT TAB(8*(L9-1))Z(K9,L9);
2080         NEXT L9
2090         PRINT
2100       NEXT K9
2110 RETURN
3000 REM ================================================= CTB1.11
3010 REM ******************>> MULT2MAT <<***********************
3020 REM =================================================
3030     PRINT "THE PRODUCT OF MATRICES X AND Y --"
3040       FOR K9 = 1 TO 8
3050         FOR L9 = 1 TO 8
3060           Z(K9,L9) = X(K9,L9) * Y(K9,L9)
3070           PRINT TAB(8*(L9-1))Z(K9,L9);
3080         NEXT L9
3090       NEXT K9
3100 RETURN
```

RUN (2Matop)

```
MATRIX X --
  1       2       3       4       5       6       7       8
  9      10      11      12      13      14      15      16
 17      18      19      20      21      22      23      24
 25      26      27      28      29      30      31      32
 33      34      35      36      37      38      39      40
 41      42      43      44      45      46      47      48
 49      50      51      52      53      54      55      56
 57      58      59      60      61      62      63      64

MATRIX Y --
101     102     103     104     105     106     107     108
109     110     111     112     113     114     115     116
117     118     119     120     121     122     123     124
125     126     127     128     129     130     131     132
133     134     135     136     137     138     139     140
141     142     143     144     145     146     147     148
149     150     151     152     153     154     155     156
157     158     159     160     161     162     163     164

THE SUM OF MATRICES X & Y --
102     104     106     108     110     112     114     116
118     120     122     124     126     128     130     132
134     136     138     140     142     144     146     148
150     152     154     156     158     160     162     164
166     168     170     172     174     176     178     180
182     184     186     188     190     192     194     196
198     200     202     204     206     208     210     212
214     216     218     220     222     224     226     228

THE PRODUCT OF MATRICES X AND Y --
101     204     309     416     525     636     749     864
981    1100    1221    1344    1469    1596    1725    1856
1989    2124    2261    2400    2541    2684    2829    2976
3125    3276    3429    3584    3741    3900    4061    4224
4389    4556    4725    4896    5069    5244    5421    5600
5781    5964    6149    6336    6525    6716    6909    7104
7301    7500    7701    7904    8109    8316    8525    8736
8949    9164    9381    9600    9821   10044   10269   10496
```

SUBROUTINE GROUP: CURVES

  ○ Lincurve   CTB1.12
  ○ Expcurve   CTB1.13
  ○ Logcurve   CTB1.14

Purpose

Generate ascending integer data sequences which conform to one of three available curves: linear, exponential, or logarithmic.

Although this group is especially appropriate for creating a smooth accelerando of tempo, a gradual increase of the volume level, or an incremental timbre shift, you can apply the curves to any compositional problem which requires discrete, continuously scaled integers for direct use or for indirect use as pointers to other sets of data.

Notes

Control parameters are S (start value), E (end value), and N (number of values to return), all of which must be positive integers.

Programming Ideas

1) Write a program which directly applies the curves to pitch, rhythm, and volume parameters.

2) Generate curves in various ranges to serve as pointers to other musical parameter arrays which contain unsorted, random-order values.

3) Modify the curve algorithms to return negative as well as positive values.

Program Listing

```
100 REM ==========================================================
110 REM                       CURVES
120 REM ==========================================================
130 REM    The subroutines LINCURVE, EXPCURVE, and LOGCURVE
140 REM    return positive values along three discrete curves:
150 REM    linear, exponential, and logarithmic.
180 REM ==========================================================
190 REM                 Variable Descriptions
200 REM    DRIVER
210 REM      S: starting curve value
220 REM      E: ending curve value
230 REM      N: number of values contained in curve
240 REM      J1: loop index, pointer to subroutines
250 REM      J2: loop index, pointer to array X()
260 REM      X(): array holding curve values
270 REM
280 REM    SUBROUTINES 1000,2000,3000
290 REM      Entering -
300 REM        S: starting curve value
```

```
310 REM          E: ending curve value
320 REM          N: number of values contained in curve
330 REM       Exiting -
340 REM          X(): array holding curve values
350 REM       Local -
360 REM          K9: loop index
370 REM          L9: loop index, pointer to array X()
380 REM ===========================================================
390 REM                         DRIVER PROGRAM
400 REM ===========================================================
410     DIM X(100)
420     S = 1
430     E = 100
440     N = 100
450       FOR J1 = 1 TO 3
460 REM >> sequentially call LINCURVE, EXPCURVE, LOGCURVE subrs.
470          ON J1 GOSUB 1000,2000,3000
480          FOR J2 = 1 TO N
490             PRINT X(J2),      '<< send curve values to screen
500          NEXT J2
510          PRINT
520       NEXT J1
530 END
1000 REM ================================================= CTB1.12
1010 REM *******************>> LINCURVE <<*******************
1020 REM ===========================================================
1030    PRINT "LINEAR CURVE:"
1040    FOR K9 = 1 TO N STEP 10
1050       FOR L9 = K9 TO K9 + 9
1060 REM >> store current computed curve value
1070          X(L9) = ABS(S + INT(((L9-1)/(N-1)) * (E-S)+.5))
1080          IF L9 = N THEN 1100
1090       NEXT L9
1100    NEXT K9
1110 RETURN
2000 REM ================================================= CTB1.13
2010 REM *******************>> EXPCURVE <<*******************
2020 REM ===========================================================
2030    PRINT "EXPONENTIAL CURVE:"
2040    FOR K9 = 1 TO N STEP 10
2050       FOR L9 = K9 TO K9 + 9
2060 REM >> store current computed curve value
2070          X(L9) = ABS(S+INT((((L9-1)^2)/((N-1)^2))*(E-S)+.5))
2080          IF L9 = N THEN 2100
2090       NEXT L9
2100    NEXT K9
2110 RETURN
3000 REM ================================================= CTB1.14
3010 REM *******************>> LOGCURVE <<*******************
3020 REM ===========================================================
3030    PRINT "LOGARITHMIC CURVE:"
3040    FOR K9 = 1 TO N STEP 10
3050       FOR L9 = K9 TO K9 + 9
3060 REM >> store current computed curve value
3070          X(L9)=ABS(S + INT(((LOG(L9))/(LOG(N)))*(E-S)+.5))
3080          IF L9 = N THEN 3100
3090       NEXT L9
3100    NEXT K9
3110 RETURN
```

RUN (Curves)

LINEAR CURVE:

1	2	3	4	5
6	7	8	9	10
11	12	13	14	15
16	17	18	19	20
21	22	23	24	25
26	27	28	29	30
31	32	33	34	35
36	37	38	39	40
41	42	43	44	45
46	47	48	49	50
51	52	53	54	55
56	57	58	59	60
61	62	63	64	65
66	67	68	69	70
71	72	73	74	75
76	77	78	79	80
81	82	83	84	85
86	87	88	89	90
91	92	93	94	95
96	97	98	99	100

EXPONENTIAL CURVE:

1	1	1	1	1
1	1	1	2	2
2	2	2	3	3
3	4	4	4	5
5	5	6	6	7
7	8	8	9	9
10	11	11	12	13
13	14	15	16	16
17	18	19	20	21
21	22	23	24	25
26	27	28	29	30
32	33	34	35	36
37	39	40	41	42
44	45	46	48	49
50	52	53	55	56
58	59	61	62	64
66	67	69	71	72
74	76	77	79	81
83	85	86	88	90
92	94	96	98	100

LOGARITHMIC CURVE:

1	16	25	31	36
40	43	46	48	51
53	54	56	58	59
61	62	63	64	65
66	67	68	69	70
71	72	73	73	74
75	76	76	77	77
78	79	79	80	80
81	81	82	82	83
83	84	84	85	85
86	86	86	87	87
88	88	88	89	89
89	90	90	90	91

91	91	92	92	92
93	93	93	94	94
94	94	95	95	95
95	96	96	96	97
97	97	97	97	98
98	98	98	99	99
99	99	100	100	100

Purpose

Sum a sequence of rhythm durations which are expressed as fraction denominators (1/2, 1/4, 1/8, 1/16, 1/32, 1/64, etc.).

It sometimes happens that a sequence of randomly generated melodic rhythm values must be reconciled to a pre-established time frame. This subroutine provides a tally of generated values which can be fed back to the program for the adjustment of individual durations.

For example, if the situation requires that:

- The melody must contain eight notes,
- The note duration values must exactly equal two whole notes 32 16th-notes in total, and
- The subroutine returns the duration sequence 1/16, 1/2, 1/16, 1/4, 1/16, 1/8, 1/4, 1/2 (29 16th-notes in total),

then the discrepancy between the tally and output requirements dictates that the shorter values be augmented by the appropriate amount—in this case, three 16th-notes spread across three randomly selected notes.

Notes

If you wish to generate duration fractions which are multivariant—3/16, 2/5, 7/8, etc.—then substitute FRACTSUM (CTB1.18 and CTB1.19) for FRACTAB.

Programming Idea

Write a program which generates random-order pitches and rhythms for a melodic line. Include FRACTAB and additional statements to reconcile the melodic rhythm duration sum to a user-input time frame.

Program Listing

```
100 REM =========================================================
110 REM                    DRIVER PROGRAM
115 REM                       (Fractab)
120 REM =========================================================
130     DIM X(50)
140     TOTAL = 50
160     PRINT "HERE IS A SERIES OF DURATION FRACTIONS:"
170        FOR J = 1 TO TOTAL
180           X(J) = J              '<<< load denominators in array
190              PRINT "1/";X(J),   '<<< send to screen as fractions
200        NEXT J
210     PRINT : PRINT
220     GOSUB 1000                       '<<< call duration tabulation
230     PRINT "SUM OF DURATIONS IS:";SUM#;"WHOLE NOTES"
```

```
 240 END
1000 REM =================================================== CTB1.15
1010 REM ******************>>  FRACTAB  <<**********************
1020 REM ===================================================
1030 REM      This subroutine tabulates rhythmic duration values
1040 REM      in cases where each value can be expressed as a
1050 REM      fraction which has 1 as the numerator (e.g., 1/8).
1060 REM      The sum of all durations is returned in decimal.
1080 REM ===================================================
1100 REM                 Variable Descriptions
1120 REM      Entering -
1140 REM        X(): array of fraction denominators to be summed
1150 REM        TOTAL: number of elements in array X()
1160 REM
1170 REM      Exiting -
1190 REM        SUM#: (double precision) decimal sum of
1200 REM              durations, expressed in whole notes
1210 REM
1220 REM      Local -
1240 REM        K9: loop index, pointer to array X()
1260 REM ===================================================
1280      SUM# = 0
1290        FOR K9 = 1 TO TOTAL
1300          SUM# = SUM# + 1 / X(K9)
1310        NEXT K9
1320 RETURN
```

RUN (Fractab)

```
HERE IS A SERIES OF DURATION FRACTIONS:
1/ 1          1/ 2          1/ 3          1/ 4          1/ 5
1/ 6          1/ 7          1/ 8          1/ 9          1/ 10
1/ 11         1/ 12         1/ 13         1/ 14         1/ 15
1/ 16         1/ 17         1/ 18         1/ 19         1/ 20
1/ 21         1/ 22         1/ 23         1/ 24         1/ 25
1/ 26         1/ 27         1/ 28         1/ 29         1/ 30
1/ 31         1/ 32         1/ 33         1/ 34         1/ 35
1/ 36         1/ 37         1/ 38         1/ 39         1/ 40
1/ 41         1/ 42         1/ 43         1/ 44         1/ 45
1/ 46         1/ 47         1/ 48         1/ 49         1/ 50
SUM OF DURATIONS IS: 4.499205391854048 WHOLE NOTES
```

Purpose

Reduce an array of rhythm duration fractions to their lowest terms (consistent with rhythm pulse subdivision); return the reduced fractions to the program as a character string array.

Notes

Circumstances arise in which computer-generated rhythms must be transcribed to conventional music notation. The process is simplified by reducing duration fractions *only* to the level of the underlying metrical pulse (or subdivision). For example, assuming a background meter of 6/8 time, it is more meaningful to a musician to see the fraction 12/16 expressed as 6/8 as opposed to 1/2, because 6/8 more adequately expresses the relationship between the background meter and the individual note durations.

If there is no need for the human user to interpret rhythm fractions—e.g., when the values are for transmission to a digital synthesizer—then use EUCREDUC (CTB1.17); it will execute more efficiently.

Programming Ideas

1) Alter the DRIVER PROGRAM to generate random-order fraction denominators as well as numerators. Observe the effect that this method of reduction has on the intelligibility of returned duration fractions.

2) Write an interactive program that allows the user to request any reasonable-length random-order melody, generates the appropriate number of rhythm durations, then adjusts the durations to conform to an input time reference.

Program Listing

```
100 REM  ===============================================================
110 REM                     DRIVER PROGRAM
115 REM                       (Durred)
120 REM  ===============================================================
130      DIM X(50),Y(50),FRACTION$(50)
140      TOTAL = 50
160      RANDOMIZE(52)
170      PRINT "RANDOM FRACTIONS, RANGE 1/50 TO 50/1 --"
180        FOR J= 1 TO TOTAL
190            X(J) = INT(RND * TOTAL)+1        '<< load numerators
200            Y(J) = 32                        '<< load denominators
210            PRINT X(J);"/";Y(J),             '<< send to screen
220        NEXT J
230      PRINT:PRINT
240      GOSUB 1000                    '<<< call fraction reduction
245      PRINT "REDUCED FRACTION SEQUENCE --"
250        FOR J = 1 TO TOTAL
260            PRINT FRACTION$(J),      '<<send fraction to screen
270        NEXT J
```

```
 280 END
1000 REM ========================================================= CTB1.16
1010 REM ****************>> DURRED <<***************************
1020 REM =========================================================
1030 REM     This subroutine reduces fractions in a manner
1040 REM     consistent with rhythmic pulse subdivision.
1110 REM =========================================================
1120 REM                   Variable Descriptions
1130 REM     Entering -
1140 REM       X(): array of fraction numerators
1150 REM       Y(): array of fraction denominators
1160 REM       TOTAL: number of fractions to be converted
1170 REM
1180 REM     Exiting -
1190 REM       FRACTION$(): character string array of fractions
1210 REM
1220 REM     Local -
1230 REM       K9: loop index, pointer to arrays X(),Y(),FRACTION$
1240 REM =========================================================
1250      FOR K9 = 1 TO TOTAL
1260         IF X(K9) / 2 <> INT(X(K9) / 2) OR Y(K9) / 2 <>
INT(Y(K9) / 2) THEN 1280
1270         X(K9) = X(K9) / 2 : Y(K9) = Y(K9) / 2 : GOTO 1260
1280         FRACTION$(K9) = STR$(X(K9)) + "/" + STR$(Y(K9))
1285      NEXT K9
1290 RETURN
```

RUN (Durred)

```
RANDOM FRACTIONS, RANGE 1/50 TO 50/1 --
  9 / 32        9 / 32       28 / 32      23 / 32      10 / 32
 16 / 32       42 / 32       41 / 32      33 / 32      24 / 32
  2 / 32       23 / 32       19 / 32      34 / 32      21 / 32
 29 / 32       22 / 32       20 / 32      45 / 32      25 / 32
 40 / 32       11 / 32       49 / 32      42 / 32      20 / 32
 44 / 32       40 / 32        6 / 32      22 / 32      20 / 32
 33 / 32       32 / 32       42 / 32      27 / 32      26 / 32
 27 / 32        2 / 32       27 / 32      48 / 32       4 / 32
 50 / 32        3 / 32       17 / 32      15 / 32      25 / 32
 19 / 32        8 / 32       38 / 32      31 / 32      42 / 32

REDUCED FRACTION SEQUENCE --
 9/ 32         9/ 32         7/ 8         23/ 32        5/ 16
 1/ 2         21/ 16        41/ 32        33/ 32        3/ 4
 1/ 16        23/ 32        19/ 32        17/ 16       21/ 32
29/ 32        11/ 16         5/ 8         45/ 32       25/ 32
 5/ 4         11/ 32        49/ 32        21/ 16        5/ 8
11/ 8          5/ 4          3/ 16        11/ 16        5/ 8
33/ 32         1/ 1         21/ 16        27/ 32       13/ 16
27/ 32         1/ 16        27/ 32         3/ 2         1/ 8
25/ 16         3/ 32        17/ 32        15/ 32       25/ 32
19/ 32         1/ 4         19/ 16        31/ 32       21/ 16
```

Purpose

Reduce rhythm duration fractions to their absolute lowest terms (for use when consistency of pulse subdivision is not a concern). Return the fractions to the program as a character string array.

Notes

Durred, CTB1.16 reduces fractions while limiting their reduction to whole-integer pulse subdivisions. (For instance, 9/12 would be reduced no further.) Eucreduc, however, relies on Euclid's Greatest Common Divisor algorithm to convert a fraction such as 9/12 to even lower terms (3/4). When durations are being directed to a synthesizer, it is preferable to use this subroutine.

If your version of BASIC lacks a SWAP statement, then substitute/insert the following code:

```
1240   IF A9 < B9 THEN 1250
1241   TEMP = A9
1242   A9 = B9
1243   B9 = TEMP
```

The WHILE . . . . WEND (do-while) loop structure can be replaced with a FOR . . . NEXT loop built around a statement to test for A9 = 0.

Programming Ideas

See Subroutine Durred.

Program Listing

```
100 REM  ============================================================
110 REM                      DRIVER PROGRAM
115 REM                        (Eucreduc)
120 REM  ============================================================
130      DIM X(50),Y(50),FRACTION$(50)
140      TOTAL = 50
160      RANDOMIZE(133)
170      PRINT "RANDOM FRACTIONS, RANGE 1/50 TO 50/1 --"
180         FOR J= 1 TO TOTAL
190            X(J) = INT(RND * TOTAL)+1        '<< load numerators
200            Y(J) = 32      '<< load denominators
210            PRINT X(J);"/";Y(J),    '<< send fraction to screen
220         NEXT J
230      PRINT
240      GOSUB 1000                     '<<< call fraction reduction
245      PRINT "REDUCED FRACTION SEQUENCE --"
250         FOR J = 1 TO TOTAL
260            PRINT FRACTION$(J),    '<< send fraction to screen
270         NEXT J
280 END
```

```
1000 REM =================================================== CTB1.17
1010 REM *******************>> EUCREDUC <<*********************
1020 REM ===================================================
1030 REM     This subroutine uses Euclid's algorithm to reduce
1040 REM     rhythmic duration fractions to absolute lowest terms.
1050 REM     It does not preserve metrical pulse consistency, in
1060 REM     that a fraction such as 9/12 will convert to 3/4.
1070 REM ===================================================
1080 REM                    Variable Descriptions
1090 REM     Entering -
1100 REM       X(): array of fraction numerators
1110 REM       Y(): array of fraction denominators
1120 REM       TOTAL: number of fractions to be reduced
1130 REM
1140 REM     Exiting -
1150 REM       FRACTION$(): character string array of fractions
1160 REM
1170 REM     Local -
1180 REM       K9: loop index, pointer to arrays X(),Y(),FRACTION$
1190 REM ===================================================
1200       FOR K9 = 1 TO TOTAL
1210           IF Y(K9) = 1 THEN 1330
1220           A9 = X(K9)
1230           B9 = Y(K9)
1240           IF A9 > B9 THEN SWAP A9,B9
1250             WHILE A9 > 0
1260               C9 = INT(B9/A9)
1270               D9 = B9-A9*C9
1280               B9 = A9
1290               A9 = D9
1300             WEND
1310 REM >> convert fraction to char string and load in array
1320           FRACTION$(K9) = STR$(X(K9)/B9) + "/" + STR$(Y(K9)/B9)
1330       NEXT K9
1340 RETURN
```

RUN (Eucreduc)

```
RANDOM FRACTIONS, RANGE 1/50 TO 50/1 --
  25 / 32       12 / 32       18 / 32        9 / 32       30 / 32
  20 / 32       41 / 32       13 / 32        8 / 32       24 / 32
  26 / 32       33 / 32       43 / 32        3 / 32        1 / 32
  33 / 32       26 / 32        8 / 32       28 / 32       32 / 32
  49 / 32       48 / 32       48 / 32       13 / 32       48 / 32
  37 / 32       34 / 32        7 / 32       23 / 32        4 / 32
  15 / 32       31 / 32       12 / 32       16 / 32        6 / 32
  45 / 32       28 / 32       13 / 32        1 / 32       15 / 32
   8 / 32        5 / 32       34 / 32       47 / 32       33 / 32
  35 / 32       45 / 32       22 / 32       46 / 32       48 / 32
REDUCED FRACTION SEQUENCE --
  25/ 32        3/ 8         9/ 16         9/ 32        15/ 16
   5/ 8        41/ 32       13/ 32         1/ 4          3/ 4
  13/ 16       33/ 32       43/ 32         3/ 32         1/ 32
  33/ 32       13/ 16        1/ 4          7/ 8          1/ 1
  49/ 32        3/ 2         3/ 2         13/ 32         3/ 2
  37/ 32       17/ 16        7/ 32        23/ 32         1/ 8
  15/ 32       31/ 32        3/ 8          1/ 2          3/ 16
  45/ 32        7/ 8        13/ 32         1/ 32        15/ 32
   1/ 4         5/ 32       17/ 16        47/ 32        33/ 32
  35/ 32       45/ 32       11/ 16        23/ 16         3/ 2
```

SUBROUTINE GROUP: FRACTSUM

- LCM   CTB1.18
- GCD   CTB1.19

Purpose

Although the subroutines in this group have a number of individual applications, they are assembled here to sum an array of multivariant rhythm duration fractions.

Notes

An alternative subroutine, FRACTAB (CTB1.15), sums fractions and expresses the result in decimal whole-note values; however, the fractions must each have the numerator 1.

Contrastingly, FRACTSUM places no restriction on the fraction, type and returns a fractional—not decimal—sum, e.g., $2/1 + 11/16 = 2 \ 11/16$. Subroutine LCM (Least Common Multiple) calls Subroutine GCD (Greatest Common Divisor) to total the sequence fractions.

There is one serious drawback to this particular fraction-summing method: When implemented for a computer with a small word-size, numeric overflow is quickly reached.

Programming Idea

Write a program which generates random-order pitches and rhythms for a melodic line. Include FRACTAB and additional code to reconcile the melodic rhythm duration sum to a user-input time frame.

Program Listing

```
100 REM ==========================================================
110 REM                     DRIVER PROGRAM
120 REM                       (Fractsum)
130 REM ==========================================================
140 REM     This subroutine group  sums an array of rhythm
150 REM     duration fractions.  The result is returned
160 REM     as a fraction.
340 REM ==========================================================
350    DIM X(20),Y(20)
360    RANDOMIZE(-139)
370    PRINT "ARRAY OF DURATION FRACTIONS TO BE TOTALED -- "
380       FOR J = 0 TO 20
390          X(J) = INT(RND * 10)+1
400          Y(J) = INT(RND * 10)+1
410          PRINT X(J);"/";Y(J),    '<< send fraction to screen
420       NEXT J
430    PRINT
440    PRINT
450       FOR J = 1 TO 20
460          GOSUB 1000
```

```
470            X(0) = NUM
480            Y(0) = DEN
490        NEXT J
495      PRINT "TOTAL --"
500      IF NUM MOD DEN = 0 THEN PRINT NUM/DEN ELSE IF NUM > DEN
THEN PRINT INT(NUM/DEN);"+";NUM MOD DEN;"/";DEN;ELSE PRINT
NUM;"/";DEN;
510 END
1000 REM ===================================================== CTB1.18
1010 REM **********************>> LCM <<***********************
1020 REM =====================================================
1030 REM     This subroutine determines the least common
1040 REM     multiple of two integers by calling the
1050 REM     greatest common divisor subroutine to supply
1060 REM     that value, then divides the product of the
1070 REM     two integers by the GCD.
1080 REM =====================================================
1090 REM                     Variable Descriptions
1100 REM     Entering -
1110 REM       X(0): current fraction numerator sum
1120 REM       X(n): next fraction numerator
1130 REM       Y(0): current fraction denominator sum
1140 REM       Y(n): next fraction denominator
1150 REM       LCM: least common multiple
1160 REM     Exiting -
1170 REM       NUM: reduced fraction numerator total
1180 REM       DEN: reduced fraction denominator total
1190 REM     Local -
1200 REM       M9: temp storage for denominator total
1210 REM       N9: temp storage for next denominator
1220 REM       GCD: greatest common divisor
1230 REM       LCM: least common multiple
1240 REM =====================================================
1250     M9 = Y(0)
1260     N9 = Y(J)
1270     GOSUB 2000                  '<< call Greatest Common Divisor
1280     LCM = M9 * N9 / GCD
1290     M9 = LCM / Y(0)
1300     N9 = LCM / Y(J)
1310     NUM = (X(0) * M9) + (X(J) * N9)
1320     DEN = LCM
1330     M9 = NUM
1340     N9 = DEN
1350     GOSUB 2000                  '<< call Greatest Common Divisor
1360     NUM = M9 / GCD
1370     DEN = N9 / GCD
1380 RETURN
2000 REM ===================================================== CTB1.19
2010 REM **********************>> GCD <<***********************
2020 REM             (EUCREDUC adapted to program specs.)
2030 REM =====================================================
2040     A9 = M9
2050     B9 = N9
2060     IF A9 > B9 THEN SWAP A9,B9
2070        WHILE A9 > 0
2080           C9=INT(B9/A9)
2090           D9 = B9 - A9 * C9
2100           B9 = A9
2110           A9 = D9
2120        WEND
```

```
2130    GCD = B9
2140 RETURN
```

RUN (FRACTSUM)

```
ARRAY OF DURATION FRACTIONS TO BE TOTALED --
3 / 7        8 / 9        4 / 9        2 / 1        6 / 9
10 / 10      7 / 4        9 / 10       4 / 3        10 / 4
6 / 9        1 / 9        10 / 4       7 / 10       7 / 4
4 / 2        3 / 2        5 / 7        1 / 6        9 / 7
9 / 9

TOTAL--
24 + 193 / 630
```

Purpose

Convert an array of decimal values (%) to fractions for use as rhythm durations.

Notes

Line 180 of the DRIVER PROGRAM fills array X( ) with decimal values which convert to relatively simple fractions. The reason for controlling decimal complexity is that some synthesizers reject fractional input smaller than 1/128th of a whole note; moreover, human perceptual limitations render extremely complex fractions useless—e.g., 121347/291385. The author sets the practical minimum duration for rhythm applications at 1/100th of a whole note because few people are able to discriminate rhythmic nuances beyond this point.

Programming Idea

Generate decimal note durations for a sequence of pitches; use computer music format (each decimal duration is printed, followed by the current total of durations in decimal to be interpreted as elapsed time). Plot the rhythm attack points and durations on graph paper, then transcribe the output to proportional graphic notation for performance by an acoustic musical instrument such as the flute.

Apply the numerators of the converted set of duration fractions as scalar values (measured in %) for the articulation or volume parameter of the piece; either map them directly or in random order.

Download the final data to a synthesizer, assign a flute timbre to the notelist, and play the electronic version.

Program Listing

```
100 REM ================================================================
110 REM                      DRIVER PROGRAM
120 REM                         (Decfrac)
130 REM ================================================================
140     DIM X(50),FRACTION$(50)
150     RANDOMIZE(22321)
160     TOTAL = 50 : PRINT "DECIMAL VALUE SEQUENCE --"
170        FOR J = 1 TO TOTAL
180           X(J)= (INT(RND * 99)+1)/100'<<< load decimal values
190           PRINT X(J),                  '<<< send to screen
200        NEXT J
210     PRINT : PRINT "SEQUENCE CONVERTED TO FRACTIONS --"
220     GOSUB 1000       '<<< call decimal to fraction conversion
230        FOR J = 1 TO TOTAL
240           PRINT FRACTION$(J),           '<<< send to screen
250        NEXT J
260 END
1000 REM =========================================== CTB1.20
1010 REM ********************>> DECFRAC <<********************
1020 REM ================================================================
```

```
1030 REM       This subroutine converts decimal values (%) to
1040 REM       fractions for use as rhythm durations.
1050 REM ======================================================
1060 REM
1070 REM                   Variable Descriptions
1080 REM
1090 REM     Entering -
1100 REM       X(): array of decimal values to be converted
1110 REM
1120 REM     Exiting -
1130 REM       FRACTION$(): character string array of fractions
1140 REM
1150 REM     Local -
1160 REM       B9: temporary storage of computation result
1170 REM       C9: holds integer computation result
1180 REM       D9: holds non-integer portion of decimal value
1190 REM       E9: temporary storage of real number result
1200 REM       F9: temporary storage of integer computation
1210 REM       K9: loop index, pointer to array X()
1220 REM ======================================================
1230     FOR K9 = 1 TO TOTAL
1240       B9= 0
1250       C9 = 1
1260       D9= ABS(X(K9)-INT(X(K9)))
1270       IF D9 = 0 THEN 1340
1280       E9 = 1 / D9
1290       F9 = C9
1300       C9 = INT(E9) * C9 + B9
1310       B9 = F9
1320       D9 = E9 - INT(E9)
1330       IF X(K9) * C9 <> INT(X(K9) * C9) THEN 1280
1340       FRACTION$(K9)=STR$(X(K9) * C9)+"/"+STR$(C9)
1350     NEXT K9
1360 RETURN
```

RUN (Decfrac)

DECIMAL VALUE SEQUENCE --

.17	.15	.77	.35	.75
.82	.69	.07	.42	.58
.32	.63	.58	.77	.99
.12	.82	.17	.7	.61
.7	.67	.99	.55	.73
.33	.1	.29	.64	.46
.33	.93	.93	.17	.73
.42	.61	.98	.97	.84
.2	.9	.45	.04	.03
.48	.72	.38	.73	.4

SEQUENCE CONVERTED TO FRACTIONS --

17/ 100	3/ 20	77/ 100	7/ 20	3/ 4
41/ 50	69/ 100	7/ 100	21/ 50	29/ 50
8/ 25	63/ 100	29/ 50	77/ 100	99/ 100
3/ 25	41/ 50	17/ 100	7/ 10	61/ 100
7/ 10	67/ 100	99/ 100	11/ 20	73/ 100
33/ 100	1/ 10	29/ 100	16/ 25	23/ 50
33/ 100	93/ 100	93/ 100	17/ 100	73/ 100
21/ 50	61/ 100	49/ 50	97/ 100	21/ 25
1/ 5	9/ 10	9/ 20	1/ 25	3/ 100
12/ 25	18/ 25	19/ 50	73/ 100	2/ 5

Purpose

Convert an array of fractional rhythm values to an array of decimal values for transference to other musical parameters.

Notes

You can translate a sequence of duration fractions—1/2, 3/7, 5/9, etc.—to decimal for mapping the rhythm parameter to another parameter. In mapping, one set of value relationships is applied at some transpositional level to another dimension of the musical texture. For instance, to map rhythm onto volume, convert the durations to decimal, then scale the decimal values to fall within the volume parameter limits. (To do this, multiply each decimal number by the correct scaling factor, then truncate the result to integer.)

Programming Idea

Generate an array of random-order, multivariant rhythm duration fractions. Convert the fractions to decimal form, then scale and truncate the values for application to the articulation parameter of a piece for a synthesizer or solo acoustic instrument.

Use the array contents, now converted and scaled, as pointers to the contents of other musical element arrays; e.g., generate the pitch, volume, and timbre parameters by applying the pointers in original or reverse order.

Program Listing

```
100 REM  ================================================================
110 REM                    DRIVER PROGRAM
115 REM                       (Fracdec)
120 REM  ================================================================
130      DIM X(50),Y(50),Z(50)
140      TOTAL = 50
160      RANDOMIZE(-12)
170        FOR J= 1 TO TOTAL
180           X(J) = INT(RND * TOTAL)+1      '<< random numerators
190           Y(J) = INT(RND * TOTAL)+1   '<< random denominators
200        NEXT J
210      GOSUB 1000           '<<< call fraction to decimal conversion
215      PRINT "FRACTION        DECIMAL VALUE"
220        FOR J = 1 TO TOTAL
230            PRINT X(J);"/";Y(J);"=";'<<send fraction to screen
240            PRINT Z(J)     '<<send decimal equivalent to screen
250        NEXT J
260      PRINT "SUM OF DURATIONS =";SUM;"WHOLE NOTES"
270 END
1000 REM  =============================================== CTB1.21
1010 REM  ******************>> FRACDEC  <<********************
1020 REM  ================================================================
1030 REM     This subroutine converts fractional values to
```

```
1040 REM     decimal for use in rhythmic applications. It also
1050 REM     computes the total of all durations in whole notes.
1060 REM ============================================================
1070 REM                 Variable Descriptions
1080 REM     Entering -
1090 REM       X(): array of fraction numerators
1100 REM       Y(): array of fraction denominators
1110 REM       TOTAL: number of fractions to be converted
1120 REM     Exiting -
1130 REM       Z(): array of decimal equivalents
1140 REM       SUM: sum of all durations in decimal
1150 REM     Local -
1160 REM       K9: loop index, pointer to arrays X(),Y()
1170 REM ============================================================
1180      SUM = 0
1190      FOR K9 = 1 TO TOTAL
1200         Z(K9) = X(K9) / Y(K9)      '<< load decimal equivalent
1210         SUM = SUM + Z(K9)
1220      NEXT K9
1230 RETURN
```

RUN (Fracdec)

```
FRACTION          DECIMAL VALUE
 50 / 16 = 3.125
 25 / 34 = .7352941
 15 / 28 = .5357143
 21 / 6 = 3.5
 28 / 15 = 1.866667
 45 / 45 = 1
 44 / 39 = 1.128205
 23 / 25 = .92
 26 / 36 = .7222222
 13 / 23 = .5652174
 37 / 49 = .755102
  2 / 34 = 5.882353E-02
 36 / 26 = 1.384615
 12 / 45 = .2666667
 44 / 31 = 1.419355
 16 / 36 = .4444445
 22 / 15 = 1.466667
 28 / 23 = 1.217391
  3 / 2 = 1.5
 39 / 35 = 1.114286
 48 / 38 = 1.263158
 29 / 34 = .8529412
  8 / 49 = .1632653
 35 / 12 = 2.916667
 49 / 14 = 3.5
 34 / 42 = .8095238
 42 / 3 = 14
 36 / 46 = .7826087
  9 / 19 = .4736842
 42 / 25 = 1.68
 44 / 14 = 3.142857
 14 / 45 = .3111111
 33 / 9 = 3.666667
  7 / 49 = .1428571
 44 / 29 = 1.517241
 10 / 15 = .6666667
```

```
26 / 50 = .52
9 / 43 = .2093023
26 / 11 = 2.363636
4 / 40 = .1
12 / 37 = .3243243
36 / 26 = 1.384615
13 / 20 = .65
42 / 2 = 21
16 / 23 = .6956522
2 / 28 = 7.142858E-02
36 / 35 = 1.028571
14 / 12 = 1.166667
35 / 45 = .7777778
25 / 18 = 1.388889
SUM OF DURATIONS = 91.29578 WHOLE NOTES
```

SUBROUTINE GROUP: DECBIDEC
○ Dec-Bin   CTB1.22
○ Bin-Dec   CTB1.23

Purpose

Convert an array of positive decimal integers to a character array of binary equivalents, and vice versa.

Notes

There are a number of significant compositional applications for binary numbers. A particularly accessible one is as note attack-point determinants within a subdivided metrical continuum. Bit patterns which represent numbers are interpreted as "on-off" signals for musical tones, normally in one of two modes—open or closed. In the open mode, a binary number is scanned from left to right. When a 1 is encountered, a tone is sounded, which may continue (if the user so chooses) until the next 1 is reached, at which point another note is attacked. In the closed mode, the instruction of each bit is literally adhered to: When a 1 is encountered, a note begins; it ends at the next bit, which will be either a new tone (1) or silence (0). Each bit of the number corresponds to a pulse unit predetermined by the composer, or to some other consistently assigned pattern.

For example, given the bit pattern 11001010, the pitches C# G Ab C, and a quarter-note pulse unit, the following relationship would be produced in the closed mode:

(R = Rest)

P(itch)	C#	G	R	R	Ab	R	C	R
R(hythm)	1/4	1/4	1/4	1/4	1/4	1/4	1/4	1/4

In the open mode, the same set of givens will produce:

P(itch)	C#	G	Ab	C
R(hythm)	1/4	3/4	1/2	1/2

Programming Idea

Write a program to apply binary numbers to the rhythm parameter using open and closed modes. Experiment with rules of your own for their application.

Program Listing

```
100 REM ============================================================
110 REM                     DRIVER PROGRAM
120 REM                      (DecBiDec)
130 REM ============================================================
```

```
140      DIM X(10),X$(10)
150      PRINT "AN ARRAY OF DECIMAL NUMBERS --"
160         FOR J = 1 TO 10
170            DECNUM = J * 10
180            X(J) = DECNUM                    '<< load decimal values
190            PRINT X(J),                           '<< send to screen
200         NEXT J
210      PRINT
220      PRINT "THE ARRAY CONVERTED TO BINARY NUMBERS --"
230      GOSUB 1000              '<< call decimal-to-binary conversion
240         FOR J = 1 TO 10
250            PRINT X$(J),                          '<< send to screen
260         NEXT J
270      PRINT
280      GOSUB 1250              '<< call binary-to-decimal conversion
290      PRINT "THE BINARY NUMBERS CONVERTED BACK TO DECIMAL --"
300         FOR J = 1 TO 10
310            PRINT X(J),                           '<< send to screen
320         NEXT J
330 END
1000 REM ================================================ CTB1.22
1010 REM *******************>> DEC-BIN <<*********************
1020 REM ================================================
1030 REM      This subroutine converts positive decimal integers
1040 REM      to their binary equivalents, which are placed in
1050 REM      a character array as successions of "0" and "1"
1060 REM      characters.
1070 REM ================================================
1080 REM                   Variable Descriptions
1090 REM      Entering -
1091 REM        X(): array holding decimal integers
1092 REM      Exiting -
1093 REM        X$(): array holding string representation of
1094 REM              binary numbers corresponding to decimal
1095 REM              integers.
1096 REM      Local -
1097 REM        P9: temporary version of decimal integer,
1098 REM            successively divided by 2.
1099 REM        Q9: quotient of P9/2
1100 REM        R9: remainder of X9/2
1101 REM        K9: loop index, pointer to array X$()
1110 REM ================================================
1120     FOR K9 = 1 TO 10
1130         P9=X(K9)
1140         BINUM$ = ""
1150         Q9 = P9
1160            WHILE Q9 > 0
1170               Q9=INT(P9/2)
1180               R9 = P9 - 2 * Q9
1190               BINUM$=MID$("01",R9+1,1)+BINUM$
1200               P9=Q9
1210            WEND
1220         X$(K9) = BINUM$
1230     NEXT K9
1240 RETURN
1250 REM ================================================ CTB1.23
1260 REM *******************>> BIN-DEC <<*********************
1270 REM ================================================
1280 REM      This subroutine converts binary numbers (stored as
1290 REM      character strings) to their decimal equivalents.
```

```
1300 REM      The INSTR function is used to ascertain the value
1310 REM      and location of each binary bit within the number
1320 REM      string. Line 1520 examines the first bit: if it
1330 REM      is "0" then DECNUM is set to 0; if it is "1",
1340 REM      DECNUM is 1. The remaining bits are scanned, and
1350 REM      as long as there is another bit, DECNUM is doubled
1360 REM      and a 1 or 0 is added to it.
1370 REM ==========================================================
1380 REM                  Variable Descriptions
1390 REM      Entering -
1400 REM        X$(): array of binary numbers stored as character
1410 REM              strings of 1s and 0s
1420 REM      Exiting -
1430 REM        X(): array of converted decimal integers
1440 REM      Local -
1450 REM        DECNUM: decimal integer
1460 REM        K9: loop index, pointer to array X()
1470 REM        L9: loop index
1480 REM ==========================================================
1490     FOR K9 = 1 TO 10
1500        DECNUM = 0
1510           FOR L9 = 1 TO LEN(X$(K9))
1520              DECNUM  = INSTR("01",MID$(X$(K9),L9,1)) - 1 +
DECNUM + DECNUM
1530           NEXT L9
1540           X(K9) = DECNUM
1550     NEXT K9
1560 RETURN
```

RUN (Decbidec)

```
AN ARRAY OF DECIMAL NUMBERS --
  10            20            30            40            50
  60            70            80            90           100

THE ARRAY CONVERTED TO BINARY NUMBERS --
1010          10100         11110         101000        110010
111100        1000110       1010000       1011010       1100100

THE BINARY NUMBERS CONVERTED BACK TO DECIMAL --
  10            20            30            40            50
  60            70            80            90           100
```

SUBROUTINE: Stirling

Purpose

To provide a "shortcut" method of calculating the factorial of an integer. Called Stirling's Approximation, the subroutine is used in statistical applications to compute probabilities, permutations, and combinations.

Notes

The algorithm computes factorials by approximating the natural logarithm for factorials greater than 10; for factorials smaller than 11, the exact log of *n!* is returned. It works quickly, and the degree of accuracy is sufficient for most situations.

Programming Ideas

See the programming ideas for the following two subroutine groups.

Program Listing

```
100 REM ============================================================
110 REM                        DRIVER PROGRAM
120 REM                          (Stirling)
130 REM ============================================================
140     FOR J = 9 TO 12
150         NUM = J
160         PRINT "INTEGER FOR WHICH FACTORIAL ";"WILL BE COMPUTED
IS";NUM
170         GOSUB 1000              '<< call Stirling's Approximation
180         PRINT "LOG OF FACTORIAL IS APPROXIMATELY";APPR
190         IF NUM < 34 THEN PRINT "FACTORIAL IS APPROXIMATELY";
INT(EXP(APPR)+.5)
200         PRINT
210     NEXT J
220     END
1000 REM ===================================================== CTB1.24
1010 REM *******************>> STIRLING <<********************
1020 REM ============================================================
1030 REM    Stirling's Approximation is useful in applications
1040 REM    which require calculation of probabilities, combi-
1050 REM    nations, and permutations.  The subroutine returns
1060 REM    the exact log of N factorial for values <= 10, and
1070 REM    returns the approximation of the log of n factorial
1080 REM    for values larger than 10.
1100 REM ============================================================
1110 REM                  Variable Descriptions
1120 REM    Entering -
1130 REM      NUM: integer for which factorial is to be computed
1140 REM    Exiting -
1150 REM      APPR: Stirling's Approximation of log of NUM
1160 REM    Local -
1170 REM      K9: loop index for factorial up to 10
1180 REM ============================================================
```

```
1190    APPR = 1
1200    IF NUM <= 0 THEN APPR = 0 : RETURN
1210       FOR K9 = 1 TO 10
1220          APPR = APPR * K9
1230          IF NUM = K9 THEN APPR = LOG(APPR) : RETURN
1240       NEXT K9
1250    APPR = LOG(6.283186)/2+LOG(NUM)*(NUM+.5)-NUM+1/(12*NUM)
1260 RETURN
```

RUN (Stirling)

```
INTEGER FOR WHICH FACTORIAL WILL BE COMPUTED IS 9
LOG OF FACTORIAL IS APPROXIMATELY 12.80183
FACTORIAL IS APPROXIMATELY 362880

INTEGER FOR WHICH FACTORIAL WILL BE COMPUTED IS 10
LOG OF FACTORIAL IS APPROXIMATELY 15.10441
FACTORIAL IS APPROXIMATELY 3628801

INTEGER FOR WHICH FACTORIAL WILL BE COMPUTED IS 11
LOG OF FACTORIAL IS APPROXIMATELY 17.50231
FACTORIAL IS APPROXIMATELY 3.991689E+07

INTEGER FOR WHICH FACTORIAL WILL BE COMPUTED IS 12
LOG OF FACTORIAL IS APPROXIMATELY 19.98722
FACTORIAL IS APPROXIMATELY 4.790015E+08
```

SUBROUTINE GROUP: PERMUTOT

- Permuts   CTB1.25
- Stirling   CTB1.24

Purpose

Compute the number of permutations (possible reorderings) of n elements taken m at a time.

Notes

Composers often wish to know the number of possible arrangements of a finite set of elements. This does not mean that all possibilities will be used within a particular composition; it is simply a point of departure for the decision-making process. In fact, a composition with all permutations of the one-octave chromatic pitch series—only 12 notes—would take a lifetime to compose and a second lifetime to perform. It would have 12! factorial—479,001,600—permutations.

The number of permutations of a given element set can be kept within human perceptual limits by taking fewer than the total number of elements at a time. For example, if one exploits all permutations of the 12-tone chromatic taken two at a time, the possibilities are reduced to 132.

Why do we need a subroutine to do this computation when a hand calculator will do the job? The answer is to provide information for the programmed structuring of data on higher organizational levels.

Programming Ideas

1) Write a program which feeds-back permutational information to an algorithm which exploits it to provide systematically permuted melodic pitch sets.

2) Write a program which "observes" various permutational possibilities of one randomly generated parameter (e.g., pitch), then returns that data to the program to control a second parameter.

Program Listing

```
100 REM =========================================================
110 REM                    DRIVER PROGRAM
120 REM                      (Permutot)
130 REM =========================================================
140    ELEMENTS = 1
150    MANY = 1
160       FOR J = 1 TO 10
170          GOSUB 1000                       '<< call permutations
180             PRINT "PERMUTATIONS OF";ELEMENTS;"THINGS TAKEN"
;MANY;"AT A TIME IS";PERMUTS
190             ELEMENTS= ELEMENTS+ 3
200             MANY = MANY + 2
```

```
210        NEXT J
220 END
1000 REM  ================================================== CTB1.25
1010 REM  *******************>> PERMUTS <<*******************
1020 REM  ==================================================
1030 REM      This subroutine computes the number of possible
1040 REM      permutations of n elements taken n at a time.
1050 REM      It relies on Stirling's Approximation to calculate
1060 REM      the requisite factorials.
1070 REM  ==================================================
1080 REM                  Variable Descriptions
1090 REM      Entering -
1100 REM        ELEMENTS: number of items
1110 REM        MANY: taken at a time
1120 REM      Exiting -
1130 REM        PERMUTS : permutation of ELEMENTS, taken MANY at
1140 REM                    a time
1150 REM      Local -
1160 REM        NUM:
1170 REM        ELEMFACT: log of ELEMENTS factorial
1180 REM        MANYFACT: log of MANY factorial
1190 REM  ==================================================
1200     NUM = ELEMENTS
1210     GOSUB 2000                    '<< call Stirling's Approximation
1220     ELEMFACT = APPR
1230     NUM = ELEMENTS - MANY
1240     GOSUB 2000                    '<< call Stirling's Approximation
1250     MANYFACT = APPR
1260     PERMUTS = INT(EXP(ELEMFACT-MANYFACT)+.5)
1270 RETURN
2000 REM  ================================================== CTB1.24
2010 REM  *******************>> STIRLING <<*******************
2020 REM  ==================================================
2030     APPR = 1
2040     IF NUM <= 0 THEN APPR = 0 : RETURN
2050        FOR K9 = 1 TO 10
2060           APPR = APPR * K9
2070           IF NUM = K9 THEN APPR = LOG(APPR) : RETURN
2080        NEXT K9
2090     APPR = LOG(6.283186)/2+LOG(NUM)*(NUM+.5)-NUM+1/(12*NUM)
2100 RETURN
```

RUN (PERMUTOT)

```
PERMUTATIONS OF 1 THINGS TAKEN 1 AT A TIME IS 1
PERMUTATIONS OF 4 THINGS TAKEN 3 AT A TIME IS 24
PERMUTATIONS OF 7 THINGS TAKEN 5 AT A TIME IS 2520
PERMUTATIONS OF 10 THINGS TAKEN 7 AT A TIME IS 604800
PERMUTATIONS OF 13 THINGS TAKEN 9 AT A TIME IS 2.594584E+08
PERMUTATIONS OF 16 THINGS TAKEN 11 AT A TIME IS 1.743566E+11
PERMUTATIONS OF 19 THINGS TAKEN 13 AT A TIME IS 1.689511E+14
PERMUTATIONS OF 22 THINGS TAKEN 15 AT A TIME IS 2.230148E+17
PERMUTATIONS OF 25 THINGS TAKEN 17 AT A TIME IS 3.847035E+20
PERMUTATIONS OF 28 THINGS TAKEN 19 AT A TIME IS 8.401887E+23
```

SUBROUTINE GROUP: COMBNTOT

  ◦ Combins   CTB1.26

  ◦ Stirling   CTB1.24

Purpose

  Computes the number of combinations of *n* elements taken *m* at a time. (The order of elements has no significance in combinations.)

Notes

  While permutations are arrangements of objects, combinations are simply selections. To illustrate, it is like asking, "How many different ways can a set of 12 pitches appear with a set of three rhythm durations?" (The answer is 220.) When you are interested only in the number of unique combinations of *n* elements taken *m* at a time, a vastly reduced set of possibilities is at hand, one which can be exploited *in toto* within the boundaries of a single composition.

  Suppose you wish to compose the pitch dimension of a process-oriented piece by generating random-order sets of six notes from the one-octave chromatic. Not considering permutations, there are only 924 different sets to be generated, each consisting of six notes, for a total of 5,544 pitches in the piece. (The maximum number of combinations for a given set of *n* elements occurs around the "taken *m*" midpoint, after which the number of combinations recedes as its complement modulo *n*; e.g., 12 elements taken seven at a time equals 792 unique combinations, as does 12 elements taken five at a time.)

Programming Idea

  Develop a program which will compute and file all the possible combinations of 12 elements after the user has selected the number to be taken at a time.

Program Listing

```
100 REM ============================================================
110 REM                        DRIVER PROGRAM
120 REM                         (Combntot)
130 REM ============================================================
140     ELEMENTS = 10
150     MANY = 2
160        FOR J = 1 TO 10
170           GOSUB 1000                        '<< call combinations
180                 PRINT  "COMBINATIONS  OF";ELEMENTS;"THINGS
TAKEN";MANY;"AT A TIME IS";COMBINS
190              ELEMENTS= ELEMENTS+ 3
200              MANY = MANY + 3
210        NEXT J
220 END
```

```
1000 REM ===================================================== CTB1.26
1010 REM *******************>> COMBINS <<***********************
1020 REM =====================================================
1030 REM     This subroutine computes the number of possible
1040 REM     combinations of n elements taken n at a time.
1050 REM     It relies on Stirling's Approximation to calculate
1060 REM     the requisite factorials.
1070 REM =====================================================
1080 REM                  Variable Descriptions
1090 REM     Entering -
1100 REM       ELEMENTS: number of items
1110 REM       MANY: taken at a time
1120 REM     Exiting -
1130 REM       COMBINS : combination of ELEMENTS, taken MANY at
1140 REM                 a time
1150 REM     Local -
1160 REM       NUM:
1170 REM       ELEMFACT: log of ELEMENTS factorial
1180 REM       MANYFACT: log of MANY factorial
1190 REM       DIFFACT : log of (ELEMFACT - MANYFACT) factorial
1200 REM =====================================================
1210     NUM = ELEMENTS
1220     GOSUB 2000                    '<< call Stirling's Approximation
1230     ELEMFACT = APPR
1240     NUM = MANY
1250     GOSUB 2000                    '<< call Stirling's Approximation
1260     MANYFACT = APPR
1270     NUM = ELEMENTS - MANY
1280     GOSUB 2000                    '<< call Stirling's Approximation
1290     DIFFACT = APPR
1300     COMBINS = INT(EXP(ELEMFACT-(MANYFACT+DIFFACT))+.5)
1310 RETURN
2000 REM ===================================================== CTB1.24
2010 REM *******************>> STIRLING <<*********************
2020 REM =====================================================
2030     APPR = 1
2040     IF NUM <= 0 THEN APPR = 0 : RETURN
2050       FOR K9 = 1 TO 10
2060         APPR = APPR * K9
2070         IF NUM = K9 THEN APPR = LOG(APPR) : RETURN
2080       NEXT K9
2090     APPR = LOG(6.283186)/2+LOG(NUM)*(NUM+.5)-NUM+1/(12*NUM)
2100 RETURN
```

RUN (Combntot)

```
COMBINATIONS OF 10 THINGS TAKEN 2 AT A TIME IS 45
COMBINATIONS OF 13 THINGS TAKEN 5 AT A TIME IS 1287
COMBINATIONS OF 16 THINGS TAKEN 8 AT A TIME IS 12870
COMBINATIONS OF 19 THINGS TAKEN 11 AT A TIME IS 75582
COMBINATIONS OF 22 THINGS TAKEN 14 AT A TIME IS 319769
COMBINATIONS OF 25 THINGS TAKEN 17 AT A TIME IS 1081578
COMBINATIONS OF 28 THINGS TAKEN 20 AT A TIME IS 3108093
COMBINATIONS OF 31 THINGS TAKEN 23 AT A TIME IS 7888647
COMBINATIONS OF 34 THINGS TAKEN 26 AT A TIME IS 1.815634E+07
COMBINATIONS OF 37 THINGS TAKEN 29 AT A TIME IS 3.860861E+07
```

SUBROUTINE GROUP: HISTO

○ Freqtabl   CTB1.27

○ Bargraph   CTB1.28

Purpose

Display the pattern produced by quantifying one attribute of a data set. (In this particular case, the random-number occurrence frequency is tabulated.)

Notes

Use a bargraph to represent any quantifiable musical dimension about which information is needed. It is coupled with Freqtabl (CTB1.27) in this subroutine for the purpose of testing random-number generator uniformity which varies according to the input start seed and the number of samples generated.

Normally, composers don't require the direct application of a large enough group of random numbers to assure uniform distribution, so it is important to experiment with various seed values to learn their influence over short-term data distributions.

A histogram also enhances analytic insight for musical parameter characteristics. Melody, rhythm, and volume data-shaping are directly experienced, thereby speeding the pattern identification process.

Programming Ideas

1) Write a program which generates a collection of random integers, displays the occurrence frequency distribution, then displays the shape of the sequence in the order it was generated.

2) Write a program which provides a graphic display of integers generated by Subroutine Group CURVES.

Program Listing

```
100 REM  ==========================================================
110 REM                    DRIVER PROGRAM
120 REM                      (Histo)
130 REM  ==========================================================
140      DIM X(20)
150      RANGE = 20              '<< set random number range 1-20
160      TOTAL = 400                    '<< return 400 values
170      RANDOMIZE(956)
180      GOSUB 1000                '<< generate frequency table
190      GOSUB 2000                 '<< call bargraph display
200 END
1000 REM ================================================= CTB1.27
1010 REM ******************>> FREQTABL <<***********************
1020 REM ==========================================================
1030 REM     This subroutine computes a table of occurrence
1040 REM     frequency for each value generated during a run.
```

```
1050 REM =========================================================
1060 REM                     Variable Descriptions
1070 REM        Entering -
1080 REM          TOTAL: number of samples to return
1090 REM          RANGE: numeric range of samples
1100 REM        Exiting -
1110 REM          X(): array holding frequency table
1120 REM        Local -
1130 REM          VALUE: random integer, pointer to array X()
1140 REM          K9: loop index
1150 REM =========================================================
1160     FOR K9 = 1 TO TOTAL
1170             VALUE = INT(RND * RANGE)+1      '<< gen random value
1180             X(VALUE)=X(VALUE)+1  '<< record occurrence of value
1190     NEXT K9
1200 RETURN
2000 REM ============================================= CTB1.28
2010 REM *****************>> BARGRAPH <<**********************
2020 REM =========================================================
2030 REM     This procedural subroutine prints a simple
2040 REM     bargraph.
2070 REM =========================================================
2080 REM                     Variable Descriptions
2090 REM        Entering -
2100 REM          X(): occurence frequency table,
2110 REM               address = random number,
2120 REM               contents = frequency of occurance
2130 REM          RANGE: range of integer values in table
2140 REM        Exiting -
2150 REM          none (subroutine is procedural)
2160 REM        Local -
2170 REM          K9: loop index, pointer to frequency table
2180 REM =========================================================
2190     FOR K9 = 1 TO RANGE
2200         PRINT K9;TAB(10);STRING$(X(K9),">")
2210     NEXT K9
2220 RETURN
```

RUN (Histo)

```
1        >>>>>>>>>>>>>>>>>>
2        >>>>>>>>>>
3        >>>>>>>>>>>>>>>>>>>>>>
4        >>>>>>>>>>>>>>>>>>>
5        >>>>>>>>>>>>>>>>>>>
6        >>>>>>>>>>>>>>>>>
7        >>>>>>>>>>>>>>>>
8        >>>>>>>>>>>>>>>>>>>>>>>>
9        >>>>>>>>>>>>>>>>>>>>>>>
10       >>>>>>>>>>>>>>>>>>>>>>>>
11       >>>>>>>>>>>>>>>>
12       >>>>>>>>>>>>>>>>>>>>>>
13       >>>>>>>>>>>>>>>>>>>>>>>>>>>>>>>
14       >>>>>>>>>>>>>>>>>
15       >>>>>>>>>>>>>>>>>>>>>>>>>>
16       >>>>>>>>>>>>>>>
17       >>>>>>>>>>>>>>>>
18       >>>>>>>>>>>>>>>>>>
19       >>>>>>>>>>>>>>>>>>>
20       >>>>>>>>>>>>>>>>>>>>
```

SUBROUTINE: Grafplot

Purpose

Compute and display functions involving two interdependent parameters. Scale input data so that any set of positive or negative data, of any range, may be graphed without concern for compression or expansion.

Notes

Musical waveforms are examples of periodic functions. A sine tone, which contains only one partial, is the simplest form of harmonic motion, and is represented by the RUN of this subroutine.

Complex waveforms are defined by the frequency, amplitude, and phase-angle of the individual sine waves which comprise them. X-Y coordinate graphs help us visualize sounds when we design new timbres; they also help us understand complicated relationships within a sound.

Of course, you can use Grafplot for many other display purposes as well. (See Subroutine Group LINEFIT, CTB1.36 and CTB1.37.)

Programming Idea

Write a program to display complex waveforms. Allow the user to input values for the number, amplitude, and phase-angle of each wave component. Limit the maximum number of wave partials to 5.

Program Listing

```
100 REM ================================================================
110 REM                         DRIVER PROGRAM
120 REM                          (Grafplot)
130 REM ================================================================
140     DIM X(50),Y(50)
150     SUM = 0
160     TOTAL = 21            '<< num of array elements in X() + Y()
170     C$ = "o"                        '<< character for graph
180       FOR J = 1 TO TOTAL
190           X(J) = SUM                  '<< load x-axis array
200           Y(J) = SIN(X(J))            '<< load y-axis array
210           SUM = SUM + .314159
220         NEXT J
230     PRINT "0 <= x <= 2pi : sin(x)"
240     GOSUB 1000                        '<< call x-y graph plotting
250 END
1000 REM ==================================================== CTB1.29
1010 REM *******************>> GRAFPLOT <<*********************
1020 REM ================================================================
1030 REM     This subroutine produces an X-Y line graph of
1040 REM     two interdependent parameters (e.g., musical waveform
1050 REM     cycle over a time period).  It performs its own
1060 REM     scaling, which means that any set of data, positive
1070 REM     negative, of any range, may be graphed without
1080 REM     concern for compression or expansion.
```

```
1090 REM ============================================================
1100 REM                  Variable Descriptions
1110 REM      Entering -
1120 REM        X(): array holding the x-axis elements
1130 REM        Y(): array holding the y-axis elements
1140 REM        TOTAL : number of elements in arrays X(),Y()
1150 REM        C$ : plotting character
1160 REM      Exiting -
1170 REM        none    (subroutine is procedural)
1180 REM      Local -
1190 REM        LOWVAL: lowest value in array Y()
1200 REM        HIGHVAL: highest value in array Y()
1210 REM        SCDISP: scale displacement between LOWVAL,HIGHVAL
1220 REM        LEFTDISP: leftmargin displacement for X position
1230 REM        K9: loop index, pointer to arrays X(),Y()
1240 REM ============================================================
1250     LOWVAL = Y(1)
1260     HIGHVAL = Y(1)
1270       FOR K9 = 2 TO TOTAL
1280           IF Y(K9) < LOWVAL THEN LOWVAL = Y(K9)
1290           IF Y(K9) < HIGHVAL THEN HIGHVAL = Y(K9)
1300       NEXT K9
1310     SCDISP = HIGHVAL - LOWVAL
1320     IF SCDISP = 0 THEN SCDISP = 1
1330       FOR K9 = 1 TO TOTAL
1340           LEFTDISP = INT(1+(Y(K9)-LOWVAL) / SCDISP * 20+.5)
1350           PRINT X(K9);TAB(15 + LEFTDISP);C$
1360       NEXT K9
1370 RETURN
```

RUN (Grafplot)

```
0 <= x <= 2pi : sin(x)
 0                                      o
 .314159                                    o
 .628318                                       o
 .942477                                        o
 1.256636                                         o
 1.570795                                          o
 1.884954                                         o
 2.199113                                       o
 2.513272                                     o
 2.827431                                  o
 3.14159                                o
 3.455749                            o
 3.769908                         o
 4.084067                       o
 4.398226                     o
 4.712385                    o
 5.026544                    o
 5.340703                     o
 5.654862                       o
 5.969021                          o
 6.283179                             o
```

SUBROUTINE GROUP: NORMHIST

- ○ Freqtabl   CTB1.27
- ○ Datanorm   CTB1.30
- ○ Bargraph   CTB1.28

Purpose

Test probability distribution functions for applicability to specific musical parameters.

Notes

To adequately test probability distribution functions, a characteristic curve must be produced by generating many samples. While we don't wish to view a detailed graph of the distribution, we do need to observe the curve's shape for comparison to the function ideal. Therefore, we must normalize data (often thousands of items) to fit within a viewable CRT range. Consequently, the displayed graph will represent each value generated during program execution, but individual bars will reflect normalization (range 0 to 1) of the integer at hand.

Programming Idea

Modify the DRIVER PROGRAM to generate data by the application of subroutines from chapter 3.

Program Listing

```
100 REM =======================================================
110 REM                     DRIVER PROGRAM
120 REM                     (Normhist)
130 REM =======================================================
140     DIM X(20)
150     RANGE = 20               '<< set random number range 1-20
160     TOTAL = 1000                    '<< return 1000 values
170     RANDOMIZE(-273)
190     PRINT "INTEGER VALUE";TAB(20); "NORM. VALUE";TAB(40);"BAR
MAP"
200     GOSUB 1000                      '<< generate frequency table
210     GOSUB 2000                      '<< call data normalization
220     GOSUB 3000                      '<< call bargraph display
230 END
1000 REM ================================================ CTB1.27
1010 REM ******************>> FREQTABL <<*********************
1020 REM =======================================================
1030     FOR K9 = 1 TO TOTAL
1040            VALUE = INT(RND * RANGE)+1      '<< gen random value
1050            X(VALUE)=X(VALUE)+1  '<< record occurrence of value
1060     NEXT K9
1070 RETURN
2000 REM ================================================ CTB1.30
```

```
2010 REM ********************>> DATANORM <<********************
2020 REM ========================================================
2030 REM      This subroutine compresses wide-range data to
2040 REM      fit within the range of 0 to 1. It is especially
2050 REM      helpful when printing histograms of huge amounts
2060 REM      of data which would otherwise cause the bars to
2070 REM      wrap-around the screen.
2150 REM ========================================================
2160 REM                  Variable Descriptions
2170 REM      Entering -
2180 REM        X(): frequency table to be normalized
2190 REM        RANGE: range of integers in frequency table
2200 REM      Exiting -
2210 REM        X(): normalized frequency table
2220 REM      Local -
2230 REM        SUM: total of values frequency table
2240 REM        K9: loop index,pointer to array X()
2250 REM ========================================================
2260    SUM = 0
2270       FOR K9 = 1 TO RANGE
2280          SUM = SUM + X(K9)
2290       NEXT K9
2300       FOR K9=1 TO RANGE
2310          X(K9) = X(K9)/ SUM
2320       NEXT K9
2330   PRINT
2340   RETURN
3000 REM ================================================= CTB1.28
3010 REM ******************>> BARGRAPH <<********************
3020 REM                 (adapted to program specs)
3030 REM ========================================================
3040    FOR K9=1 TO RANGE
3050       MAP = INT(100*X(K9)+.5)
3060       PRINT K9;"=";TAB(20);X(K9);TAB(40);STRING$(MAP,">")
3070    NEXT K9
3080 RETURN
```

RUN (Normhist)

INTEGER VALUE	NORM. VALUE	BAR MAP
1 =	.044	>>>>
2 =	.052	>>>>>
3 =	.04	>>>>
4 =	.05	>>>>>
5 =	.041	>>>>
6 =	.055	>>>>>>
7 =	.051	>>>>>
8 =	.058	>>>>>>
9 =	.049	>>>>>
10 =	.047	>>>>>
11 =	.045	>>>>>
12 =	.057	>>>>>>
13 =	.046	>>>>>
14 =	.052	>>>>>
15 =	.058	>>>>>>
16 =	.053	>>>>>
17 =	.049	>>>>>
18 =	.058	>>>>>>
19 =	.048	>>>>>
20 =	.047	>>>>>

SUBROUTINE GROUP: STATS

○ Freqtabl	CTB1.27
○ Bargraph	CTB1.28
○ Maxval	CTB1.31
○ Minval	CTB1.32
○ Mean	CTB1.33
○ Variance	CTB1.34
○ Stdev	CTB1.35

Purpose

Ascertain statistical characteristics of a data set for use in analytic-synthetic procedures.

Notes

There are a number of important applications of this subroutine group to musical parameter data. To name a few:

- The analysis of probability distribution functions for conformity to idealized curves.
- The development and testing of algorithms.
- Channeling run-time intelligence to other program subroutines.

Programming Ideas

Devise a hypothetical probability distribution function—sheer speculation is fine! Plug it into a driver program, include Subroutine Group STATS, and gather intelligence about the function. Adjust the function parameters to coincide closely with your goals.

Program Listing

```
100 REM ==============================================================
110 REM                      DRIVER PROGRAM
120 REM                        (Stats)
130 REM ==============================================================
140     DIM X(200),Y(15)'<< sequence array, frequency table array
150     RANGE = 15              '<< set random number range 1-15
160     TOTAL = 200                     '<< return 200 values
170     RANDOMIZE(213)
180     GOSUB 1000  '<< generate sequence array & frequency table
190     GOSUB 2000                      '<< call bargraph display
200     GOSUB 3000           '<< call statistical mode (maxval)
210     GOSUB 4000           '<< call least frequent (minval)
220     GOSUB 5000                  '<< call arithmetic mean
230     GOSUB 6000               '<< call statistical variance
240     GOSUB 7000               '<< call standard deviation
```

```
 250 END
1000 REM ==================================================== CTB1.27
1010 REM ******************>> FREQTABL <<************************
1020 REM ====================================================
1030     FOR K9 = 1 TO TOTAL
1040          VALUE = INT(RND * RANGE)+1     '<< gen random value
1050          X(K9) = VALUE                  '<< load sequence array
1060          Y(VALUE)=Y(VALUE)+1  '<< record occurrence of value
1070     NEXT K9
1080 RETURN
2000 REM ==================================================== CTB1.28
2010 REM ******************>> BARGRAPH <<************************
2020 REM ====================================================
2030     FOR K9 = 1 TO RANGE
2040        PRINT K9;TAB(10);STRING$(Y(K9),">")
2050     NEXT K9
2060 RETURN
3000 REM ==================================================== CTB1.31
3010 REM ********************>> MAXVAL <<************************
3020 REM ====================================================
3030 REM      This subroutine finds the statistical mode of
3040 REM      a collection of values. It scans the integer
3050 REM      frequency table, then records the address and
3060 REM      number of occurrence of the most frequent value(s).
3070 REM ====================================================
3080 REM                 Variable Descriptions
3090 REM      Entering -
3100 REM       Y(): occurrence frequency table
3110 REM       RANGE: range of integer values in table
3120 REM      Exiting -
3130 REM       none   (subroutine is procedural)
3140 REM      Local -
3150 REM       MAX: statistical mode
3160 REM       K9: loop index, pointer to frequency table
3170 REM ====================================================
3180     MAX = Y(1)
3190      FOR K9 = 2 TO RANGE
3200         IF MAX < Y(K9) THEN MAX = Y(K9)
3210      NEXT K9
3220      FOR K9 = 1 TO RANGE
3230          IF Y(K9) = MAX THEN PRINT "THE INTEGER";K9;  ":
MODE;";" FREQ =";MAX
3240      NEXT K9
3250 RETURN
4000 REM ==================================================== CTB1.32
4010 REM ******************>> MINVAL <<*************************
4020 REM ====================================================
4030 REM      This subroutine scans the occurrence frequency
4040 REM      table, then records the address and number of
4050 REM      occurrences of the least frequent value.
4060 REM ====================================================
4070 REM                 Variable Descriptions
4080 REM      Entering -
4090 REM       Y(): occurrence frequency table
4100 REM       RANGE: range of integer values in table
4110 REM      Exiting -
4120 REM       none   (subroutine is procedural)
4130 REM      Local -
4140 REM       MIN: least frequent integer
4150 REM       K9: loop index, pointer to array Y()
```

```
4160 REM ==============================================================
4170    MIN = Y(1)
4180       FOR K9 = 2 TO RANGE
4190          IF MIN > Y(K9) THEN MIN = Y(K9)
4200       NEXT K9
4210       FOR K9 = 1 TO RANGE
4220          IF Y(K9) = MIN THEN PRINT "THE INTEGER";K9; " =
LEAST FREQUENT;";" FREQ =";MIN
4230       NEXT K9
4240 RETURN
5000 REM ============================================== CTB1.33
5010 REM *********************>> MEAN <<***********************
5020 REM ==============================================================
5030 REM     This subroutine finds the arithmetic mean of
5040 REM     a sample collection.
5050 REM ==============================================================
5060 REM                 Variable Descriptions
5070 REM     Entering -
5080 REM      TOTAL: length of sequence
5090 REM     Exiting -
5100 REM      none   (subroutine is procedural)
5110 REM     Local -
5120 REM      SUM: sum of sequence values
5130 REM      MEAN: arithmetic mean of values
5140 REM      K9: loop index, pointer to sequence array X()
5150 REM ==============================================================
5160    SUM = 0
5170       FOR K9 = 1 TO TOTAL
5180          SUM = SUM + X(K9)
5190       NEXT K9
5200    MEAN = SUM / TOTAL
5210    PRINT "MEAN =";MEAN;" ";
5220 RETURN
6000 REM ============================================== CTB1.34
6010 REM ******************>> VARIANCE <<**********************
6020 REM ==============================================================
6030 REM     This subroutine computes statistical variance of
6040 REM     a collection of samples.
6050 REM ==============================================================
6060 REM                 Variable Descriptions
6070 REM     Entering -
6080 REM      TOTAL: length of sequence
6090 REM      MEAN: arithmetic mean of sequence values
6100 REM     Exiting -
6110 REM      none   (subroutine is procedural)
6120 REM     Local -
6130 REM      VARIANCE: statistical variance
6140 REM      TEMP: temporary storage of computation
6150 REM      K9: loop index, pointer to sequence array X()
6160 REM ==============================================================
6170    VARIANCE = 0
6180       FOR K9 = 1 TO TOTAL
6190          TEMP = (X(K9) - MEAN) ^ 2
6200          VARIANCE = VARIANCE + TEMP
6210       NEXT K9
6220    VARIANCE = VARIANCE / (TOTAL - 1)
6230    PRINT "VARIANCE = ";VARIANCE
6240 RETURN
7000 REM ============================================== CTB1.35
7010 REM ******************>> STDEV <<**********************
```

```
7020 REM ========================================================
7030 REM      This subroutine computes standard deviation and
7040 REM      standard error of the mean.
7050 REM ========================================================
7060 REM                   Variable Descriptions
7070 REM      Entering -
7080 REM        VARIANCE: statistical variance
7090 REM      Exiting -
7100 REM        none     (subroutine is procedural)
7110 REM      Local -
7120 REM        DEV: standard deviation
7130 REM        STDERR: standard error of the mean
7140 REM ========================================================
7150      DEV = SQR(VARIANCE)
7160      STDERR = DEV / SQR(TOTAL)
7170      PRINT "STANDARD DEVIATION = ";DEV
7180      PRINT "STANDARD ERROR OF THE MEAN = ";STDERR
7190 RETURN
```

RUN (STATS)

```
1        >>>>>>>>>>>>>>>>
2        >>>>>>>>>>>>>
3        >>>>>>>
4        >>>>>>>>>>>
5        >>>>>>>>>>>>
6        >>>>>>>>>>>>
7        >>>>>>>>>>
8        >>>>>>>>>>>>>>>>>>>
9        >>>>>>>>>>
10       >>>>>>>>>>>>>>>>>>>>
11       >>>>>>>>>>>>>>>>>
12       >>>>>>>>>>>>
13       >>>>>>>>>>>>>>
14       >>>>>>>>>>>>>>>>
15       >>>>>>>>>>>
THE INTEGER 10 = MODE; FREQ = 20
THE INTEGER 3  = LEAST FREQUENT; FREQ = 7
MEAN = 8.18   VARIANCE =  18.55036
STANDARD DEVIATION =  4.307013
STANDARD ERROR OF THE MEAN =  .3045518
```

SUBROUTINE GROUP: LINEGEN

- ○ Linefit   CTB1.36
- ○ Grafplot   CTB1.29

Purpose

Compute and display a straight line that represents the directional tendency of a random-order collection of pitch, rhythm, or volume parameter data.

Notes

Linefit (CTB1.36) is the Linear Least Squares Fit algorithm. It is used in business trend analyses to predict the future behavior of the stock market, sales, profits, etc.

Applied to the musical elements, the algorithm gives a quick look at data sequence directionality for testing function arguments and random-number generator seeds. The most obvious parameter to lineate is pitch, but you will find additional uses for it.

Programming Ideas

Generate an array of random integers scaled for application to the pitch parameter. Run the array through the Linefit subroutine and consider the musical consequences of assigning the data to pitches. If undesirable as pitches, rescale the data first as rhythm durations, then as volume data.

Program Listing

```
100 REM ==================================================
110 REM                   DRIVER PROGRAM
120 REM                     (Linegen)
130 REM ==================================================
140    DIM X(100),Y(100)
150    RANDOMIZE(-2438)
160    C$ = "o"                            '<< character for graph
170    TOTAL = 50
180    PRINT TOTAL;"RANDOM NUMBERS"
190    PRINT
200       FOR J = 1 TO TOTAL
210          X(J)=J                         '<< data point ordinate
220          Y(J)= INT(RND * 88) + 1     '<< data point coordinate
230          PRINT Y(J),                '<< random-order data to screen
240       NEXT J
250    GOSUB 1000                     '<< call linear least squares fit
260    PRINT
270    PRINT "STRAIGHT LINE THAT BEST FITS THE DATA:"
280    PRINT
290    PRINT "Y=";SLOPE;"X";
300    IF INTERCEPT < 0 THEN PRINT "-";ELSE PRINT "+";
310    PRINT ABS(INTERCEPT)
```

```
320          FOR K9 = 1 TO TOTAL     '<< scale line for graph plotting
330              Y(K9) = SLOPE * K9 + INTERCEPT
340          NEXT K9
350       GOSUB 2000                          '<< call x-y graph plot
360 END
1000 REM ================================================= CTB1.36
1010 REM ******************>> LINEFIT <<********************
1020 REM =================================================
1030 REM      This subroutine calculates the equation of the
1040 REM      straight line that best fits a set of data.
1050 REM      Its proper name is the Linear Least Squares Fit.
1100 REM =================================================
1110 REM                      Variable Descriptions
1120 REM      Entering-
1130 REM        X(): array of ordinate increments
1140 REM        Y(): array of random integers for coordinate
1150 REM        TOTAL: number of data points
1160 REM      Exiting -
1170 REM        SLOPE: slope of linear least squares fit
1180 REM        INTERCEPT: (coordinate) intercept of linear least
1190 REM                     squares fit line
1200 REM      Local -
1210 REM        XERR: sum of X errors
1220 REM        XSQERR: sum of X-squared errors
1230 REM        YERR: sum of Y errors
1240 REM        XYPRODERR: sum of X-Y (cross-product) errors
1250 REM        K9: loop index, pointer to X(),Y()
1260 REM =================================================
1270      XERR = 0
1280      XSQERR = 0
1290      YERR = 0
1300      XYPRODERR = 0
1310         FOR K9 = 1 TO TOTAL
1320             XERR = XERR + X(K9)
1330             XSQERR = XSQERR + X(K9) ^ 2
1340             YERR = YERR + Y(K9)
1350             XYPRODERR = XYPRODERR + X(K9) * Y(K9)
1360         NEXT K9
1370      SLOPE=(TOTAL * XYPRODERR - XERR * YERR) / (TOTAL * XSQERR
 - XERR ^ 2)
1380      INTERCEPT = (XSQERR * YERR - XERR * XYPRODERR) / (TOTAL *
XSQERR - XERR ^ 2)
1390 RETURN
2000 REM ================================================= CTB1.29
2010 REM ******************>> GRAFPLOT <<*******************
2020 REM =================================================
2030      LOWVAL = Y(1)
2040      HIGHVAL = Y(1)
2050         FOR K9 = 2 TO TOTAL
2060             IF Y(K9) < LOWVAL THEN LOWVAL = Y(K9)
2070             IF Y(K9) < HIGHVAL THEN HIGHVAL = Y(K9)
2080         NEXT K9
2090      SCDISP = HIGHVAL - LOWVAL
2100      IF SCDISP = 0 THEN SCDISP = 1
2110         FOR K9 = 1 TO TOTAL
2120             LEFTDISP = INT(1+(Y(K9)-LOWVAL) / SCDISP * 2+.5)
2130             PRINT X(K9);TAB(5+LEFTDISP);C$
2140         NEXT K9
2150 RETURN
```

RUN (Linegen)

50 RANDOM NUMBERS

61	36	46	49	67
78	25	88	47	54
25	64	41	65	35
11	19	74	18	53
36	59	69	79	53
5	84	61	54	12
52	34	88	73	25
21	71	43	24	58
57	78	46	70	80
39	13	29	25	53

STRAIGHT LINE THAT BEST FITS THE DATA:

Y=-9.330132E-02 X+ 51.31918
```
 1                 o
 2                 o
 3                 o
 4                  o
 5                o
 6                o
 7                o
 8                o
 9                o
10              o
11              o
12              o
13              o
14              o
15              o
16             o
17             o
18             o
19             o
20             o
21           o
22           o
23           o
24           o
25           o
26          o
27          o
28          o
29          o
30          o
31          o
32         o
33         o
34         o
35         o
36         o
37        o
38        o
39        o
40        o
41        o
```

```
42    o
43    o
44    o
45    o
46    o
47    o
48  o
49  o
50  o
```

2
Series and Motive Operations

SUBROUTINE GROUP: MOTFORMS

- Pitchtab   CTB1.3
- Matprint   CTB1.6
- Motretro   CTB2.1
- Motinvrt   CTB2.2
- Motrnpz   CTB2.3

Purpose

Process pitch sequences (motifs) of varying lengths by any of three standard methods:

1) Retrograde order
2) Intervallic inversion
3) Intervallic transposition

Notes

The DRIVER PROGRAM variable TOTAL can be changed to accommodate any length sequence, but the array dimension statement in Line 140 must also be altered accordingly.

Take care to prevent an overrun of the pitch element table range limits when modifying the driver program to allow for user input of melodic sequences. To prevent program failure, insert additional code to reset output data within pitch limits if an overrun occurs.

Programming Ideas

1) Convert the DRIVER PROGRAM to an interactive main routine; i.e., allow the user to input pitch sequences and to select program options.

2) Alter the program to read pitch data from a source file, process the data in various ways, then send the output to a destination file.

Program Listing

```
100 REM ==============================================================
110 REM                     DRIVER PROGRAM
120 REM                        (Motforms)
130 REM ==============================================================
140     DIM X(15),Y(15),P$(84)
150     RANDOMIZE(967)
160     GOSUB 1000                          '<< call pitch table
170     TOTAL = 15
180     PRINT "ORIGINAL PITCH MOTIF --"
190        FOR J = 1 TO TOTAL
200            X(J) = INT(RND * 12) + 1
210            PRINT P$(X(J));" ";        '<< random motif to screen
220        NEXT J
230     PRINT
240     GOSUB 3000                             '<< call retrograde
250     PRINT "THE RETROGRADE MOTIF --"
260     GOSUB 2000                             '<< call table print
270     PRINT
280     GOSUB 4000                          '<< call motif inversion
290     PRINT "THE INVERTED MOTIF --"
300     GOSUB 2000                             '<< call table print
310     PRINT
320     INTVAL = 1                      '<< (set transposition interval
330     PRINT "ORIGINAL MOTIF TRANSPOSITIONS"
340        FOR J = 1 TO 11
350            PRINT "NUMBER ";J
360            GOSUB 5000               '<< call motif transposition
370            GOSUB 2000                       '<< call table print
380            PRINT
390            INTVAL = INTVAL + 1
400        NEXT J
410 END
1000  REM ================================================ CTB1.3
1010  REM ******************>> PITCHTAB <<*******************
1020  REM ================================================
1030      NOTE$ = " CC# DD# E FF# GG# AA# B"
1040      OCTAVE$ = "1234567"
1050         FOR K9 = 1 TO 7
1060            FOR L9 = 1 TO 12
1070               P$(L9+(K9-1)*12)    =    MID$(NOTE$,(L9*2-1),2)
+MID$(OCTAVE$,K9,1)
1080            NEXT L9
```

```
1090        NEXT K9
1100    RETURN
2000 REM ================================================ CTB1.6
2010 REM *******************>> MATPRINT <<*********************
2020 REM ================================================
2030        FOR K9 = 1 TO TOTAL
2040            PRINT P$(Y(K9));" ";
2050        NEXT K9
2060 RETURN
3000 REM ================================================ CTB2.1
3010 REM *******************>> MOTRETRO <<*******************
3020 REM ================================================
3030 REM     This subroutine accepts an input pitch sequence
3040 REM     and outputs its retrograde form.
3050 REM ================================================
3060 REM                 Variable Descriptions
3070 REM     Entering -
3080 REM       X(): prime motif array
3090 REM       TOTAL: motif length
3100 REM     Exiting -
3110 REM       Y(): retrograde motif array
3120 REM     Local -
3130 REM       L: pointer to Y()
3140 REM       K9; loop index, pointer to X()
3150 REM ================================================
3160    FOR K9 = 1 TO TOTAL
3170        L = TOTAL-K9+1
3180        Y(L)=X(K9)
3190    NEXT K9
3200 RETURN
4000 REM ================================================ CTB2.2
4010 REM *******************>> MOTINVRT <<*******************
4020 REM ================================================
4030 REM     This subroutine accepts an input pitch sequence
4040 REM     and outputs its mirror-image form.
4050 REM ================================================
4060 REM                 Variable Descriptions
4070 REM     Entering -
4080 REM       X(): prime motif array
4090 REM       TOTAL: motif length
4100 REM     Exiting -
4110 REM       Y(): inverted motif array
4120 REM     Local -
4130 REM       K9: loop index, pointer to X(),Y()
4140 REM ================================================
4150    Y(1)=X(1)
4160        FOR K9 = 2 TO TOTAL
4170            Y(K9) = Y(K9-1)-(X(K9)-X(K9-1))
4180        NEXT K9
4190 RETURN
5000 REM ================================================ CTB2.3
5010 REM *******************>> MOTRNPZ <<*******************
5020 REM ================================================
5030 REM     This subroutine transposes an input motif by
5040 REM     a specified number of 1/2-steps. Transposition
5050 REM     direction is determined by the sign of the
5060 REM     transposition interval.
5070 REM ================================================
5080 REM                 Variable Descriptions
5090 REM       Entering -
```

```
5100 REM        X(): array holding random motif
5110 REM        TOTAL: motif length
5120 REM        INTVAL: interval of transposition in 1/2-steps
5130 REM     Exiting -
5140 REM        Y(): array holding transposed motif
5150 REM     Local -
5160 REM        K9: loop index, pointer to Y()
5170 REM ========================================================
5180    FOR K9 = 1 TO TOTAL
5190       Y(K9) = X(K9) + INTVAL
5200    NEXT K9
5210 RETURN
```

RUN (Motforms)

```
ORIGINAL PITCH MOTIF --
 B1 C#1  E1  A1  G1 C#1  B1  C1  F1  B1  A1 F#1  D1  B1  F1
THE RETROGRADE MOTIF --
 F1  B1  D1 F#1  A1  B1  F1  C1  B1 C#1  G1  A1  E1 C#1  B1
THE INVERTED MOTIF --
 B1  A2 F#2 C#2 D#2  A2  B1 A#2  F2  B1 C#2  E2 G#2  B1  F2
ORIGINAL MOTIF TRANSPOSITIONS
NUMBER  1
 C2  D1  F1 A#1 G#1  D1  C2 C#1 F#1  C2 A#1  G1 D#1  C2 F#1
NUMBER  2
C#2 D#1 F#1  B1  A1 D#1 C#2  D1  G1 C#2  B1 G#1  E1 C#2  G1
NUMBER  3
 D2  E1  G1  C2 A#1  E1  D2 D#1 G#1  D2  C2  A1  F1  D2 G#1
NUMBER  4
D#2  F1 G#1 C#2  B1  F1 D#2  E1  A1 D#2 C#2 A#1 F#1 D#2  A1
NUMBER  5
 E2 F#1  A1  D2  C2 F#1  E2  F1 A#1  E2  D2  B1  G1  E2 A#1
NUMBER  6
 F2  G1 A#1 D#2 C#2  G1  F2 F#1  B1  F2 D#2  C2 G#1  F2  B1
NUMBER  7
F#2 G#1  B1  E2  D2 G#1 F#2  G1  C2 F#2  E2 C#2  A1 F#2  C2
NUMBER  8
 G2  A1  C2  F2 D#2  A1  G2 G#1 C#2  G2  F2  D2 A#1  G2 C#2
NUMBER  9
G#2 A#1 C#2 F#2  E2 A#1 G#2  A1  D2 G#2 F#2 D#2  B1 G#2  D2
NUMBER  10
 A2  B1  D2  G2  F2  B1  A2 A#1 D#2  A2  G2  E2  C2  A2 D#2
NUMBER  11
A#2  C2 D#2 G#2 F#2  C2 A#2  B1  E2 A#2 G#2  F2 C#2 A#2  E2
```

SUBROUTINE GROUP: DISPLACE

- ○ Displace   CTB2.4
- ○ Pitchtab   CTB1.3

Purpose

Vary registrated pitch sequences by individually displacing notes a specific number of octaves.

Notes

The DRIVER PROGRAM can be converted to an interactive main routine by dimensioning arrays X( ), Y( ), and DISP( ) to accommodate longer pitch sequences. Replace Lines 210 and 220 with an input loop which prompts the user to enter the pitch sequence and corresponding octave displacements.

Programming Ideas

1) Convert the DRIVER PROGRAM to an interactive main routine which will accept any length pitch sequence up to 100 notes.

2) Write a program which uses an array of random-order rhythm values (range 1 to 6) to displace a pitch sequence. Avoid parametric unity, i.e., duration 1 (a whole note) should not result in displacement by one octave. (Hint: use the durations as pointers to the addresses of an array which contains random-order octave displacements.)

3) Write an interactive program which offers the user options to invert, retrograde, transpose, and displace an input melodic sequence.

4) Convert the integers of the octave-displaced sequence to binary form; map the binary numbers to the rhythm parameter in an interesting way.

Program Listing

```
100 REM ============================================================
110 REM                       DRIVER PROGRAM
120 REM                         (Displace)
130 REM ============================================================
140    DIM P$(84)
150    DIM X(20),Y(20)
160    DIM DISP(20)
170    RANDOMIZE(1324)
180    GOSUB 530                              '<< call pitch table
190    TOTAL = 10
200       FOR J= 1 TO TOTAL
210          X(J) = INT(RND * 12) + 1     '<< load random pitches
220          DISP(J) = INT(RND * 6)+1'<<load random octave displ.
230          PRINT P$(X(J));" WILL BE DISPLACED BY ";DISP(J);"
OCTAVE(S)"
240       NEXT J
250    GOSUB 300                        '<< call registral displacement
```

```
260          FOR J = 1 TO TOTAL
270          PRINT P$(Y(J));" ";
280          NEXT J
290 END
300 REM ================================================= CTB2.4
310 REM ******************>> DISPLACE <<********************
320 REM =================================================
330 REM     This subroutine (individually) displaces the pitches
340 REM     of an input sequence by a specific number of octaves.
350 REM =================================================
360 REM                    Variable Descriptions
370 REM     Entering -
380 REM       X(): array holding undisplaced pitch sequence
390 REM       DISP(): array holding individual pitch displacements
400 REM       TOTAL: sequence length
430 REM     Exiting -
440 REM       Y(): array containing octave-displaced pitches
450 REM     Local -
460 REM       K9: loop index, pointer to DISP(),X(),Y()
470 REM =================================================
480 REM
490    FOR K9 = 1 TO TOTAL
500        Y(K9)=X(K9) + 12 * DISP(K9)
510    NEXT K9
520 RETURN
530 REM ================================================= CTB1.3
540 REM ******************>> PITCHTAB <<********************
550 REM =================================================
560    NOTE$ = " CC# DD# E FF# GG# AA# B"
570    OCTAVE$ = "1234567"
600        FOR K9 = 1 TO 7
610            FOR L9 = 1 TO 12
620                P$(L9+(K9-1)*12) = MID$(NOTE$,(L9*2-1),2)+MID$
(OCTAVE$,K9,1)
630            NEXT L9
640        NEXT K9
650 RETURN
```

RUN (Displace)

```
 A1 WILL BE DISPLACED BY  2 OCTAVE(S)
F#1 WILL BE DISPLACED BY  5 OCTAVE(S)
G#1 WILL BE DISPLACED BY  4 OCTAVE(S)
 B1 WILL BE DISPLACED BY  6 OCTAVE(S)
 D1 WILL BE DISPLACED BY  5 OCTAVE(S)
 D1 WILL BE DISPLACED BY  2 OCTAVE(S)
 A1 WILL BE DISPLACED BY  3 OCTAVE(S)
 F1 WILL BE DISPLACED BY  6 OCTAVE(S)
D#1 WILL BE DISPLACED BY  4 OCTAVE(S)
D#1 WILL BE DISPLACED BY  5 OCTAVE(S)
 A3 F#6 G#5  B7  D6  D3  A4  F7 D#5 D#6
```

SUBROUTINE: Alterseq

Purpose

Modify a pitch sequence via interval expansion or contraction by a constant factor.

Notes

Variable INTSIZE, if negative, contracts the melodic interval (measured in 1/2 steps) between adjacent notes of the pitch sequence. If INTSIZE is positive, the interval is expanded.

There is built-in protection against repeated tones resulting from compression; Line 1250 prevents the return of intervals smaller than a minor second. However, repeated tones contained in the original sequence are allowed to remain.

Programming Ideas

1) Convert the DRIVER PROGRAM to an interactive main routine which allows the user to input a sequence of integers representing registered pitches. Run the program several times using the same pitch sequence, but expand or contract the intervals by a markedly different factor during each run. Map the prime order output data to the pitch parameter, then map the same data in retrograde form to the rhythm parameter.

2) Run the interactive program version three times using the same input integer sequence, but alter the interval of expansion/contraction with each run. Apply the original integer sequence to the pitch parameter; map the three altered output integer sequences to the rhythm, volume, and articulation parameters.

Program Listing

```
100 REM ============================================================
110 REM .                     DRIVER PROGRAM
120 REM                          (Alterseq)
130 REM ============================================================
140    DIM X(12),Y(12)
150    RANDOMIZE(-368)
160    TOTAL = 12
170    LOW = 22
180    HIGH = 66
190    RANGE = HIGH - LOW + 1
200    INTSIZE = 5          '<< expand intervals by five 1/2-steps
210    PRINT "A RANDOM-ORDER SEQUENCE --"
220       FOR J = 1 TO TOTAL
230          X(J) = INT(RND * RANGE)+ LOW
240          PRINT X(J);          '<< send prime sequence to screen
250       NEXT J
260    PRINT : PRINT
270       FOR J = 1 TO 2
```

```
280             PRINT "PASS";J
290             PRINT "ALTERATION INTEGER =";INTSIZE"
300             PRINT "ALTERED SEQUENCE --"
310             GOSUB 1000              '<< call sequence alteration
320             FOR J1 = 1 TO TOTAL
330               PRINT Y(J1);  '<< send altered sequence to screen
340             NEXT J1
350             INTSIZE = - 5                '<< contract intervals
360             PRINT
370           NEXT J
380 END
1000 REM ======================================================= CTB2.5
1010 REM ********************>> ALTERSEQ <<********************
1020 REM =======================================================
1030 REM      This subroutine alters a value sequence by interval
1040 REM      expansion or contraction. Positive integers expand
1050 REM      the sequence, negative integers contract it.
1060 REM =======================================================
1070 REM                    Variable Descriptions
1080 REM      Entering -
1090 REM        X(): primary value sequence
1100 REM        TOTAL: length of sequence
1110 REM        INTSIZE: size of alteration interval in units
1120 REM      Exiting -
1130 REM        X(): primary value sequence
1140 REM        Y(): altered value sequence
1150 REM      Local -
1160 REM        INTDIR: direction of alteration
1170 REM        INTVAL: altered interval
1180 REM        K9: loop index, pointer to X(),Y()
1190 REM =======================================================
1200     Y(1) = X(1)
1210       FOR K9 = 2 TO TOTAL
1220          IF X(K9) <> X(K9-1) THEN 1230 ELSE Y(K9) = Y(K9-1)
: GOTO 1270
1230             INTDIR = SGN(X(K9)-X(K9-1))
1240             INTVAL=ABS(X(K9)-X(K9-1)+INTSIZE
1250             IF INTVAL <1 THEN INTVAL = 1
1260             Y(K9)=Y(K9-1)+INTDIR * INTVAL
1270          NEXT K9
1280 RETURN
```

RUN   (Alterseq)

```
A RANDOM-ORDER SEQUENCE --
 41   50   42   66   58   54   60   65   40   39   44   34

PASS 1
ALTERATION INTEGER = 5
ALTERED SEQUENCE --
 41   55   42   71   58   49   60   70   40   34   44   29
PASS 2
ALTERATION INTEGER =-5
ALTERED SEQUENCE --
 41   45   42   61   58   57   58   59   39   38   39   34
```

SUBROUTINE: Setflag

Purpose

Generate a random-order integer series by the array flag method; repeated invocation returns random-order permutations.

Notes

This sampling-without-replacement subroutine is inefficient, but works well when the number of elements to be serialized is relatively small. It generates a random number within range limits, then checks the contents of the array CUM( ) address pointed to by the random number to determine whether a flag (1) is present. If the address is empty, it receives the flag, and the random integer is placed in array SET( ) as a series member. If the address already has the flag, the number is discarded and another is generated.

Repeated invocation of this subroutine for the purpose of generating series permutations requires adapting Subroutine Zeromat (CTB1.9) to reset to 0 the flags in array CUM( ) prior to each call.

Depending upon programming circumstances, it may be more appropriate to invoke either of the two shuffling subroutines (CTB2.7 or CTB2.8) to generate permutations of an element set.

Programming Ideas

1) Write an interactive main routine that allows the user to input LOW and HIGH element values. Run the program several times, setting LOW to 1 and HIGH to various values (try 500) to get a feeling for the limited usefulness of the algorithm.

2) Generate series containing noncontinuous scalar components (12, 14, 23, 45, 47, 61, etc.) by treating the subroutine output as a set of pointers to an element table.

Program Listing

```
100 REM ============================================================
110 REM                      DRIVER PROGRAM
115 REM                        (Setflag)
120 REM ============================================================
130     DIM SET(12),CUM(12)
140     RANDOMIZE(291)
150     TOTAL = 12
160     LOW = 1
170     HIGH = 12
180     RANGE = HIGH-LOW+1
190     GOSUB 1000
200        FOR J = 1 TO TOTAL
210           PRINT  SET(J);" ";        '<< send series to screen
220        NEXT J
230 END
```

```
1000 REM ================================================== CTB2.6
1010 REM *******************>> SETFLAG <<********************
1020 REM ==================================================
1030 REM      This subroutine generates random-order series by
1040 REM      the array flag method.
1120 REM ==================================================
1130 REM                     Variable Descriptions
1140 REM      Entering -
1150 REM        TOTAL: length of set
1160 REM        LOW: lowest value
1170 REM        RANGE: set value range
1180 REM      Exiting -
1190 REM        SET(): final set of values
1200 REM      Local -
1210 REM        CUM(): array holding occurrence flags
1220 REM        R9: random value to be tested for occurrence
1230 REM        K9: loop index, pointer to array SET()
1240 REM ==================================================
1250       FOR K9 = 1 TO TOTAL
1260          R9 = INT(RND * RANGE) + LOW
1270          IF CUM(R9) = 1 THEN 1260
1280          CUM(R9) = 1
1290          SET(K9) = R9
1300       NEXT K9
1310 RETURN
```

RUN (Setflag)

6   9   5   1   10   4   3   7   2   8   11   12

SUBROUTINE: Conshufl   CTB2.7

Purpose

Randomly reorder (shuffle) the contents of an element table array.

Notes

This algorithm shuffles an element table by first generating a random sequence of pointers and then swaps the corresponding array address contents. However, after shuffling, the prime order element table is no longer available to the program. (See Subroutine Addshufl (CTB2.8) for a nondisruptive randomization of array addresses.)

Programming Ideas

1) Write a program that will randomize (shuffle) any reasonable-length list of parameter values. Provide options for accessing any of four element tables: pitch, rhythm, articulation, and volume.

2) Add Subroutine Group VECTORS to the above program to organize the output data into event vectors.

3) Write a program to randomize a data table containing numbers corresponding to a six-octave microtonal scale (CTB1.1). Use the output of four runs to generate a four-voice texture whose rhythms are also derived from a shuffled duration element table.

Program Listing

```
100  REM  ===========================================================
110  REM                       DRIVER PROGRAM
120  REM                        (Conshufl)
130  REM  ===========================================================
140     DIM X(20)
145     RANDOMIZE(56)
150     TOTAL = 20
155     PRINT "INTEGER SEQUENCE ARRAY -- "
160        FOR J = 1 TO TOTAL
170           X(J) = J            '<< fill array with number sequence
175           PRINT X(J),
180        NEXT J
190     GOSUB 1000
195     PRINT "SHUFFLED ARRAY --"
200        FOR J = 1 TO TOTAL
210           PRINT X(J),            '<< send shuffled array to screen
220        NEXT J
230  END
1000 REM  ====================================================== CTB2.7
1010 REM  *******************>> CONSHUFL <<*********************
1015 REM                     (Disruptive Shuffle)
1020 REM  ===========================================================
1100 REM                    Variable Descriptions
```

```
1110 REM        Entering -
1120 REM          X(): array of sequential values
1130 REM          TOTAL: length of list (array)
1140 REM        Exiting -
1150 REM          X(): randomized array of values
1160 REM        Local -
1170 REM          R9: random number
1180 REM          S9: temporary storage variable
1190 REM          K9: loop index, pointer to array X()
1200 REM ==========================================================
1220        FOR K9 = 1 TO TOTAL
1230            R9 = INT(RND * TOTAL) + 1
1300            S9 = X(K9)
1310            X(K9) = X(R9)
1320            X(R9) = S9
1330        NEXT K9
1340 RETURN
```

RUN (Conshufl)

INTEGER SEQUENCE ARRAY --

1	2	3	4	5
6	7	8	9	10
11	12	13	14	15
16	17	18	19	20

SHUFFLED ARRAY --

20	12	3	18	8
11	19	9	13	15
1	7	14	16	5
2	4	10	6	17

Purpose

Randomly reorder (shuffle) a list of pointers to an element table.

Notes

This subroutine differs from Conshufl (CTB2.7), in that it is nondisruptive; that is, pointers to an array are shuffled instead of the array contents, thereby leaving the original list intact for future access by the program main routine.

Programming Ideas

1) Write a program that intersperses the four standard pitch modification operations (retrograde, inversion, retrograde-inversion, and transpositions) with random-order permutations of a prime order pitch sequence.

2) Write a program based upon Subroutine Group CURVES (CTB1.12, CTB1.13, and CTB1.14) to generate random-order permutations of parameter data tables consisting of linearly, exponentially, and logarithmically scaled value sequences.

Program Listing

```
100  REM =============================================================
110  REM                      DRIVER PROGRAM
111  REM                        (Addshufl)
120  REM =============================================================
130      DIM TABLE(20),PNTR(20)
135      RANDOMIZE(323)
140      TOTAL = 20
145      PRINT "INTEGER SEQUENCE ARRAY --"
150        FOR J = 1 TO TOTAL
160           TABLE(J) = J       '<< fill array with number sequence
165           PNTR(J) = J                    '<< load pointer array
170           PRINT TABLE(J),
180        NEXT J
190      GOSUB 1000
195      PRINT "TABLE REFERENCED BY ARRAY OF SHUFFLED POINTERS --"
200        FOR J = 1 TO TOTAL
210           PRINT TABLE(PNTR(J)),'<<send shuffled table to screen
220        NEXT J
230  END
1000 REM ================================================= CTB2.8
1010 REM ********************>> ADDSHUFL <<********************
1015 REM                   (Nondisruptive Shuffle)
1020 REM =============================================================
1090 REM                    Variable Descriptions
1100 REM
1110 REM     Entering -
1120 REM        TOTAL: number of values in the list
```

```
1130 REM        X(): array of ordered address pointers
1140 REM    Exiting -
1150 REM        X(): randomized array of pointers to list
1160 REM    Local -
1170 REM        R9: random number
1180 REM        S9: temporary storage variable
1190 REM        K9: loop index, pointer to array X()
1200 REM
1210 REM  ========================================================
1220    RANDOMIZE
1230       FOR K9 = 1 TO TOTAL
1240          R9 = INT(RND * TOTAL) + 1
1250          S9 = PNTR(K9)
1260          PNTR(K9) = PNTR(R9)
1270          PNTR(R9) = S9
1280       NEXT K9
1290 RETURN
```

RUN (Addshufl)

```
INTEGER SEQUENCE ARRAY --
    1               2               3               4               5
    6               7               8               9              10
   11              12              13              14              15
   16              17              18              19              20
TABLE REFERENCED BY ARRAY OF SHUFFLED POINTERS --
    8               6               1              16               4
    9               7              19              11              12
   10               2              15               5              18
    3              13              20              17              14
```

SUBROUTINE GROUP: ROWFORMS

○ Pitchtab	CTB1.3
○ Conshufl	CTB2.7
○ Rowretro	CTB2.9
○ Rowinvrt	CTB2.10
○ Rowtrnpz	CTB2.11

Purpose

Generate commonly found 12-tone row forms: original, retrograde, inversion, and transpositions.

Notes

The 12-tone row forms produced by this set of subroutines are not register-specific. However, octave assignments may be derived from the row in a number of ways, or they may be randomly generated as the result of a separate, unrelated process.

Programming Ideas

1) Write a program that generates random-order 12-tone rows, then maps pitch octave assignments from a compressed scale representing the interval-sizes between the row pitches. (Hint: Since the largest possible interval in 1/2 steps is 11 and the normal pitch range is one to six octaves, one obvious method is to "wraparound" the interval scale on the octave range scale.)

2) Expand the above program to generate rhythm durations derived from the random-order 12-tone rows (add Subroutine Timpoint, CTB2.20).

3) Use Subroutine Displace (CTB2.4) to generate pitch octave assignments.

Program Listing

```
100 REM ================================================================
110 REM                    DRIVER PROGRAM
120 REM                      (Rowforms)
130 REM ================================================================
140 REM     This set of subroutines produces commonly found
150 REM     12-tone row forms - original, retrograde, inversion,
160 REM     and transpositions.  Because the processes are well
170 REM     known and simple, variable descriptions have been
180 REM     dispensed with.
190 REM ================================================================
200     DIM P$(12)
210     DIM X(12),Y(12)
220     INTVAL = 4                      '<< transposition interval
230     RANDOMIZE(654)
240     GOSUB 1000                       '<< load element tables
```

```
250      GOSUB 2000                                '<< call random shuffle
260      PRINT
270      PRINT "RANDOM-ORDER 12-TONE ROW --"
280        FOR J = 0 TO 11
290          PRINT P$(X(J));" "; '<< random 12-tone row to screen
300        NEXT J
310      PRINT : PRINT
320        FOR J = 1 TO 3
330          ON J GOSUB 3000,4000,5000 '<< call retro,invrt,trnpz
340            FOR J1 = 0 TO 11
350              PRINT P$(Y(J1));" ";    '<< row forms to screen
360            NEXT J1
370          PRINT : PRINT
380        NEXT J
390 END
1000 REM ============================================= CTB1.3
1010 REM ******************>> PITCHTAB <<**********************
1020 REM             (modified to program specs)
1030 REM =================================================
1040    FOR J = 0 TO 11
1050      X(J) = J                          '<< load row elements
1060      READ P$(J)              '<< load pitch class equivalents
1070    NEXT J
1080 REM++++++++++++++++++++++++++++++++++++
1090    DATA C,C#,D,D#,E,F,F#,G,G#,A,A#,B
1100 REM++++++++++++++++++++++++++++++++++++
1110 RETURN
2000 REM ============================================= CTB2.7
2010 REM ******************>> CONSHUFL <<*********************
2020 REM =================================================
2030    FOR K9 = 0 TO 11
2040      R9 = INT(RND * 12)
2050      S9 = X(K9)
2060      X(K9) = X(R9)
2070      X(R9) = S9
2080    NEXT K9
2090 RETURN
3000 REM ============================================= CTB2.9
3010 REM ********************>> ROWRETRO <<*******************
3020 REM =================================================
3030 REM      This subroutine outputs retrograde form.
3040 REM =================================================
3050    PRINT "RETROGRADE ORDER --"
3060      FOR K9 = 0 TO 11
3070        L = (11 - K9) MOD 12
3080        Y(L) = X(K9)
3090      NEXT K9
3100 RETURN
4000 REM ============================================= CTB2.10
4010 REM ******************>> ROWINVRT <<*********************
4020 REM =================================================
4030 REM      This subroutine outputs inverted form.
4040 REM =================================================
4050 PRINT "INVERTED ORDER --"
4060    FOR K9 = 0 TO 11
4070      Y(K9) = (12 - X(K9)) MOD 12
4080    NEXT K9
4090 RETURN
5000 REM ============================================= CTB2.11
5010 REM ******************>> ROWTRNPZ <<*********************
```

```
5020 REM ==============================================================
5030 REM      This subroutine outputs row form transpositions.
5040 REM ==============================================================
5050    PRINT "TRANSPOSED (UP MAJOR 3RD) ORIGINAL FORM --"
5060       FOR K9 = 0 TO 11
5070          Y(K9) = (X(K9) + INTVAL) MOD 12
5080       NEXT K9
5090 RETURN
```

RUN (Rowforms)

RANDOM-ORDER 12-TONE ROW --
D B C A A# G F G# D# C# F# E

RETROGRADE ORDER --
E F# C# D# G# F G A# A C B D

INVERTED ORDER --
A# C# C D# D F G E A B F# G#

TRANSPOSED (UP MAJOR 3RD) ORIGINAL FORM --
F# D# E C# D B A C G F A# G#

SUBROUTINE GROUP: ROWSQUARE

- Pitchtab   CTB1.3
- Setflag   CTB2.6
- Rowmat   CTB2.12

Purpose

Generate and display a square matrix containing all forms and transpositions of a random-order 12-tone row.

Notes

Composers who use serial techniques sometimes like to visualize combinatorial pitch row possibilities by printing a compressed version of the 48 transpositions of a particular set. It may seem awkward to shift one's reading style from the unidirectional to multidirectional mode, but the serial matrix affords one an uncluttered view of compositional potential.

The matrix row has also been adapted to nonserial applications by composers. Although the traditional 12-tone technique interprets the matrix in a rigid, literal fashion, one might imagine many conceptual extensions which simply use the square as a pretext for a musical event. For example, each of the 12 chromatic pitches could represent a complex of sounds rather than a single note; or, indeterminacy might be introduced into a performance by giving individual players different serial matrices to read in a presribed manner.

Programming Ideas

1) Convert the DRIVER PROGRAM to an interactive main routine which allows the user to input pitch rows.

2) Modify the above program to store the matrix in a two-dimensional array, then add code to generate a random four-directional walk through the matrix (see Subroutine Matwalk, CTB6.9).

3) Devise other strategies for traversing the matrix.

Program Listing

```
100 REM ============================================================
110 REM                      DRIVER PROGRAM
120 REM                        (Rowsquare)
130 REM ============================================================
140     DIM P$(12),CUM(12),X(12),Y(12)
150     RANDOMIZE(-1322)
160     GOSUB 1000                            '<< call pitch table
170     GOSUB 2000                            '<< call set generator
180     GOSUB 3000              '<< call composite row form printout
190 END
1000 REM ============================================== CTB1.3
1010 REM *******************>> PITCHTAB <<*******************
```

```
1020 REM              (modified to load pitch classes only)
1030 REM ========================================================
1040    FOR J = 0 TO 11
1050       READ P$(J)                          '<< load pitch table
1060    NEXT J
1070 REM+++++++++++++++++++++++++++++++++++++++++++++++
1080    DATA "C  ","C# ","D  ","D# ","E  ","F  "
1090    DATA "F# ","G  ","G# ","A  ","A# ","B  "
1100 REM+++++++++++++++++++++++++++++++++++++++++++++++
1110 RETURN
2000 REM ===================================================== CTB2.6
2010 REM *********************>> SETFLAG <<*********************
2020 REM               (modified to program specs)
2030 REM ========================================================
2040    FOR K9 = 0 TO 11
2050       F = INT(RND*12)
2060       IF CUM(F) = 1 THEN 2050
2070       CUM(F) = 1
2080       IF K9 = 0 THEN TRANS = F
2090       IF F-TRANS < 0 THEN X(K9) = F-TRANS+ 12 ELSE X(K9) =
F-TRANS
2100       Y(K9) = (12-X(K9)) MOD 12
2110    NEXT K9
2120 RETURN
3000 REM ==================================================== CTB2.12
3010 REM *******************>> ROWMAT <<*********************
3020 REM ========================================================
3030 REM    This subroutine prints a square matrix containing
3040 REM    composite 12-tone row forms: Original (Prime),
3050 REM    Retrograde, Inversion, and Retrograde-Inversion.
3060 REM ========================================================
3070 REM                   Variable Descriptions
3080 REM    Entering -
3090 REM      X(): original order set array
3100 REM      Y(): inverted order set array
3110 REM      P$(): pitch table array
3120 REM    Exiting -
3130 REM      none  (subroutine is procedural)
3140 REM    Local -
3150 REM      INTVAL: transposition interval
3160 REM      K9: loop index, pointer to Y()
3170 REM      L9: loop index, pointer to X()
3180 REM ========================================================
3200    PRINT "    MATRIX OF TRANSPOSITIONS YIELDING O,RO,I,RI    "
3210    PRINT "++++++++++++++++++++++++++++++++++++++++++++++++++"
3220    PRINT "+                                   ORIGINAL ---->   +"
3230    PRINT "+ | INVERSION                                     +"
3240    PRINT "+ V                                              +"
3250    FOR K9= 0 TO 11
3260       PRINT "+";TAB(8);
3270          INTVAL = Y(K9)
3280          FOR L9= 0 TO 11
3290             PRINT P$((X(L9) + INTVAL) MOD 12);
3300          NEXT L9
3310       PRINT TAB(50);"+"
3320    NEXT K9
3330    PRINT "+ ^                                              +"
3340    PRINT "+ | RETROGRADE INVERSION                         +"
3350    PRINT "+                         <--- RETROGRADE        +"
```

```
3360    PRINT "+++++++++++++++++++++++++++++++++++++++++++++++++"
3370 RETURN
```

RUN (Rowsquare)

```
     MATRIX OF TRANSPOSITIONS YIELDING O,RO,I,RI
+++++++++++++++++++++++++++++++++++++++++++++++++
+                                   ORIGINAL ---->    +
+  | INVERSION                                        +
+  V                                                  +
+      C   B   A#  G#  A   E   G   D   D#  F   F#  C#  +
+      C#  C   B   A   A#  F   G#  D#  E   F#  G   D   +
+      D   C#  C   A#  B   F#  A   E   F   G   G#  D#  +
+      E   D#  D   C   C#  G#  B   F#  G   A   A#  F   +
+      D#  D   C#  B   C   G   A#  F   F#  G#  A   E   +
+      G#  G   F#  E   F   C   D#  A#  B   C#  D   A   +
+      F   E   D#  C#  D   A   C   G   G#  A#  B   F#  +
+      A#  A   G#  F#  G   D   F   C   C#  D#  E   B   +
+      A   G#  G   F   F#  C#  E   B   C   D   D#  A#  +
+      G   F#  F   D#  E   B   D   A   A#  C   C#  G#  +
+      F#  F   E   D   D#  A#  C#  G#  A   B   C   G   +
+      B   A#  A   G   G#  D#  F#  C#  D   E   F   C   +
+  ^                                                  +
+  | RETROGRADE INVERSION                             +
+                      <--- RETROGRADE                +
+++++++++++++++++++++++++++++++++++++++++++++++++
```

SUBROUTINE GROUP: MODOPS

○ Pitchtab	CTB1.3
○ Conshufl	CTB2.7
○ M5setM7	CTB2.13

Purpose

Generate related transformations of a 12-tone series via multiplicative operations.

Notes

Although the M5 and M7 operations are said to produce transformations of a tone row, in a broader sense they generate nonrandom-order permutations of the 12 notes of the chromatic scale (just as intervallic transposition produces series-related nonrandom permutations of the chromatic set). The distinction between a simple permutation and a transformation lies in the orderly propagation of new sets from a reference set in a manner that preserves some of the characteristics of the original (or model) set. The "relatedness" in multiplicative operations is manifest by virtue of the fact that ordered pairs of notes within the series exchange their positions. Moreover, the M5 operation represents a mapping of a chromatic scale ordering onto the cycle of fourths, while the M7 operation is a mapping onto the cycle of fifths.

Programming Ideas

1) Explore other multiplication factors for Mod 12. What happens to series integrity?

2) Experiment with various-length series using different multiplication factors.

Program Listing

```
100 REM =============================================================
110 REM                      DRIVER PROGRAM
120 REM                        (Modops)
130 REM =============================================================
140    DIM P$(12)
150    DIM X(12),Y(12)
160    RANDOMIZE(923)
170    TOTAL = 12
180    OP = 5                          '<< value for m5 operation
190    GOSUB 1000                          '<< call pitch table
200    GOSUB 2000                          '<< call random shuffle
210    PRINT
220    PRINT "RANDOM-ORDER 12-TONE SET --"
230       FOR J = 0 TO TOTAL-1
240          PRINT P$(X(J));" "; '<< random 12-tone set to screen
250       NEXT J
```

```
260    PRINT : PRINT
270       FOR J = 1 TO 2
280          GOSUB 3000                      '<< call m5/m7 permutation
290          PRINT "THE PERMUTATION RESULTING FROM ";"M";OP;"
OPERATION"
300             FOR J1 = 0 TO TOTAL-1
310                PRINT P$(Y(J1));" ";   '<< send perm to screen
320             NEXT J1
330          PRINT : PRINT
340          OP = 7                          '<< value for m7 operation
350       NEXT J
360 END
1000 REM ==================================================== CTB1.3
1010 REM ******************>> PITCHTAB <<***********************
1020 REM          (modified to load pitch classes only)
1030 REM ====================================================
1040    FOR J = 0 TO TOTAL-1
1050       X(J) = J                          '<< load set elements
1060       READ P$(J)                '<< load pitch class equivalents
1070    NEXT J
1080 REM+++++++++++++++++++++++++++++++++++++
1090    DATA C,C#,D,D#,E,F,F#,G,G#,A,A#,B
1100 REM+++++++++++++++++++++++++++++++++++++
1110 RETURN
2000 REM ==================================================== CTB2.7
2010 REM ******************>> CONSHUFL <<**********************
2020 REM ====================================================
2030    FOR K9 = 0 TO TOTAL-1
2040       R9 = INT(RND * TOTAL)
2050       S9 = X(K9)
2060       X(K9) = X(R9)
2070       X(R9) = S9
2080    NEXT K9
2090 RETURN
3000 REM ==================================================== CTB2.13
3010 REM ******************>> M5SETM7 <<***********************
3020 REM ====================================================
3030 REM    This subroutine outputs a permutation of an input
3040 REM    set (series) by the "M5" or "M7" operation.
3050 REM ====================================================
3060 REM                 Variable Descriptions
3070 REM    Entering -
3080 REM      X(): array holding random 12-tone set
3090 REM      OP: value for m5 or m7 operation
3100 REM    Exiting -
3110 REM      Y(): array holding m5 or m7 permutation
3120 REM    Local -
3130 REM      K9: loop index, pointer to X(),Y()
3140 REM ====================================================
3150    FOR K9 = 0 TO 11
3160       Y(K9) = (X(K9) * OP) MOD 12
3170    NEXT
3180 RETURN
```

RUN (Modops)

RANDOM-ORDER 12-TONE SET --
C# G A D# E D C A# B F F# G#

THE PERMUTATION RESULTING FROM M 5   OPERATION
F B A D# G# A# C D G C# F# E

THE PERMUTATION RESULTING FROM M 7   OPERATION
G C# D# A E D C A# F B F# G#

SUBROUTINE GROUP: PSTNPERM
  ○ Setflag   CTB2.6
  ○ Pstnperm   CTB2.14

Purpose

Permute a prime order 12-tone series by swapping pitch-class numbers with position-in-set numbers.

Notes

A member of the class of permutations consisting of derived series transformations, this algorithm has an interesting special case: When the ascending or descending chromatic scale is the prime order series, its retrograde is returned.

This method of systematic set permutation may be applied to value series of any reasonable length. The derived set propagation is nearly endless if one submits every transposition of all four forms for each permuted set to the swapping process.

Programming Ideas

1) Modify the DRIVER PROGRAM to allow the user to input numeric series of variable lengths; add the necessary lines of code to generate the retrograde, inversion, and retrograde-inversion forms, as well as all chromatic transpositions. Include a user option to submit any or all forms and transpositions to the PSTNPERM subroutine.

2) Write an interactive program using CTB2.15 which interprets the permuted output series as pointers to values contained in the data tables of other musical parameters.

Program Listing

```
100 REM ========================================================
110 REM                      DRIVER PROGRAM
120 REM                        (Pstnperm)
130 REM ========================================================
140     DIM SET(12),POSIT(12),CUM(12)
150     RANDOMIZE(-56)
160     TOTAL = 12
170     LOW = 1 : HIGH = 12
190     RANGE = HIGH-LOW+1
200     GOSUB 1000                      '<< call series generator
210     PRINT "PRIME ORDER SERIES --"
220        FOR J = 1 TO TOTAL
230           PRINT  SET(J);" ";        '<< send series to screen
240        NEXT J
250     GOSUB 2000                      '<< call position permutator
260     PRINT
270     PRINT "SET PERMUTATION RESULTING FROM ";" SWAP OF PC NMBR
```

```
AND POSITION"
280         FOR J = 1 TO TOTAL
290             PRINT POSIT(J);" "; '<< send permutation to screen
300         NEXT J
310 END
1000 REM ===================================================== CTB2.6
1010 REM ********************>> SETFLAG <<********************
1020 REM =====================================================
1030         FOR K9 = 1 TO TOTAL
1040             R9 = INT(RND * RANGE) + LOW
1050             IF CUM(R9) = 1 THEN 1040
1060             CUM(R9) = 1
1070             SET(K9) = R9
1080         NEXT K9
1090 RETURN
2000 REM ===================================================== CTB2.14
2010 REM ********************>> PSTNPERM <<********************
2020 REM =====================================================
2030 REM     This subroutine generates a permutation of a
2040 REM     prime order series by swapping pitch class numbers
2050 REM     with position-in-set numbers. (If the series is
2060 REM     the chromatic scale, then, of course, no alteration
2070 REM     of the set will take place - the retrograde will
2080 REM     be returned.)
2090 REM =====================================================
2100 REM                 Variable Descriptions
2110 REM     Entering -
2120 REM       SET(): array containing series, pointer to POSIT()
2130 REM       TOTAL: length of series
2140 REM     Exiting -
2150 REM       POSIT(): array containing set permutation
2160 REM     Local -
2170 REM       K9: loop index, pointer to SET()
2180 REM =====================================================
2190     FOR K9 = 1 TO TOTAL
2200         POSIT(SET(K9)) = K9
2210     NEXT K9
2220 RETURN
```

RUN (Pstnperm)

```
PRIME ORDER SERIES --
 4    6   12   11    1    7    3    8   10    5    9    2
SET PERMUTATION RESULTING FROM SWAP OF PC NMBR AND POSITION
 5   12    7    1   10    2    6    8   11    9    4    3
```

SUBROUTINE: Samplset

Purpose

Generate permutations of a number series via cyclical, exhaustive sampling of the source set at a selected interval (start at set member n and place the nth set member in a destination set, looping back through the series until all values have been transferred).

Notes

This algorithm is derived from the classic Josephus' Problem, which is:

1) Arrange a group of men in a circle
2) Move around the circle
3) Shoot and remove every nth man
4) Repeat steps 2 and 3 until all men are dead.

Although there are other methods of accomplishing exhaustive sampling, this subroutine works by using two "bounce" arrays to hold transient versions of the set which is being sampled. During the sampling process, each member of the destination series is sent to the screen as it is removed from a copy of the source set. The source set is not disrupted.

If this subroutine is called by a program that requires run-time storage of the set permutations, then another array must be included to receive the destination series as they are printed to the screen (Lines 1390 and 1460).

Programming Ideas

1) Write a program using CTB2.15 which generates and files permutations of a user-input value series. (Treat the destination series as a set of pointers to element tables holding pitch, rhythm, articulation, or volume data.)
2) Write a program which derives sampling factors for a group of set permutations from the input series, thereby systematizing the generation of new series from a source set.

Program Listing

```
100 REM ============================================================
110 REM                      DRIVER PROGRAM
120 REM                       (Samplset)
130 REM ============================================================
140     DIM SET(100),A(100),B(100)
150     PERMUT = 5
160     TOTAL = 12
170     PRINT "A SEQUENTIAL SET -"
180       FOR J = 1 TO TOTAL
190          SET(J) = J : PRINT SET(J);
200       NEXT J
210     PRINT
```

```
220     FACTOR = 2
230       FOR CYCLE = 1 TO PERMUT
240         PRINT "PERMUTATION ";CYCLE
250         TARGET = 1
260         PRINT "SET START POSITION = ";TARGET;"; " "SET TARGET
FACTOR= ";FACTOR
270         GOSUB 1000                        '<< call sampling
280         FACTOR = FACTOR + 2
290       NEXT CYCLE
300 END
1000 REM ===================================================== CTB2.15
1010 REM ******************>> SAMPLSET <<********************
1020 REM =====================================================
1030 REM     This subroutine produces numeric series permutations
1040 REM     by cyclical set sampling at a selected interval.
1050 REM     (Start at set member n and remove every nth element,
1060 REM     looping back through the series until reordered.)
1150 REM =====================================================
1160 REM                     Variable Descriptions
1170 REM       Entering -
1180 REM        SET(): initial value series
1190 REM        TOTAL: series length
1200 REM        TARGET: current set sample
1210 REM        FACTOR: sampling interval
1220 REM       Exiting -
1230 REM        none: (subroutine is procedural)
1240 REM       Local -
1250 REM        SETL: current set length (shrinks every iteration)
1270 REM        A(): bounce array 1
1280 REM        B(): bounce array 2
1290 REM        ACNT: pointer to A()
1300 REM        BCNT: pointer to B()
1310 REM        K9: loop index, pointer to A(),B()
1320 REM =====================================================
1330     SETL = TOTAL
1340       FOR K9 = 1 TO SETL
1350         A(K9)=SET(K9)
1360       NEXT K9
1370     BCNT = 0
1380       FOR K9 = 1 TO SETL
1390         IF K9 = TARGET THEN PRINT A(K9); : TARGET = TARGET +
FACTOR ELSE BCNT = BCNT + 1 : B(BCNT) = A(K9)
1400       NEXT K9
1410     IF BCNT < 1 THEN 1530
1420     TARGET = TARGET - SETL
1430     ACNT = 0
1440      IF TARGET MOD BCNT <> 0 THEN TARGET = TARGET MOD  BCNT
ELSE TARGET = BCNT
1450       FOR K9 = 1 TO BCNT
1460         IF K9 = TARGET THEN PRINT B(K9); : TARGET = TARGET
+ FACTOR ELSE ACNT = ACNT + 1 : A(ACNT) = B(K9)
1470       NEXT K9
1480     IF ACNT < 1 THEN 1530
1490     SETL = ACNT
1500     TARGET = TARGET - BCNT
1510     IF TARGET MOD SETL <> 0 THEN TARGET = TARGET MOD  SETL
ELSE TARGET = SETL
1520     GOTO 1370
1530     PRINT
1540 RETURN
```

RUN (Samplset)

```
A SEQUENTIAL SET -
  1   2   3   4   5   6   7   8   9   10   11   12
PERMUTATION   1
SET START POSITION =   1 ; SET TARGET FACTOR=   2
  1   3   5   7   9   11   2   6   10   4   12   8
PERMUTATION   2
SET START POSITION =   1 ; SET TARGET FACTOR=   4
  1   5   9   2   7   12   8   4   3   6   11   10
PERMUTATION   3
SET START POSITION =   1 ; SET TARGET FACTOR=   6
  1   7   2   9   5   3   12   4   8   6   11   10
PERMUTATION   4
SET START POSITION =   1 ; SET TARGET FACTOR=   8
  1   9   6   4   3   5   8   12   11   7   2   10
PERMUTATION   5
SET START POSITION =   1 ; SET TARGET FACTOR=   10
  1   11   10   12   3   6   2   9   5   7   4   8
```

SUBROUTINE: Systperm CTB2.16

Internal secondary procedures related only to Systperm which do not receive individual subroutine numbers are PUSH, POP, and PRINT.

Purpose

Generate permutations of a number series by a systematic, nonrandom process external to the input series.

Notes

This algorithm invokes a set of internal procedures—PUSH and POP—to compensate for BASIC's lack of a user-accessible stack. It is an adaptation of a table-searching procedure written in Pascal, which explains its rather fragmented appearance.

The permutations returned by the subroutine are not related to the internal characteristics of a source series; they are simply abstract, systematic reorderings of the scalar numbers 1 through n. However, the DRIVER PROGRAM may be modified to allow the user to enter values in array A( ), or the subroutine output may be interpreted as pointers to other musical element tables.

Notice (in the program run following the listing) that the permutation process works from left to right; i.e., exhaustive permutations are cumulatively generated from expanding subsets of the total series.

For many musical applications, this procedure is too arbitrarily systematic; however, it lends itself very nicely to pattern/process-based compositional methods.

Programming Idea

Modify the subroutine to generate pitch sequences which (interestingly) exploit repetition of a gradually expanding, permuted set. Project the pitch structure onto other parameter elements through the use of permuted data pointers.

Program Listing

```
100 REM ================================================================
110 REM                   DRIVER PROGRAM
111 REM                     (Systperm)
112 REM ================================================================
120 REM    This subroutine is a set of subroutines which
130 REM    produce systematic(as opposed to random-order)
140 REM    permutations of a series of values.
180 REM ================================================================
190      DIM A(12), S(500),T(500)
220      PRINT "ENTER NUMBER OF SET MEMBERS TO BE PERMUTATED:"
230      INPUT N
240      PRINT "HOW MANY PERMUTATIONS TO BE RETURNED?"
250      INPUT T
260      K = N
```

```
270        FOR I = 1 TO N
280          A(I) = I
290        NEXT I
300        GOSUB 1030                          '<< call permute
310 END
1000 REM ============================================== CTB2.16
1010 REM ******************>> SYSTPERM <<************************
1020 REM ============================================================
1030       IF K = 1 THEN 4010                  '<< call print
1040       GOSUB 2010                          '<< call stack push
1050       K = K - 1
1060       GOSUB 1030                          '<< call permute
1070       I = 1
1080       IF I = K THEN 1200
1090       X = A(I)
1100       A(I) = A(K)
1110       A(K) = X
1120       GOSUB 2010                          '<< call stack push
1130       K = K - 1
1140       GOSUB 1030                          '<< call permute
1150       X = A(I)
1160       A(I) = A(K)
1170       A(K) = X
1180       I = I + 1
1190       GOTO 1080
1200       GOSUB 3010                          '<< call stack pop
1210 RETURN
1220 REM:
2000 REM ==========================================================
2010 REM *******************>> PUSH <<************************
2020 REM ==========================================================
2030     P = P + 1
2040     S(P) = K
2050     T(P) = I
2060 RETURN
3000 REM ==========================================================
3010 REM *******************>> POP <<***********************
3020 REM ==========================================================
3030     K = S(P)
3040     I = T(P)
3050     P = P - 1
3060 RETURN
4000 REM ==========================================================
4010 REM * ****************>> PRINT <<************************
4020 REM ==========================================================
4030       FOR J = 1 TO N
4040          PRINT A(J);
4050       NEXT J
4060       PRINT
4070       Z = Z + 1
4080       IF Z = T THEN END  ELSE 1200
```

RUN (Systperm)

```
ENTER NUMBER OF SET MEMBERS TO BE PERMUTATED:
? 8
HOW MANY PERMUTATIONS TO BE RETURNED?
? 10
 1  2  3  4  5  6  7  8
```

```
2   1   3   4   5   6   7   8
3   2   1   4   5   6   7   8
2   3   1   4   5   6   7   8
1   3   2   4   5   6   7   8
3   1   2   4   5   6   7   8
4   2   3   1   5   6   7   8
2   4   3   1   5   6   7   8
3   2   4   1   5   6   7   8
2   3   4   1   5   6   7   8
```

SUBROUTINE GROUP: ROTATION

- Setflag   CTB2.6
- Setrotat   CTB2.17
- Zerotrnpz   CTB2.18
- Segrotat   CTB2.19
- GCD   CTB1.19

Purpose

Perform rotational and transpositional operations on a 12-element set of values.

Notes

A set member rotation is a common 12-tone row transformation operation. In this group of procedures, integers are output instead of pitch classes to underscore applications to other musical parameters. (The set members can also serve as array pointers.) The numbers 0 to 11 symbolize the 12 pitch classes of the chromatic scale in a form suitable for further modulo operations as in CTB2.13, but the subroutine can be easily rewritten using the numbers 1 to 12.

Subroutine Setrotat functions by moving a given number of consecutive set members from the front to the end of the series. It also calculates the number of unique transformations of the row before repetition occurs and prevents the program from continuing beyond that point. The rotations are placed in array MAT1 for printout and later use by subroutine Zerotrnpz.

Subroutine Segrotat rotates partitioned-set segment members. Segments must equally subdivide the row (two groups of six notes, three groups of four notes, etc.). After the number of unique transformations is calculated, the rotations are placed in array MAT3 for printout.

Programming Idea

Write an interactive program based on ROTATION which prompts the user to input source series, performs set rotations, then calls Pstnperm (CTB2.5) to derive the next set to be subjected to rotations.

Program Listing

```
100 REM  ============================================================
110 REM                     DRIVER PROGRAM
120 REM                       (Rotation)
130 REM  ============================================================
140 REM     This set of subroutines performs rotation and
150 REM     transposition operations on a 12-element set
160 REM     of values.
210 REM  ============================================================
```

```
220      DIM CUM(12),SET(12),MAT1(12,12),MAT2(12,12),MAT3(12,12)
230      RANDOMIZE(2130)
240      SET = 12
250      PRINT "A RANDOM-ORDER SET -->"
260      GOSUB 1000                      '<< call set generator
270         FOR J = 0 TO SET-1
280            PRINT SET(J);" ";
290         NEXT J
300      PRINT : PRINT
320      ROTEGROUP = 4
330      PRINT "UNPARTITIONED ARRAY, ELEMENT/GROUP ROTATION -->"
340      PRINT "(";ROTEGROUP;"SET MEMBERS PER CYCLE ROTATED )"
350      GOSUB 5000                      '<< call Euclid's Algorithm
360      PRINT "TOTAL NUMBER OF UNIQUE CYCLES =";CYCLES
370      GOSUB 2000      '<< call unpartitioned set group rotation
380         FOR J1 = 0 TO CYCLES-1
390            FOR J2 = 0 TO SET-1
400               PRINT MAT1(J1,J2);
410            NEXT J2
420            PRINT
430            PRINT
440         NEXT J1
450      PRINT "'0' START POINT TRANSPOSITION -->"
460      GOSUB 3000                          '<< call set transposition
470         FOR J1 = 0 TO CYCLES-1
480            FOR J2 = 0 TO SET-1
490               PRINT MAT2(J1,J2);
500            NEXT J2
510            PRINT
520            PRINT
530         NEXT J1
540      NUMSEGS = 4
550      SEGMEMS = SET/NUMSEGS
560      PRINT "PARTITIONED ARRAY, ROTATION WITHIN SEGMENT -->"
570      PRINT "(DIVIDED INTO";NUMSEGS;"EQUAL SEGMENTS)"
580      GOSUB 4000           '<< call set segment member rotation
590         FOR J1 = 0 TO SEGMEMS - 1
600            PRINT "|";
610            FOR J2 = 0 TO SET - 1
620               PRINT MAT3(J1,J2);
630               IF (J2+1) MOD SEGMEMS = 0 THEN PRINT "|";
640            NEXT J2
650            PRINT
660            PRINT
670         NEXT J1
680 END
1000 REM ================================================ CTB2.5
1010 REM *********************>> SETFLAG <<*********************
1020 REM ================================================
1030    FOR K9 = 0 TO SET - 1
1040       R9 = INT(RND * SET)
1050       IF CUM(R9) = 1 THEN 1040
1060       CUM(R9) = 1
1070       SET(K9) = R9
1080    NEXT K9
1090 RETURN
2000 REM ================================================ CTB2.17
2010 REM *******************>> SETROTAT <<*********************
2020 REM ================================================
2030 REM    This subroutine rotates set members by moving a
```

```
2040 REM      specified group of notes from the beginning to the
2050 REM      end of the series.
2060 REM ===============================================================
2070 REM                    Variable Descriptions
2080 REM        Entering -
2090 REM          SET: length of series
2100 REM          ROTEGROUP: # of contiguous set members to rotate
2110 REM        Exiting -
2120 REM          MAT1: matrix of rotated sets
2130 REM        Local -
2140 REM          R9: rotation factor marker
2150 REM          S9: counter, pointer to MAT1(n,n)
2160 REM          T9: pointer to SET()
2170 REM          K9: loop index
2180 REM          L9: loop index, pointer to MAT(n,n)
2190 REM ===============================================================
2200     ROTEGROUP = ROTEGROUP - 1
2210     R9 = 0
2220     S9 = 0
2230        FOR K9 = ROTEGROUP TO SET-1 + ROTEGROUP
2240           FOR L9 = 1 TO SET
2250              T9 = (K9+L9+R9) MOD SET
2260              MAT1(S9,L9-1) = SET(T9)
2270           NEXT L9
2280           R9 = R9 + ROTEGROUP
2290           S9 = S9 + 1
2295 IF S9 = CYCLES THEN RETURN
2300        NEXT K9
2310 RETURN
3000 REM ====================================================== CTB2.1
3010 REM ******************>> ZEROTRNP <<*********************
3020 REM ===============================================================
3030 REM     This subroutine transposes a collection of sets
3040 REM     sets to '0' start point.
3050 REM ===============================================================
3060 REM                    Variable Descriptions
3070 REM        Entering -
3080 REM          MAT1(n,n): matrix of rotated sets
3090 REM          SET: length of series
3100 REM        Exiting -
3110 REM          MAT2(n,n): matrix of transposed sets
3120 REM        Local -
3130 REM          INTVAL: interval of transposition
3140 REM          S9: set member after transposition
3150 REM          K9: loop index, pointer to MAT1(n,n) & MAT2(n,n)
3160 REM          L9: loop index, pointer to MAT1(n,n) & MAT2(n,n)
3170 REM ===============================================================
3180     FOR K9 = 0 TO CYCLES-1
3190        INTVAL = MAT1(K9,0)
3200           FOR L9 = 0 TO SET-1
3210              S9 = MAT1(K9,L9)-INTVAL
3220              IF S9 < 0 THEN S9 = S9 + 12
3230              MAT2(K9,L9) = S9
3240           NEXT L9
3250     NEXT K9
3260 RETURN
4000 REM ====================================================== CTB2.19
4010 REM *********************>> SEGROTAT <<*******************
4020 REM ===============================================================
4030 REM     This subroutine rotates partitioned-set segment
```

```
4040 REM     members.
4050 REM ============================================================
4060 REM                    Variable Descriptions
4070 REM     Entering -
4080 REM       SET(): prime set
4090 REM       SET: length of series
4100 REM       NUMSEGS: symmetrical set partitioning
4110 REM     Exiting -
4120 REM       MAT3(n,n): matrix of sets after internal rotation
4130 REM     Local -
4140 REM       SEGMEMS: number of members in each segment
4150 REM       S9: counter, pointer to MAT(n,n)
4160 REM       T9: counter, pointer to MAT(n,n)
4170 REM       K9: loop index
4180 REM       L9: loop index, pointer to SET()
4190 REM       M9: loop index, pointer to SET()
4200 REM ============================================================
4210     S9 = 0
4220     SEGMEMS = SET/NUMSEGS
4230        FOR K9 = 1 TO SEGMEMS
4240           T9 = 0
4250           FOR L9 = 0 TO SET-1 STEP SEGMEMS
4260              FOR M9 = S9 + 1 TO SEGMEMS + S9
4270                 MAT3(S9,T9) = SET(M9 MOD SEGMEMS + L9)
4280                 T9 = T9 + 1
4290              NEXT M9
4300           NEXT L9
4310           S9 = S9 + 1
4320        NEXT K9
4330  RETURN
5000 REM ================================================= CTB1.19
5010 REM ********************>> GCD <<**************************
5020 REM               (modified to meet program specs)
5030 REM ============================================================
5040     A9 = SET
5050     B9 = ROTEGROUP
5060     IF A9 > B9 THEN SWAP A9,B9
5070        WHILE A9 > 0
5080           C9 = INT(B9/A9)
5090           D9 = B9-A9*C9
5100           B9 = A9
5110           A9 = D9
5120        WEND
5130     CYCLES = SET/B9
5140 RETURN
```

RUN (Rotation)

```
Random Number Seed (-32768 to 32767)? 2130
A RANDOM-ORDER SET -->
  10   9   8  11   5   3   2   7   4   0   6   1

UNPARTITIONED ARRAY, ELEMENT/GROUP ROTATION -->
( 4 SET MEMBERS PER CYCLE ROTATED )
TOTAL NUMBER OF UNIQUE CYCLES = 3
   5   3   2   7   4   0   6   1  10   9   8  11

   4   0   6   1  10   9   8  11   5   3   2   7

  10   9   8  11   5   3   2   7   4   0   6   1
```

```
'0' START POINT TRANSPOSITION -->
 0  10  9  2  11  7  1  8  5  4  3  6

 0  8  2  9  6  5  4  7  1  11  10  3

 0  11  10  1  7  5  4  9  6  2  8  3
```

PARTITIONED ARRAY, ROTATION WITHIN SEGMENT -->
(DIVIDED INTO 4 EQUAL SEGMENTS)

```
| 9   8   10 | 5   3   11 | 7   4   2 | 6   1   0 |

| 8   10  9  | 3   11  5  | 4   2   7 | 1   0   6 |

| 10  9   8  | 11  5   3  | 2   7   4 | 0   6   1 |
```

SUBROUTINE GROUP: TIMPOINT

○ Pitchtab	CTB1.3
○ Setflag	CTB2.6
○ Timpoint	CTB2.20

Purpose

Derive a rhythm duration series from a 12-tone pitch series using the timepoint system.

Notes

Sometimes, composers wish to map the internal interval relations of a 12-tone series onto the rhythm domain. The timepoint system is commonly used to produce a one-to-one correspondence between the pitch interval-size and note attack-point. As it is the time intervals between pitch attacks that are of importance to this system, the sound-to-silence ratio between pitch onsets may be determined by an independent articulation parameter. A modulus is often used to keep numeric series computation within the one-octave pitch class boundaries (0 to 11, mod 12); similarly, a time modulus is employed to match the pitch modulus when correlation is desirable.

This subroutine first computes the distance in 1/2-steps between consecutive set members; it then returns a series of durations, articulated by a modulus which determines the number of metrical pulses allowed within each bar.

Programming Ideas

1) Write a program that allows the user to input a 12-tone series and then transforms the original row via cyclical sampling (Samplset, CTB2.15). Map the pitch series to attack timepoints.

2) Modify the above program to include the set rotation and transposition subroutines CTB2.17, CTB2.18, and CTB2.19. Allow the user to derive articulation and volume parameters from the input series transformations as well as the ryhthm.

3) Write a program to automatically generate random-order 12-tone rows, produce transformations, and then file data for four musical parameters.

Program Listing

```
100 REM ================================================================
110 REM                       DRIVER PROGRAM
120 REM                         (Timpoint)
130 REM ================================================================
140     DIM SET(12),CUM(12)
150     DIM P$(12),FRACTION$(12)
160     RANDOMIZE(-111)
170     MEDIAN = 16
```

```
180      GOSUB 1000                              '<< call pitch class table
190        FOR J = 1 TO 4
200          GOSUB 2000                              '<< call set generator
210          PRINT "RANDOM-ORDER 12-TONE ROW #";J;"MOD";MDLS;"--"
220            FOR J1 =  0 TO 11
230              PRINT P$(SET(J1));" ";     '<< series to screen
240            NEXT J1
250          PRINT
260          PRINT "THE NUMERIC EQUIVALENT --"
270            FOR J1 = 0 TO 11
280              PRINT SET(J1);
290            NEXT J1
300          PRINT
310          PRINT "DURATIONS REPRESENTING THE DISTANCE";"
BETWEEN TIME POINTS --"
320          PRINT "(USING A 16TH-NOTE PULSE BASE ";"AND A
MEASURE OF ";MDLS;"-16THS)"
330          GOSUB 3000              '<< call timepoint generator
340            FOR J1 = 0 TO 11
350              PRINT FRACTION$(J1);  '<< timepoints to screen
360            NEXT J1
370          PRINT "TOTAL OF DURATIONS =";TALLY;
380          PRINT
390          PRINT
400        NEXT J
410 END
1000 REM ===================================================== CTB1.3
1010 REM *******************>> PITCHTAB <<*********************
1020 REM            (modified to load pitch classes only)
1030 REM =====================================================
1040      FOR J = 0 TO 11
1050          READ P$(J)                     '<< load pitch classes
1060        NEXT J
1070 REM++++++++++++++++++++++++++++++++++
1080    DATA C,C#,D,D#,E,F,F#,G,G#,A,A#,B
1090 REM++++++++++++++++++++++++++++++++++
1100 RETURN
2000 REM ===================================================== CTB2.5
2010 REM *******************>> SETFLAG <<*********************
2020 REM            (modified to generate modulus-converted
2030 REM                series and reset flag array)
2040 REM =====================================================
2050    MDLS = 12/J         '<< change modulus for each new series
2060        FOR K9 = 0 TO 11
2070          R9 = INT(RND * 12)
2080          IF CUM(R9) = 1 THEN 2070
2090          CUM(R9) = 1
2100          SET(K9) = R9 MOD MDLS
2110        NEXT K9
2120        FOR K9 = 0 TO 12
2130          CUM(K9) = 0          '<< zero flags prior to next call
2140 NEXT K9
2150 RETURN
3000 REM ===================================================== CTB2.20
3010 REM *******************>> TIMPOINT <<*********************
3020 REM =====================================================
3030 REM      This subroutine produces rhythm duration values
3040 REM      using the serial 'timepoint system'.  That is,
3050 REM      a sequence of time durations,mod n,is derived
3060 REM      from the distance between consecutive set
```

```
3070 REM       members.  The modulus determines the number of
3080 REM       metrical pulses contained within one measure.
3090 REM ===========================================================
3100 REM                    Variable Descriptions
3110 REM       Entering -
3120 REM         SET(): array of series values
3130 REM         MDLS: modulus for computation
3140 REM         MEDIAN: basic pulse unit
3150 REM       Exiting -
3160 REM         FRACTION$(): character array of time durations
3170 REM         TALLY: total of time durations
3180 REM       Local -
3190 REM         DUR: fraction numerator
3200 REM         K9: loop index, pointer to SET()
3210 REM ===========================================================
3220     TALLY = 0
3230        FOR K9 = 0 TO 10
3240           IF SET(K9+1) <= SET(K9) THEN DUR = MDLS - SET(K9) +
SET(K9+1) ELSE DUR = SET(K9+1) - SET(K9)
3250           TALLY = TALLY + DUR
3260           FRACTION$(K9) = STR$(DUR) + "/" + STR$(MEDIAN)
3270        NEXT K9
3280     DUR = MDLS - SET(K9)
3290     TALLY = TALLY + DUR
3300     FRACTION$(11) = STR$(DUR) + "/" + STR$(MEDIAN)
3310 RETURN
```

RUN (Timpoint)

```
RANDOM-ORDER 12-TONE ROW # 1 MOD 12 --
G# C F# G F D# A C# B D E A#
THE NUMERIC EQUIVALENT --
 8   0   6   7   5   3   9   1   11   2   4   10
DURATIONS REPRESENTING THE DISTANCE BETWEEN TIME POINTS --
(USING A 16TH-NOTE PULSE BASE AND A MEASURE OF  12 -16THS)
 4/ 16 6/ 16 1/ 16 10/ 16 10/ 16 6/ 16 4/ 16 10/ 16 3/ 16
 2/ 16 6/ 16 2/ 16
TOTAL OF DURATIONS = 64

RANDOM-ORDER 12-TONE ROW # 2 MOD 6 --
D F C F E C E D# C# C# D D#
THE NUMERIC EQUIVALENT --
 2   5   0   5   4   0   4   3   1   1   2   3
DURATIONS REPRESENTING THE DISTANCE BETWEEN TIME POINTS --
(USING A 16TH-NOTE PULSE BASE AND A MEASURE OF  6 -16THS)
 3/ 16 1/ 16 5/ 16 5/ 16 2/ 16 4/ 16 5/ 16 4/ 16 6/ 16
 1/ 16 1/ 16 3/ 16
TOTAL OF DURATIONS = 40

RANDOM-ORDER 12-TONE ROW # 3 MOD 4 --
D# C D D C D# D# C# C# D C C#
THE NUMERIC EQUIVALENT --
 3   0   2   2   0   3   3   1   1   2   0   1
DURATIONS REPRESENTING THE DISTANCE BETWEEN TIME POINTS --
(USING A 16TH-NOTE PULSE BASE AND A MEASURE OF  4 -16THS)
 1/ 16 2/ 16 4/ 16 2/ 16 3/ 16 4/ 16 2/ 16 4/ 16 1/ 16
 2/ 16 1/ 16 3/ 16
TOTAL OF DURATIONS = 29
```

```
RANDOM-ORDER 12-TONE ROW # 4 MOD 3 --
C C# C# C C D D D C# C C#
THE NUMERIC EQUIVALENT --
 0  1  1  0  0  2  2  2  2  1  0  1
DURATIONS REPRESENTING THE DISTANCE BETWEEN TIME POINTS --
(USING A 16TH-NOTE PULSE BASE AND A MEASURE OF  3 -16THS)
 1/ 16 3/ 16 2/ 16 3/ 16 2/ 16 3/ 16 3/ 16 3/ 16 2/ 16
 2/ 16 1/ 16 2/ 16
TOTAL OF DURATIONS = 27
```

SUBROUTINE GROUP: ALINTSEQ

○ Alintseq   CTB2.21
○ Conshufl   CTB2.7

Purpose

Map a set of 11 unique numeric intervals (sizes 1 to 11) to chromatic scale pitch classes.

Notes

Although the random-order interval set generated by the program contains only one of each interval, it is quite likely that the mapping process will result in the repetition of one or more pitch classes. (The production of an all-interval pitch class series requires a more laborious algorithm.) Nevertheless, the repetition of tones in an all-interval sequence can be used intentionally to achieve tonal emphasis through pitch omission and redundancy.

The tones of numeric pitch class, interval-derived series and sequences can be octave-displaced without destroying the basic internal relationships; all that need be done is to convert an interval to its octave-contained complement when displacement causes a change of direction (e.g., a minor 3rd upward interval becomes a major 6th downward interval.

Programming Ideas

1) Write a program to test a randomly generated interval series for pitch class omissions and redundancy. Tabulate the total number of absent pitches, specific pitch omissions, total number of pitch redundancies, and specific pitch repetitions.

2) Augment the above program to increase its intelligence; i.e., give it conditional guidelines for creating a continuity factor when testing and selecting rows for placement in a file of tonally related series.

3) Use the file generated in number 2 as a set of pointers for pitch, rhythm, articulation, and volume parameters.

4) Modify ALINTSEQ to include a subroutine for pitch octave-displacement which uses interval complementation to deal with line direction change.

Program Listing

```
100 REM  ============================================================
110 REM                      DRIVER PROGRAM
120 REM                        (Alintseq)
130 REM  ============================================================
140    DIM INTSET(11),PCLASS(12)
150    TOTAL = 5
160    RANDOMIZE(212)
170      FOR J = 1 TO 11
180        INTSET(J) = (J)              '<< load interval set array
```

```
190             NEXT J
200             FOR J = 1 TO TOTAL
210                 GOSUB 2000            '<< call interval array shuffler
220                 PRINT "RANDOM-ORDER INTERVAL CLASS SERIES # ";J ":"
230                     FOR J1 = 1 TO 11
240                         PRINT INTSET(J1);
250                     NEXT J1
260                 PRINT
270                 GOSUB 1000 '<<  call interval to pitch class mapping
280                 PRINT "--- MAPPED TO PITCH CLASS NUMBERS ---"
290                     FOR J1 = 0 TO 11
300                         PRINT PCLASS(J1);
310                     NEXT J1
320                 PRINT
330 NEXT J
340 END
1000 REM ================================================= CTB2.21
1010 REM *******************>> ALINTSEQ <<*********************
1020 REM =====================================================
1030 REM     This subroutine maps a set of 11 unique intervals
1040 REM     (in semitones, size 1-11) to the pitch classes of
1050 REM     the chromatic scale.  Although the interval set is
1060 REM     non-redundant, there is a high probability that
1070 REM     the resultant pitch class sequence will contain at
1080 REM     least one repeated tone, thus producing a 12-note
1090 REM     sequence rather than a 12-note series.
1100 REM =====================================================
1110 REM                 Variable Descriptions
1120 REM     Entering -
1130 REM       INTSET(): array of unique interval-sizes 1-11
1140 REM     Exiting -
1150 REM       PCLASS(): pitch class sequence array
1160 REM     Local -
1170 REM       K9: loop index, pointer to intset(),PCLASS()
1180 REM =====================================================
1190    PCLASS(0)=0
1200      FOR K9 = 1 TO 11
1210          PCLASS(K9) = (PCLASS(K9-1) + INTSET(K9)) MOD 12
1220      NEXT K9
1230 RETURN
2000 REM ================================================= CTB2.6
2010 REM *******************>> CONSHUFL) <<********************
2020 REM                 (adapted to program specs)
2030 REM =====================================================
2040    FOR K9 = 1 TO 11
2050        R9 = INT(RND * 11) + 1
2060        S9 = INTSET(K9)
2070        INTSET(K9) = INTSET(R9)
2080        INTSET(R9) = S9
2090    NEXT K9
2100 RETURN
```

RUN (Alintseq)

```
RANDOM-ORDER INTERVAL CLASS SERIES #  1 :
 1   3   10   11   7   8   2   6   9   4   5
--- MAPPED TO PITCH CLASS NUMBERS ---
 0   1   4   2   1   8   4   6   0   9   1   6
```

```
RANDOM-ORDER INTERVAL CLASS SERIES #  2 :
  8  11  9  4  6  5  10  1  7  2  3
--- MAPPED TO PITCH CLASS NUMBERS ---
  0  8  7  4  8  2  7  5  6  1  3  6
RANDOM-ORDER INTERVAL CLASS SERIES #  3 :
  4  6  1  11  9  10  2  5  8  7  3
--- MAPPED TO PITCH CLASS NUMBERS ---
  0  4  10  11  10  7  5  7  0  8  3  6
RANDOM-ORDER INTERVAL CLASS SERIES #  4 :
  7  1  4  5  11  6  8  9  3  10  2
--- MAPPED TO PITCH CLASS NUMBERS ---
  0  7  8  0  5  4  10  6  3  6  4  6
RANDOM-ORDER INTERVAL CLASS SERIES #  5 :
  4  7  1  3  2  8  5  9  10  6  11
--- MAPPED TO PITCH CLASS NUMBERS ---
  0  4  11  0  3  5  1  6  3  1  7  6
```

SUBROUTINE GROUP: ALINTSET

- ○ Alintset   CTB2.22
- ○ Zeromat   CTB1.9
- ○ Setstore   CTB2.23

Purpose

Generate all-interval 12-tone series. (Pitch-class repetition is disallowed.)

Notes

The algorithm in Subroutine Alintset relies on the computer's ability to sample/test and then discard/keep huge amounts of data in a short period of time. Although the method employed is one of "brute force," it is similar to the way composers go about discovering all-interval pitch series. As the computer randomly generates the tones of the series, it tests the pitch classes and melodic intervals for uniqueness. If redundancy is encountered, the offending pitch is discarded and progress resumes. The catch is that, as more and more pitches are added to the series, it becomes increasingly difficult to find tones that pass the redundancy tests. In fact, many trial sets have to be abandoned near the end because no solution can be found (given the previous choices). Nevertheless, execution of the algorithm on a 16-bit micro using interpreted BASIC will generate an average of four all-interval series per minute. If this is too slow, then a compiled version of the program must be run.

Upon completion of each valid series, ALINTSET calls Subroutine SET-STORE to compare the current series with those previously generated. If the set is unique, it is stored in array ALSET$( ).

Programming Ideas

1) Alter the program to include Pitchtab (CTB1.3).

2) Write a program to rotate the intervals of the all-interval series returned by the program; note the effects of interval rotation on pitch redundancy, and then find ways to exploit row characteristics.

3) Modify Subroutine Group ALINTSET to include a procedure for pitch octave-displacement which uses interval complementation to deal with line direction changes.

Program Listing

```
100 REM ============================================================
110 REM                     DRIVER PROGRAM
120 REM                      (Alintset)
130 REM ============================================================
140     DIM PCLASS(12),PCUM(12),ICUM(12),TEMP(12),ALSET$(10)
150     TOTAL = 10
160     SETCOUNT = 0
```

```
170      RANDOMIZE(-1923)
180        FOR J = 1 TO TOTAL
190          PRINT "COMPUTING -- ALL-INTERVAL 12-TONE SET #";J
200          GOSUB 1000
210        IF FLAG = 1 THEN PRINT ALSET$(SETCOUNT) ELSE GOSUB 1000
220        NEXT J
230 END
1000 REM ================================================= CTB2.22
1010 REM ******************>> ALINTSET <<*********************
1020 REM =================================================
1030 REM    This subroutine generates all-interval 12-note
1040 REM    series by the sample-test-discard/keep method.
1100 REM =================================================
1110 REM                  Variable Descriptions
1120 REM    Entering -
1130 REM       none
1140 REM    Exiting -
1150 REM       PCLASS(): array holding all-interval series
1160 REM    Local -
1170 REM       PCUM(): array of note redundancy flags
1180 REM       ICUM(): array of interval redundancy flags
1190 REM       TEMP(): array holding temporary trial series
1200 REM       INTSIZE: interval (in 1/2-steps) between notes
1210 REM       R9: random integer for test series
1220 REM       K9: loop index, pointer to TEMP()
1230 REM       L9: loop index, pointer to TEMP(), PCLASS()
1240 REM       M9: loop index, pointer to TEMP(), PCLASS()
1250 REM =================================================
1260     PCLASS(1) = 1 : PCLASS(12) = 7
1270        FOR K9 = 2 TO 11
1280          R9 = INT(RND * 11) + 2
1290          IF R9 = 7 THEN 1280
1300          IF PCUM(R9) = 1 THEN 1280
1310          TEMP(K9) = R9
1320          PCUM(R9) = 1
1330        NEXT K9
1340        FOR L9 = 2 TO 12
1350          FOR M9 = 2 TO 11
1360            IF TEMP(M9) > 0 THEN INTSIZE = TEMP(M9) - PCLASS
(L9-1)ELSE 1390
1370            IF INTSIZE < 0 THEN INTSIZE = 12 + INTSIZE
1380            IF ICUM(INTSIZE) < 1 THEN PCLASS(L9) = TEMP(M9):
TEMP(M9) = 0 : ICUM(INTSIZE) = 1 : GOTO 1410 ELSE 1390
1390          NEXT M9
1400          IF PCLASS(L9) = 0 THEN GOSUB 2000 : GOTO 1200
1410        NEXT L9
1420     GOSUB 3000 : GOSUB 2000
1430 RETURN 210
2000 REM ================================================= CTB1.9
2010 REM ******************>> ZEROMAT <<*********************
2020 REM =================================================
2030     FOR L9 = 1 TO 12
2040        PCUM(L9) = 0 : ICUM(L9) = 0 : PCLASS(L9) = 0
2050     NEXT L9
2060 RETURN
3000 REM ================================================= CTB2.23
3010 REM ******************>> SETSTORE <<*********************
3020 REM =================================================
3030 REM    This subroutine stores and maintains an identity
3040 REM    check on the all-interval series generated by the
```

```
3050 REM     subroutine ALINTSET.  Each output set is converted
3060 REM     to a character string, tested against all prev-
3070 REM     iously stored sets for uniqueness, then put in
3080 REM     an character string array.
3090 REM ==========================================================
3100 REM                  Variable Descriptions
3110 REM     Entering -
3120 REM       PCLASS(): holds current pitch class (integer) set
3130 REM     Exiting -
3140 REM       ALSET$(): string array holding all unique sets
3150 REM       SETCOUNT: index of unique all-interval sets
3160 REM       FLAG: indicator of set uniqueness
3170 REM     Local -
3180 REM       L9: loop index, pointer to PCLASS()
3190 REM       CURSET$: string buffer holding current set
3200 REM ==========================================================
3210    CURSET$ = ""
3220       FOR L9=1 TO 12
3230          CURSET$ = CURSET$ + STR$(PCLASS(L9)-1)
3240       NEXT L9
3250    SETCOUNT = SETCOUNT + 1
3260       FOR L9 = 1 TO SETCOUNT - 1
3270          IF ALSET$(L9) = CURSET$ THEN FLAG = 0 : RETURN
3280       NEXT L9
3290    ALSET$(SETCOUNT)=CURSET$
3300    FLAG = 1
3310 RETURN
```

RUN (Alintset)

```
COMPUTING -- ALL-INTERVAL 12-TONE SET # 1
 0  5  7 11  2  3  1  8  4 10  9  6
COMPUTING -- ALL-INTERVAL 12-TONE SET # 2
 0  2 11  4  8  7  1  9 10  5  3  6
COMPUTING -- ALL-INTERVAL 12-TONE SET # 3
 0  5  2  9  1  3  4 10  8 11  7  6
COMPUTING -- ALL-INTERVAL 12-TONE SET # 4
 0  3 11 10  5  9  2  4  1  7  8  6
COMPUTING -- ALL-INTERVAL 12-TONE SET # 5
 0  9  8  1  7 11  2 10  5  3  4  6
COMPUTING -- ALL-INTERVAL 12-TONE SET # 6
 0  4 10  3  1  9 11  8  7  2  5  6
COMPUTING -- ALL-INTERVAL 12-TONE SET # 7
 0  7 11  4  5  2 10  1  3  9  8  6
COMPUTING -- ALL-INTERVAL 12-TONE SET # 8
 0  2  3  7  5  1  8 11 10  4  9  6
COMPUTING -- ALL-INTERVAL 12-TONE SET # 9
 0  1 10  3  7  2  8 11  9  5  4  6
COMPUTING -- ALL-INTERVAL 12-TONE SET # 10
 0  7  8  2 11  9  1  4  3  5 10  6
```

SUBROUTINE GROUP: INTLINK

- ○ Intlink   CTB2.24
- ○ Matprint   CTB1.6
- ○ Zeromat   CTB1.9

Purpose

Generate a stream of 12-tone series linked at the point of interval redundancy.

Notes

This group of subroutines represents one of the most unrigorous serial procedures imaginable. First, INTLINK builds a random-order number series (1 to 12). It then locates the set position at which interval redundancy occurs and uses the remaining tones in the row (in order) as the nucleus of the next series to be generated; the values needed to complete the new row are then randomly generated. Thus, pitch-group repetitions of various lengths are produced—within an overall serial context—as a method of generating new, obliquely related series for use as pointers to any or all musical element tables.

Although it is theoretically possible that an order correspondence of from two to 12 pitches will be maintained between consecutively generated series, probabilities are skewed toward the carry-over of smaller groups of tones.

Programming Idea

Write a program that:

- Derives rhythm parameter timepoints from each series returned.
- Randomly assigns octave-displacements to the series tones.
- Invokes Alterseq (CTB2.4) to expand or contract the lines resulting from the previous step.
- Files the pitch and rhythm data.

Program Listing

```
100 REM  ========================================================
110 REM                      DRIVER PROGRAM
120 REM                        (Intlink)
130 REM  ========================================================
140     DIM PCUM(12),ICUM(12),PCLASS(12)
150     RANDOMIZE(1)
160     TOTAL = 10
170     GOSUB 1000      '<< call interval-linked PC series generator
180 END
1000 REM  ================================================= CTB2.24
1010 REM  *******************>> INTLINK <<********************
1020 REM  ========================================================
```

```
1030 REM      This subroutine generates a random-order series,
1040 REM      locates the series position at which interval-size
1050 REM      redundancy occurs, then links subsequent set
1060 REM      permutations by moving remaining values from flag-
1070 REM      point in the current series to the beginning of the
1080 REM      next series to form its nucleus. Appropriate values
1090 REM      are then permutated to complete the (now) current
1100 REM      series. Thus, value-group repetitions of various
1110 REM      lengths are produced - within an overall serial
1120 REM      context - as a method of generating new related
1130 REM      sequences for use as pointers to pitch, rhythm,
1140 REM      volume, articulation, or other parameter elements.
1150 REM ============================================================
1160 REM                    Variable Descriptions
1170 REM      Entering -
1180 REM        TOTAL: number of series to generate & link
1190 REM      Exiting -
1200 REM        (to ZEROMAT)
1210 REM          PCUM: array of pitchclass flags
1220 REM          ICUM: array of intervalclass flags
1230 REM        (to MATPRINT)
1240 REM          PCLASS(): array holding current series
1250 REM          REDPT: interval redundancy point marker
1260 REM      Local -
1270 REM        INTSIZE: interval between consecutive pitchclasses
1280 REM        SHIFT: number of places to shift remaining setmems
1290 REM        R9: random integer
1300 REM        K9: loop index
1310 REM        L9: loop index, pointer to PCLASS()
1320 REM ============================================================
1330     REDPT = 1
1340       FOR K9 = 1 TO TOTAL   '<< flag carried-over set members
1350         FOR L9 = 1 TO 12
1360           IF PCLASS(L9) > 0 THEN PCUM(PCLASS(L9)) = 1
1370         NEXT L9
1380         FOR L9 = 1 TO 12     '<< gen required new setmembers
1390           IF PCLASS(L9) > 0 THEN 1440
1400           R9 = INT(RND * 12) + 1
1410           IF PCUM(R9) = 1 THEN 1400
1420           PCUM(R9) = 1
1430           PCLASS(L9) = R9
1440         NEXT L9
1450         FOR L9 = 1 TO 11 '<< find intervals btwn setmembers
1460           INTSIZE = PCLASS(L9+1) - PCLASS(L9)
1470           IF INTSIZE < 0 THEN INTSIZE = 12 - ABS(INTSIZE)
1480           IF ICUM(INTSIZE) = 1 THEN 1510'<<mark redundancy
1490           ICUM(INTSIZE) = 1
1500         NEXT L9
1510         REDPT = L9 + 1
1520         PRINT "INTERVAL REDUNDANCY OCCURS";
1530         PRINT " AT POSITION -->";REDPT
1540         GOSUB 2000
1550         GOSUB 3000
1560         SHIFT = 1
1570         FOR L9 = REDPT  TO 12 '<< shift set balance forward
1580           PCLASS(SHIFT) = PCLASS(L9)
1590           SHIFT = SHIFT + 1
1600         NEXT L9
1610         FOR L9 = SHIFT TO 12'<< zero remaining array places
1620           PCLASS(L9) = 0
```

```
1630          NEXT L9
1640        NEXT K9
1650 RETURN
2000 REM ======================================================= CTB1.6
2010 REM *********************>> MATPRINT <<*********************
2020 REM                 (adapted to program specs)
2030 REM =======================================================
2040    PRINT "PC SET: ";
2050       FOR M9 = 1 TO 12
2060          PRINT PCLASS(M9);
2070          IF M9 = REDPT - 1 THEN PRINT "||";
2080       NEXT M9
2090    PRINT
2100 RETURN
3000 REM ======================================================= CTB1.9
3010 REM *********************>> ZEROMAT <<*********************
3020 REM                 (adapted to program specs)
3030 REM =======================================================
3040    FOR N9 = 1 TO 12
3050       PCUM(N9) = 0 : ICUM(N9) = 0
3060    NEXT N9
3070 RETURN
```

RUN (Intlink)

```
INTERVAL REDUNDANCY OCCURS AT POSITION --> 4
PC SET:  6  8  9 || 10  1  4  7  3  5  2 11  12
INTERVAL REDUNDANCY OCCURS AT POSITION --> 3
PC SET: 10  1 || 4  7  3  5  2 11 12  8  9  6
INTERVAL REDUNDANCY OCCURS AT POSITION --> 6
PC SET:  4  7  3  5  2 || 11 12  8  9  6 10  1
INTERVAL REDUNDANCY OCCURS AT POSITION --> 4
PC SET: 11 12  8 || 9  6 10  1  2  4  5  7  3
INTERVAL REDUNDANCY OCCURS AT POSITION --> 7
PC SET:  9  6 10  1  2  4 || 5  7  3 11  8 12
INTERVAL REDUNDANCY OCCURS AT POSITION --> 4
PC SET:  5  7  3 || 11  8 12 10  6  4  9  2  1
INTERVAL REDUNDANCY OCCURS AT POSITION --> 6
PC SET: 11  8 12 10  6 || 4  9  2  1  3  5  7
INTERVAL REDUNDANCY OCCURS AT POSITION --> 3
PC SET:  4  9 || 2  1  3  5  7 11  8 12  6 10
INTERVAL REDUNDANCY OCCURS AT POSITION --> 4
PC SET:  2  1  3 || 5  7 11  8 12  6 10  9  4
INTERVAL REDUNDANCY OCCURS AT POSITION --> 5
PC SET:  5  7 11  8 || 12  6 10  9  4  1  3  2
```

Purpose

Control the ratio of repeated integers to unique integers in a random-order stream of values.

Notes

The algorithm imposes a kind of "sliding series" on a continuously gener-ated sequence of bounded values. It works by preventing the repetition of any number falling within an arbitrary window of a predetermined size. For instance, if 100 random numbers within the range 1 to 10 are to be returned, and a window of 9 is specified, then the output sequence will be a nonrepeat-ing set. However, if a smaller window is entered, say 4, then redundancy will only be disallowed within any group of four adjacent numbers.

Programming Ideas

1) Modify the DRIVER PROGRAM to allow user input of TOTAL, RANGE, and WINDO values.

2) Write a program based on Valratio which returns (over separate runs) pointers to pitch, octave-displacement, rhythm duration, volume, and articulation element tables.

3) Expand program 2 above to include Alterseq (CTB2.4). Add file-writing code to send the output of multiple program executions to four separate files, each of which should contain pitch, rhythm, articulation, and volume data for a single musical line. Perform the four files concurrently on a digi-tal synthesizer.

Program Listing

```
100 REM =============================================================
110 REM                         DRIVER PROGRAM
115 REM                           (Valratio)
120 REM =============================================================
130     DIM P(12),X(100)
140     RANDOMIZE(-29312)
150     TOTAL = 100
160     RANGE = 12                     '<< range of random integers
170     WINDO = 4            ' << size of repetition prevent window
180     GOSUB 1000                      '<< call value ratio control
185     PRINT "SIZE OF VALUE WINDOW IS ";WINDO
190        FOR J = 1 TO 100
200           PRINT X(J),
210        NEXT J
220 END
1000 REM ============================================== CTB2.25
1010 REM ****************>> VALRATIO <<************************
1020 REM ============================================================
1030 REM    This algorithm prevents repetition of values which
```

```
1040 REM      fall within a specified 'window' of predetermined
1050 REM      size.  For instance, if 100 values are to be
1060 REM      returned, a window of 9 is specified, and a
1070 REM      random number value range of 1-10 is entered,
1080 REM      then the sequence which is generated will be a
1090 REM      non-repeating series (set).  However, if a smaller
1100 REM      window is entered, then only the values falling
1110 REM      within the sliding 'window' will be prevented
1120 REM      from containing repetitions.
1130 REM ========================================================
1140 REM                  Variable Descriptions
1150 REM
1160 REM      Entering -
1170 REM        TOTAL: number of values to be returned
1180 REM        RANGE: 1-n inclusive limits for random numbers
1190 REM        WINDO: size of window for repetition prevention
1200 REM      Exiting -
1210 REM        X(): array holding sequence of values
1220 REM      Local -
1230 REM        U: random number, pointer to array P()
1240 REM        P(): array which records value occurence
1250 REM        K9: loop index, pointer to array X()
1260 REM
1270 REM ========================================================
1280          FOR K9 = 1 TO TOTAL
1290            U = INT(RND * RANGE)+1
1300            IF P(U) = 1 THEN 1290
1310            P(U) = 1
1320            X(K9) = U
1330            IF K9 <= WINDO THEN 1350
1340            P(X(K9-WINDO)) = 0
1350          NEXT K9
1360 RETURN
```

RUN (Valratio)

SIZE OF VALUE WINDOW IS 4

7	2	8	3	11
4	12	10	2	1
4	3	5	2	11
1	7	3	4	12
9	8	11	4	1
6	3	11	4	9
2	7	10	12	1
6	11	4	2	3
5	12	6	8	10
1	2	4	7	8
10	5	4	11	9
1	12	5	8	10
6	2	4	1	5
6	11	7	12	9
3	5	10	2	7
1	5	10	8	12
2	4	11	3	1
8	6	9	12	5
7	8	9	2	1
6	11	7	4	9

Purpose

Generate a Markovian integer summation residue cycle that conforms to parameters passed from the driver program; provide a table of integer occurrence frequencies.

Notes

This subroutine was adapted from an algorithm devised by composer Peter Armstrong. Peter's goal was to harness various kinds of numeric series (other than 12-tone) for application to musical elements such as microtonal pitch scales, rhythm tables, etc.

Control parameters ORDER and APPLY$ provide the beautiful flexibility of this algorithm. You can generate many types of ascending integer series, depending upon the number and value of "seeds" input and the summation application mode (if APPLY$ is set to "EXCLUSIVE" then only the outer pair of seed terms is added to generate the next; if APPLY$ is set to "INCLUSIVE" then all seeds are summed to produce the next term). The simplest cases of this Markovian concept are the Fibonacci and Lucas series.

Control variable MODULUS converts the ascending number series to a manageable form (series generated in this manner quickly transcend musical element table bounds). It has been set to 12 for the runs produced by the DRIVER PROGRAM; output falls within the range 0 to 11 to accommodate the numbering system used in several chapter 2 programs which deal with the 12 pitch classes of the chromatic scale. Other MODULUS values may be substituted to "wraparound" the integer output on any desirable range.

A word of caution: If you enter a large number of start seeds and a large modulus, the subroutine can take a long time to execute on a microcomputer running interpreted BASIC.

Programming Idea

Write an interactive program that includes Markov (CTB2.26) and Tunings (CTB1.1) to generate a number of different octave-repeating microtonal series on a digital synthesizer. (The variable MODULUS sets the number of pitches per octave.)

Program Listing

```
100 REM ===========================================================
110 REM                    DRIVER PROGRAM
120 REM                      (Markov)
130 REM ===========================================================
140    DIM CYCLE(5000), SEED(88), FREQ(88)
150    ORDER = 2   '<<nmbr of preceding terms to sum for next term
160    MODULUS = 12            '<< set modulus of residue cycle
170    APPLY$ = "INCLUSIVE"             '<< apply to all seeds
```

```
180          FOR J = 1 TO 2              '<< generate 2 separate cycles
190             PRINT APPLY$;" ADDITION; SEEDS ARE :";
200                FOR J1 = 1 TO ORDER
210                   READ SEED(J1)
220                   PRINT SEED(J1);         '<< send seeds to screen
230                NEXT J1
240 REM +++++++++++++++++++
250 DATA 0,1,1,4,5
260 REM +++++++++++++++++++
270             PRINT
280             GOSUB 1000     '<< call Markovian summation subroutine
290             PRINT
300             PRINT TOTAL; " - MEMBER CYCLE:"
310             PRINT
320                FOR J1 = 1 TO TOTAL
330                   PRINT CYCLE(J1),    '<< display completed cycle
340                NEXT J1
350             PRINT : PRINT
360             PRINT "FREQUENCY TABLE:"
370             PRINT
380                FOR J1 = 1 TO MODULUS
390                   PRINT (J1-1); ":"; FREQ(J1),
400                NEXT J1
410             ORDER = 3          '<< number of preceding terms to sum
420             APPLY$ = "EXCLUSIVE" '<< add outside seed pairs only
430             PRINT
440             PRINT
450          NEXT J
460 END
1000 REM ==================================================== CTB2.26
1010 REM *******************>>  MARKOV  <<*********************
1020 REM ====================================================
1030 REM    Markovian Integer Summation Residual Cycle Generator
1040 REM ====================================================
1050 REM                      Variable Descriptions
1060 REM     Entering -
1070 REM        ORDER:  number of immediately preceding terms
1080 REM                whose sum determines next term
1090 REM        MODULUS: Integer-range modulus; cycle-creating
1100 REM                factor to be imposed on each sum
1110 REM        SEED(): array of seeds (initial "Order" number
1120 REM                of integers to be summed)
1130 REM        APPLY$: string to signal inclusive or exclusive
1140 REM                addition of series seeds
1150 REM     Exiting -
1160 REM        CYCLE(): array holding generated integer cycle
1170 REM        FREQ(): array of integer occurrence frequencies
1180 REM     Local -
1190 REM        NXTERM:  next term to be computed
1200 REM        TOTAL: total number of terms generated
1210 REM        K9: loop index
1220 REM        L9: loop index
1230 REM ====================================================
1240    FOR K9 = 1 TO ORDER
1250       CYCLE(K9) = SEED(K9)              '<< start cycle with seeds
1260    NEXT K9
1270    TOTAL = ORDER
1280    FOR K9 = 1 TO 5000                   '<< compute next new term
1290       NXTERM = SEED(ORDER)
1300          FOR L9 = 1 TO (ORDER-1)
```

```
1310                NXTERM = NXTERM + SEED(L9)
1320            NEXT L9
1330        IF APPLY$ = "EXCLUSIVE" THEN NXTERM = SEED(ORDER) +
SEED(1)
1340        NXTERM = NXTERM - INT(NXTERM/MODULUS) * MODULUS
1350        CYCLE(K9+ORDER) = NXTERM
1360           FOR L9 = 1 TO (ORDER-1)
1370              SEED(L9) = SEED(L9+1)   '<< update seeds
1380           NEXT L9
1390        SEED(ORDER) = NXTERM
1400        TOTAL = TOTAL + 1
1410           FOR L9 = 1 TO ORDER
1420            IF SEED(L9) <> CYCLE(L9) THEN  1470  '<< finished?
1430           NEXT L9
1440        L9 = ORDER
1450        K9 = 5000
1460        TOTAL = TOTAL - ORDER
1470     NEXT K9
1475     GOSUB 2000                              ' << call zeromat
1480     FOR K9 = 1 TO MODULUS   '<< compute occurrence frequencies
1490        FOR L9 = 1 TO TOTAL
1500           IF CYCLE(L9) + 1 = K9 THEN FREQ(K9) = FREQ(K9) + 1
1510        NEXT L9
1520     NEXT K9
1530 RETURN
2000 REM=============================================== CTB1.9
2010 REM ******************>> ZEROMAT <<**********************
2020 REM ====================================================
2030     FOR K9 = 1 TO MODULUS
2040        FREQ(K9) = 0
2050     NEXT K9
2060 RETURN
```

RUN (Markov)

```
INCLUSIVE ADDITION; SEEDS ARE :  0   1

  24  - MEMBER CYCLE:

0              1              1              2              3
5              8              1              9              10
7              5              0              5              5
10             3              1              4              5
9              2              11             1

FREQUENCY TABLE:

0 : 2          1 : 5          2 : 2          3 : 2          4 : 1
5 : 5          6 : 0          7 : 1          8 : 1          9 : 2
10 : 2         11 : 1

EXCLUSIVE ADDITION; SEEDS ARE : 1   4   5

  56  - MEMBER CYCLE:

1              4              5              6              10
3              9              7              10             7
2              0              7              9              9
4              1              10             2              3
```

1	3	6	7	10
4	11	9	1	0
9	10	10	7	5
3	10	3	6	4
7	1	5	0	1
6	6	7	1	7
2	3	10	0	3
1				

FREQUENCY TABLE:

0 : 4	1 : 8	2 : 3	3 : 7	4 : 4
5 : 3	6 : 5	7 : 8	8 : 0	9 : 5
10 : 8	11 : 1			

3
Probability Distribution Functions

PRELIMINARIES

Many compositional algorithms entail testing large amounts of data derived from the uniform random number generator found on mainframes and micros. Music based on sets of syntactical rules and constraints often requires many calls to the integerized RND function by way of the sample-test/keep-discard method, which can be viewed as a process of "filtering" non-conforming values from a stream of data destined for a given musical parameter. Normally, textures composed in this manner are arrived at most efficiently via the computer's intrinsic uniform random distribution algorithm.

Nonuniform probability distributions, on the other hand, are fundamental to an important method of composition in which the details of selected musical parameters are directly calculated without reference to table-based syntactical rules. Often, the goal of this approach is to map the characteristic curve exhibited by the function onto one or more musical parameters. There is no further contextual or historical contingency other than to appropriately scale data to meet parameter range requirements. The collection of algorithms presented in this chapter is by no means exhaustive; it is, however, broad enough to cover most compositional situations.

Each subroutine deals with either a continuous or discrete random variable. Random variables normally assume their values as the result of a random process based on probabilities of occurrence. A continuous random variable can take on an infinite number of states—subject to the precision of the computer word—and is normally expressed as a real number falling between zero and one. A discrete random variable can only take on a limited number of (normally integer) states.

The sum of all the probabilities of all possible outcomes of a random process is always equal to one, and is customarily expressed as a line or bargraph. The continuous random variable graph is typified by a solid line curve. The discrete random variable graph resembles a histogram, but differs in that a histogram records actual frequencies of occurrence of specific values during a program run, whereas the probability distribution graph represents the likelihood of the occurrence of points along an infinite or discrete scale of values during a hypothetical program run. Comparing an occurrence frequency histogram with a probability distribution graph for a particular algorithm provides a method of verifying correct subroutine operation. It also clarifies the correlation between the number of generated samples and fidelity to the ideal probability distribution. (Usually, many data must be generated before the characteristic curve develops.)

Real number values of continuous variables may be converted to integer and mapped to any numerical range by taking the integer portion (the BASIC INT function) after multiplication by the appropriate scaling factor.

Purpose

Generate a random number data set exhibiting Beta Probability Distribution characteristics.

Notes

The algorithm returns continous, random-order real numbers > 0 and $< = 1$. The shape of its curve changes with the values of its controlling parameters—PROB0 and PROB1. PROB0 determines the probability of values nearest zero; PROB1 determines probabilities nearest one. Smaller parameter values produce higher probabilities at the respective boundary; if PROB0 and PROB1 are equal, the curve is symmetric around .5, otherwise the curve tilts in favor of the boundary controlled by the smaller parameter. The mean is

$$PROB0/(PROB0 + PROB1)$$

The curve produced by this function can be made to resemble the bell-shaped (so-called normal) Gaussian curve by setting both PROB0 and PROB1 greater than one. It can be toggled to output uniform distribution by setting PROB0 and PROB1 equal to one.

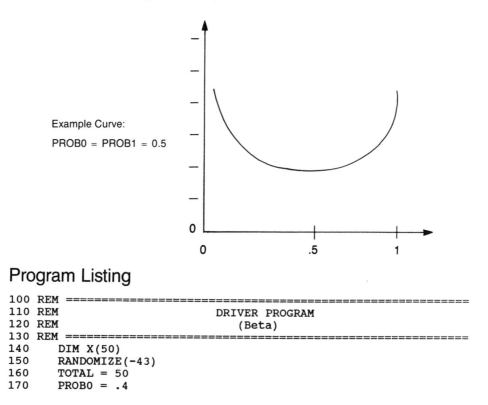

Example Curve:

PROB0 = PROB1 = 0.5

Program Listing

```
100 REM  ===============================================================
110 REM                        DRIVER PROGRAM
120 REM                           (Beta)
130 REM  ===============================================================
140     DIM X(50)
150     RANDOMIZE(-43)
160     TOTAL = 50
170     PROB0 = .4
```

```
180     PROB1 = .2
190     GOSUB 1000                  '<< call Eulerian Beta distribution
200         FOR J = 1 TO TOTAL
210             PRINT X(J);" ";                  '<< sequence to screen
215         IF J MOD 4 = 0 THEN PRINT
220         NEXT J
230 END
1000 REM ================================================== CTB3.1
1010 REM ********************>> BETA <<************************
1020 REM ==================================================
1030 REM            Eulerian Beta Distribution Function
1080 REM ==================================================
1090 REM                   Variable Descriptions
1100 REM
1110 REM       Entering -
1120 REM         TOTAL: length of sequence
1130 REM         PROB0: controls occurrence of values nearer to 0
1140 REM         PROB1: controls occurrence of values nearer to 1
1150 REM       Exiting -
1160 REM         X(): array holding BETA distribution
1170 REM       Local -
1180 REM         R8: random number 1
1190 REM         R9: random number 2
1200 REM         T1: computed probability 1
1210 REM         T2: computed probability 2
1220 REM         SUM: total of probabilities 1 & 2
1230 REM         K9: loop index, pointer to array X()
1240 REM ==================================================
1250     PROB0 = 1 / PROB0
1260     PROB1 = 1 / PROB1
1270         FOR K9 = 1 TO TOTAL
1280             R8 = RND
1290             R9 = RND
1300             T1 = R8 ^ PROB0
1310             T2 = R9 ^ PROB1
1320             SUM = T1 + T2
1330             IF SUM > 1 THEN 1280 ELSE X(K9) = T1 / SUM
1340         NEXT K9
1350 RETURN
```

RUN (Beta)

.7374235	1.508907E-02	.1982958	.5404798
.8092735	.9839786	.787956	.4500791
.6320743	2.327007E-03	.9993017	.9867567
.1578648	4.570445E-03	1.895223E-03	.9999836
.8675156	.9173698	.1980324	.8315632
.9817003	.9999928	.9758412	1.191727E-04
.8533422	.9871663	.9999993	2.200857E-02
.2931527	.7608284	1	2.641087E-02
.9750708	.8355502	.9999956	.9960837
.7803568	.2853642	.9946657	.9999932
.9996375	.9984575	1	.7613421
.2004554	1.390761E-02	.9994531	.3365564
.6699975	.9900687		

Purpose

Generate a random-number data set exhibiting Bilateral Exponential Probability Distribution characteristics.

Notes

This function returns continuous, random-order numbers centered about zero. The negative to positive values are distributed exponentially on either side of the mean (0) and its range is unbounded both above and below the mean. Sometimes referred to as the First Law of LaPlace, the distribution is controlled by the parameter SPREAD, which increases the range of generated values in inverse proportion to its magnitude (must be > 0).

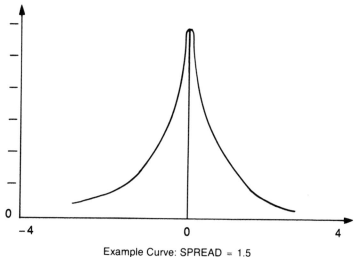

Example Curve: SPREAD = 1.5

Program Listing

```
100 REM ================================================================
110 REM                          DRIVER PROGRAM
120 REM                            (Bilexp)
130 REM ================================================================
140     DIM X(100)
150     RANDOMIZE(-232)
160     TOTAL = 100
170     SPREAD = 1.5
180     GOSUB 1010        '<< call Bilateral Exponential Distribution
190        FOR J = 1 TO TOTAL
200           PRINT X(J);"  ";                '<< sequence to screen
205           IF J MOD 4 = 0 THEN PRINT
210        NEXT J
220 END
```

```
1000 REM ================================================ CTB3.2
1010 REM ********************>> BILEXP <<********************
1020 REM ================================================
1030 REM          Bilateral Exponential Distribution Function
1090 REM ================================================
1100 REM                   Variable Descriptions
1110 REM      Entering -
1120 REM        TOTAL: sequence length
1130 REM        SPREAD: horizontal scaling value
1140 REM      Exiting -
1150 REM        X(): array holding BILEXP real numbers sequence
1160 REM      Local -
1170 REM        R9: random number > 0 & < 2
1180 REM        K9: loop index, pointer to array X()
1190 REM ================================================
1200      FOR K9 = 1 TO TOTAL
1210          R9 = 2 * RND
1220       IF R9 > 1 THEN R9 = 2 - R9 : X(K0) = - LOG(R0) / SPREAD
ELSE X(K9) = LOG(R9) / SPREAD
1230          X(K9) = LOG(R9)/SPREAD
1240      NEXT K9
1250 RETURN
```

RUN (Bilexp)

-7.527557E-02	-1.048221	-.501609	-.2519994
-1.250644	-2.077493	-.6291791	-.1350027
-.3317514	-.6676554	-.4461632	-.1836391
-.5460463	-1.90607	-.3781001	-4.221345E-03
-1.867456	-3.551681E-02	-3.140455	-2.288614
-.1653103	-.2016787	-1.06775	-.3859044
-.1347419	-.3660186	-.2937816	-.2585062
-1.02371	-.5031054	-9.857698E-03	-2.48315
-.8699966	-2.763871E-02	-2.032015	-.8029451
-9.554353E-02	-.664152	-.209433	-.3556865
-.0413544	-6.037871E-03	-.2083645	-1.270443
-1.196018E-02	-.5717624	-2.156488	-1.815228
-.9352418	-.7964256	-1.026462	-.3324287
-1.685562	-1.424225	-1.177418	-.1132024
-.4870833	-1.280384	-.520645	-1.106162
-.1751037	-.173508	-2.140626	-4.139423E-02
-4.881247E-03	-2.0667	-.5787996	-.5220735
-2.864639	-6.984135E-02	-.1644743	-.8086827
-.1401253	-.1342839	-.1037712	-1.231441
-.8923945	-9.915353E-02	-.0458915	-.1809691
-2.627466	-.3321272	-.8375581	-1.060364
-.2185364	-1.804743E-02	-4.740762E-02	-.4196546
-.5685414	-.2167344	-.1957427	-.2934903
-1.691944	-.4002831	-.1195477	-1.082456
-.2708417	-.3499161	-.2475746	-.1130062

Purpose

Generate a random-number data set exhibiting Cauchy Probability Distribution characteristics.

Notes

This subroutine returns continuous real numbers in a symmetrical, positive-to-negative distribution centered around the mean. It is similar to Gaussian distribution in that it is unbounded above and below the mean (0), but it approaches zero probabilities more slowly at the extremes. In practical terms, this causes values quite remote from the mean to have a higher probability of occurrence than in a Gaussian distribution. The control parameter SPREAD determines the horizontal dispersion of values along the curve.

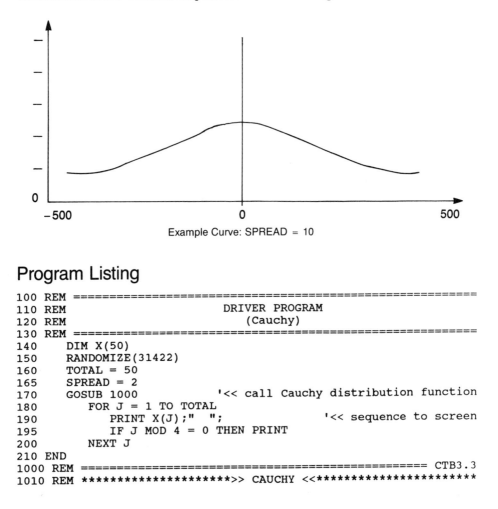

Example Curve: SPREAD = 10

Program Listing

```
100 REM  ==========================================================
110 REM                       DRIVER PROGRAM
120 REM                         (Cauchy)
130 REM  ==========================================================
140     DIM X(50)
150     RANDOMIZE(31422)
160     TOTAL = 50
165     SPREAD = 2
170     GOSUB 1000              '<< call Cauchy distribution function
180        FOR J = 1 TO TOTAL
190           PRINT X(J);"  ";            '<< sequence to screen
195           IF J MOD 4 = 0 THEN PRINT
200        NEXT J
210 END
1000 REM ============================================= CTB3.3
1010 REM ******************>> CAUCHY <<********************
```

```
1020 REM  ============================================================
1030 REM              Cauchy Probability Distribution Function
1070 REM  ============================================================
1080 REM                    Variable Descriptions
1090 REM      Entering -
1100 REM        TOTAL: length of sequence
1110 REM        SPREAD: scaling parameter
1120 REM      Exiting -
1130 REM        X(): array holding cauchy distribution
1140 REM      Local -
1150 REM        R9: uniform random number
1160 REM        K9: loop index, pointer to array X()
1170 REM  ============================================================
1171      PI = 3.1415927#
1180         FOR K9 = 1 TO TOTAL
1200            R9# = RND
1210            IF R9# = .5 THEN 1200
1220            R9# = R9# * PI
1230            X(K9) = SPREAD * TAN(R9#)
1240         NEXT K9
1250 RETURN
```

RUN (Cauchy)

```
  1.435218    -3.135468     2.058527    -3.762384
-27.95866      6.063459     2.358028     3.062942
 -5.187778      .9340848    1.803345     1.071952
  1.506539     2.615161     2.263138    -1.337906
  1.42068     -2.862467     1.341476     -.4193819
 12.46916      3.395561     3.760365   -35.02975
 -1.565518     2.57346     -1.586209    37.2678
  2.275438     -.2182467   -4.067533   371.3344
 -2.783898    -61.7626     -1.701122      .4014113
  5.449896    -16.25256    -4.052299    -1.155056
  1.304845      .5203197   31.81785      1.457217
 -2.350121    -1.610642    -4.015357      .787217
  -.2709108     4.526322
```

Purpose

Generate a random-number data set exhibiting Exponential Probability Distribution characteristics.

Notes

This algorithm returns continuous, random-order real numbers > 0. Samples closer to zero are most likely to occur, with the probabilities of higher numbers falling off exponentially.

The control parameter SPREAD determines the dispersion of values along the curve; larger values for SPREAD increase the probability of returning a small-number result. Although there is no upper limit to the size of an individual sample, it is very unlikely that a large number will be generated. The distribution mean is .69315/SPREAD.

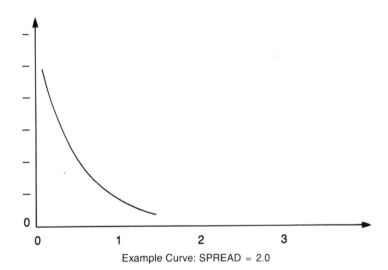

Example Curve: SPREAD = 2.0

Program Listing

```
100 REM ================================================================
110 REM                         DRIVER PROGRAM
120 REM                           (Expon)
130 REM ================================================================
140     DIM X(50)
150     RANDOMIZE(1296)
160     TOTAL = 50
170     SPREAD = 2
180     GOSUB 1000        '<< call exponential distribution function
190        FOR J = 1 TO TOTAL
200           PRINT X(J),                  '<< sequence to screen
210        NEXT J
220 END
```

```
1000 REM ================================================= CTB3.4
1010 REM *********************>> EXPON <<*********************
1020 REM =================================================
1030 REM      Exponential Probability Distribution Function
1040 REM =================================================
1100 REM                Variable Descriptions
1110 REM      Entering -
1120 REM        SPREAD: horizontal scaling parameter
1130 REM        TOTAL: length of sequence
1140 REM      Exiting -
1150 REM        X(): array holding exponential distribution
1160 REM      Local -
1170 REM        R9 : uniform random number
1180 REM        K9: loop index, pointer to array X()
1190 REM =================================================
1200    FOR K9 = 1 TO TOTAL
1210       R9 = RND
1220       X(K9) = -LOG(R9) / SPREAD
1230    NEXT K9
1240 RETURN
```

RUN (Expon)

.1917903	.6090066	5.155992E-02	4.022093E-02	.1240665
.996584	.7575346	.1768736	.3523805	1.213248
.5519703	.1693524	.1969187	.9126783	.324524
.9116937	.3338148	.5374395	.9643518	1.46772
.1065933	.113965	2.275808	2.001591	.3667951
.5592505	1.798156	.4686218	.5429181	1.321781
1.179796	.3076696	1.194048	.3912797	.7134883
.4083722	.2364688	.4502663	2.169933	.3349404
.3498687	.1204267	1.045777	.1909255	.1589727
1.090397	.5495311	.1563222	.1134708	.3398349

Purpose

Generate a random-number data set exhibiting Gamma Probability Distribution characteristics.

Notes

This algorithm returns continuous, random-order real numbers over an asymmetrical curve. It is often used in rhythmic applications to provide a sense of "rubato." The shape of the curve is drastically altered by the value of control parameter SPREAD. Generally, SPREAD values larger than 10 are not used because the algorithm tends toward a Gaussian distribution as the value rises.

Since there are several possible special cases (radically altered curve shapes), it will pay to experiment with a diversity of SPREAD values and to tally actual occurrence frequencies on a bargraph.

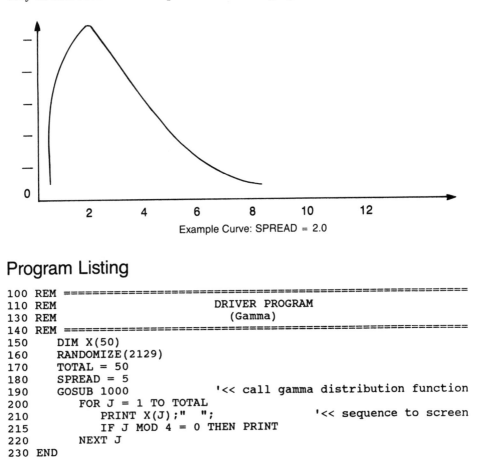

Example Curve: SPREAD = 2.0

Program Listing

```
100 REM ===========================================================
110 REM                       DRIVER PROGRAM
130 REM                         (Gamma)
140 REM ===========================================================
150     DIM X(50)
160     RANDOMIZE(2129)
170     TOTAL = 50
180     SPREAD = 5
190     GOSUB 1000               '<< call gamma distribution function
200        FOR J = 1 TO TOTAL
210           PRINT X(J);"   ";             '<< sequence to screen
215           IF J MOD 4 = 0 THEN PRINT
220        NEXT J
230 END
```

```
1000 REM ======================================================= CTB3.5
1010 REM *********************>> GAMMA <<*********************
1020 REM =======================================================
1030 REM          Gamma Probability Distribution Function
1080 REM =======================================================
1090 REM                  Variable Descriptions
1100 REM      Entering -
1110 REM        TOTAL: length of sequence
1120 REM        SPREAD: control parameter
1130 REM      Exiting -
1140 REM        X(): array holding gamma distribution
1150 REM      Local -
1160 REM        SUM: accumulator
1170 REM        GAMMA: current distribution value
1180 REM        K9: loop index, pointer to array X()
1190 REM =======================================================
1200      FOR K9 = 1 TO TOTAL
1210         SUM = 1
1220            FOR L9 = 1 TO SPREAD
1230               SUM = SUM * RND
1240            NEXT L9
1250         X(K9) = -LOG(SUM)
1260      NEXT K9
1270 RETURN
```

RUN (Gamma)

5.089768	8.643037	2.553714	2.8501
5.857388	5.625569	4.866669	5.657082
5.55371	2.709609	3.830674	6.412706
6.234925	6.495875	9.030503	8.116611
10.25226	5.494516	4.849351	4.14915
5.946736	1.501904	6.848026	3.143872
5.304213	3.56936	3.304387	5.779018
5.831986	3.818624	8.635681	3.598258
5.242219	5.57136	5.954569	8.304726
3.802275	2.755267	2.896282	2.168865
4.891008	2.406916	5.833667	3.90302
5.33627	7.537259	7.276123	2.267955
2.631941	9.904975		

SUBROUTINE: Gauss

Purpose

Generate a random-number data set exhibiting Gaussian Probability Distribution characteristics.

Notes

Also referred to as the "normal distribution" and the Gauss-LaPlace Distribution, this algorithm generates a bell-shaped curve comprised of random-order real numbers larger than zero and centered about the mean. The distribution is arrived at via the summation of uniform random numbers. The standard deviation—DEV—and the mean—MEAN—are the control parameters.

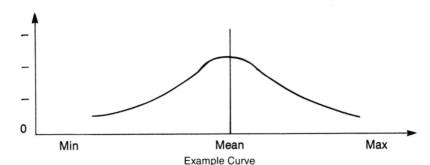

Example Curve

Program Listing

```
100 REM  ===========================================================
110 REM                       DRIVER PROGRAM
120 REM                          (Gauss)
130 REM  ===========================================================
140     DIM X(50)
150     RANDOMIZE(-30261)
160     TOTAL = 50
170     DEV = 2
180     MEAN = 10
190     GOSUB 1000        '<< call gaussian distribution function
200        FOR J = 1 TO TOTAL
210           PRINT X(J);"  ";            '<< sequence to screen
215           IF J MOD 4 = 0 THEN PRINT
220        NEXT J
230 END
1000 REM  ================================================= CTB3.6
1010 REM  *******************>> GAUSS <<*********************
1020 REM  ===========================================================
1030 REM           Gaussian Probability Distribution Function
1110 REM  ===========================================================
1120 REM                    Variable Descriptions
1130 REM        Entering -
1140 REM          TOTAL: length of sequence
```

```
1150 REM          DEV: statistical standard deviation
1160 REM          MEAN: statistical mean
1170 REM      Exiting -
1180 REM        X(): array holding gaussian distribution
1190 REM      Local -
1200 REM        NUM: number of random values used in computation
1210 REM        HALFNUM: NUM / 2
1220 REM        SCALE: scaling factor    (varies with NUM as
1230 REM              SCALE =  1 / SQR(NUM/12)
1240 REM        K9: loop index, pointer to array X()
1250 REM =========================================================
1260     NUM = 12
1270     HALFNUM = NUM/2
1280     SCALE=1
1290       FOR K9= 1 TO TOTAL
1300          SUM=0
1310            FOR L9 = 1 TO NUM
1320               SUM = SUM + RND
1330            NEXT L9
1340          X(K9) = DEV * SCALE * (SUM - HALFNUM) + MEAN
1350       NEXT K9
1360 RETURN
```

RUN (Gauss)

13.30657	11.70571	12.39236	9.985172
7.704356	11.74669	9.660515	10.72073
8.303805	10.26276	13.3022	7.353261
13.94866	8.597688	9.161171	10.22651
11.48268	10.09521	9.081176	11.68424
9.749614	12.09908	8.905967	8.070188
7.593204	9.953041	10.47929	9.728108
5.857204	9.000855	11.6449	9.001751
11.38536	10.58627	10.24655	8.234867
11.02143	10.05303	12.12798	9.771207
7.609164	8.744881	5.132949	11.95452
9.992305	8.005586	7.105201	9.128552
7.014606	9.178887		

SUBROUTINE: Hypcosin

Purpose

Generate a random-number data set exhibiting Hyperbolic Cosine Probability Distribution characteristics.

Notes

This algorithm produces a symmetrical curve comprised of random-order, continuous, positive-to-negative real numbers. Although centered on zero, the mean is missing.

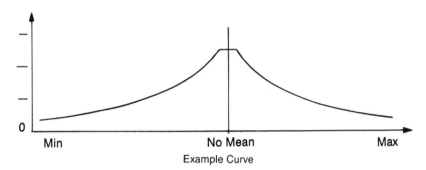

Example Curve

Program Listing

```
100 REM ============================================================
110 REM                        DRIVER PROGRAM
120 REM                          (Hypcosin)
130 REM ============================================================
140     DIM X(50)
150     RANDOMIZE(602)
160     TOTAL = 50
170     GOSUB 1000            '<< call hyperbolic cosine distribution
180       FOR J = 1 TO TOTAL
190         PRINT X(J);" ";                 '<< sequence to screen
195         IF J MOD 4 = 0 THEN PRINT
200       NEXT J
210 END
1000 REM ==================================================== CTB3.7
1010 REM *****************>> HYPCOSIN <<************************
1020 REM ============================================================
1030 REM           Hyperbolic Cosine Probability Distribution
1060 REM ============================================================
1070 REM                   Variable Descriptions
1080 REM         Entering -
1090 REM           TOTAL: length of sequence
1100 REM         Exiting -
1110 REM           X(): array holding Hypercosine distribution
1120 REM         Local -
1130 REM           R9: uniform random number
1140 REM           K9: loop index, pointer to array X()
```

```
1150 REM ============================================================
1160    FOR K9 = 1 TO TOTAL
1170       R9 = RND
1180       X(K9) = LOG(TAN(3.14159 * R9 /2))+4
1190    NEXT K9
1200 RETURN
```

RUN (Hypcosin)

1.384163	5.255279	4.94751	3.376151
7.912003	4.645272	3.445628	3.459728
8.797903	4.65001	4.022547	4.073108
4.135764	6.956409	2.780773	3.162475
3.290484	2.140438	5.982318	6.489809
5.409669	5.25776	5.138133	3.442506
5.058158	7.514055	4.489821	1.931654
6.027468	4.731007	3.460616	4.365874
5.065785	6.15111	3.890722	2.773518
3.904885	7.527119	3.147088	2.816621
4.169889	4.521966	4.610699	5.011795
3.775745	3.536135	5.536147	4.500287
5.091225	4.142592		

Purpose

Generate a random-number data set exhibiting Linear Probability Distribution characteristics.

Notes

This function returns continuous, random-order real numbers > 0 and < 1. Results closer to zero are most likely to occur. The range of the variable R8 will be the same as the BASIC RND function, with a mean of .2929; however, by substituting as follows—

```
1210 R8 = INT (RND * RANGE)
1220 R9 = INT (RND * RANGE)
```

—and defining the variable RANGE, the output can be converted to integer and scaled to meet program requirements.

A reverse linear distribution can be achieved by altering the algorithm to select the larger rather than smaller random value in Line 1230. In this case, results farther removed from zero will be more likely to occur.

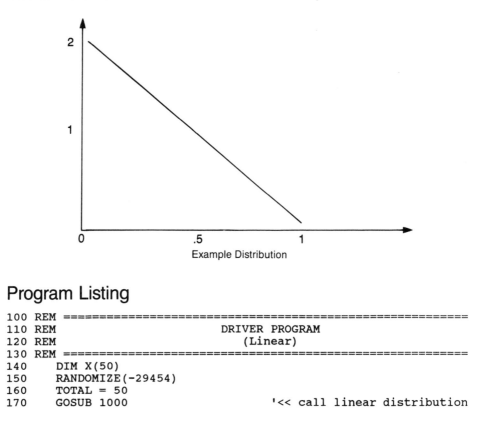

Example Distribution

Program Listing

```
100 REM ===========================================================
110 REM                        DRIVER PROGRAM
120 REM                          (Linear)
130 REM ===========================================================
140     DIM X(50)
150     RANDOMIZE(-29454)
160     TOTAL = 50
170     GOSUB 1000                    '<< call linear distribution
```

```
180        FOR J = 1 TO TOTAL
190          PRINT X(J);"  ";                    '<< sequence to screen
195          IF J MOD 4 = 0 THEN PRINT
200        NEXT J
210 END
1000 REM ================================================ CTB3.9
1010 REM ********************>> LINEAR <<********************
1020 REM ================================================
1030 REM            Linear Distribution Function
1090 REM ================================================
1100 REM                  Variable Descriptions
1110 REM       Entering -
1120 REM        TOTAL: length of sequence
1130 REM       Exiting -
1140 REM        X(): array holding LINEAR real number sequence
1150 REM       Local -
1160 REM        R8: random number 1
1170 REM        R9: random number 2
1180 REM        K9: loop index, pointer to array X()
1190 REM ================================================
1200    FOR K9 = 1 TO TOTAL
1210       R8 = RND
1220       R9 = RND
1230       IF R9 < R8 THEN R8=R9
1240       X(K9) = R8
1250    NEXT K9
1260 RETURN
```

RUN (Linear)

.4456887	.2722291	.3064838	.3420551
.351074	.4640859	.7553751	.1060918
.1278117	.193983	.1276593	7.395947E-02
.2792682	.1303772	.3700039	.2647041
.2115452	1.985061E-02	.2108588	.6762706
8.201766E-02	.1416531	.3802015	.1715714
.3024199	3.498828E-02	.1224885	.2874659
.5373027	.5444416	.2117493	.197436
3.475803E-02	.3495422	.2150704	.7970608
.4743383	.3625273	9.280014E-02	.4293836
.6929202	2.369869E-02	.3738582	.5406035
.1870632	5.152357E-02	.29202	.1851393
.8570027	.6911503		

Purpose

Generate a random-number data set exhibiting Logistic Probability Distribution characteristics.

Notes

This subroutine returns continuous, random-order, negative-to-positive real numbers. The control parameters PAR1 and PAR2 determine the mean and dispersion of values along the curve.

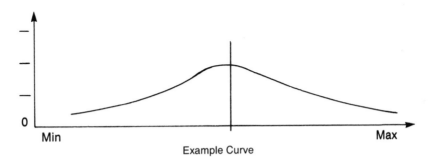

Example Curve

Program Listing

```
100 REM ==============================================================
110 REM                        DRIVER PROGRAM
120 REM                          (Logistic)
130 REM ==============================================================
140    DIM X(50)
150    RANDOMIZE(742)
160    TOTAL = 50
170    PAR1 =  1
180    PAR2 =  5
190    GOSUB 1000         '<< call logistic distribution function
200       FOR J = 1 TO TOTAL
210          PRINT X(J);"  ";            '<< sequence to screen
215          IF J MOD 4 = 0 THEN PRINT
220       NEXT J
230 END
1000 REM ================================================= CTB3.10
1010 REM *******************>> LOGISTIC <<*******************
1020 REM ==================================================
1030 REM         Logistic Probability Distribution Function
1090 REM ==================================================
1100 REM                     Variable Descriptions
1110 REM        Entering -
1120 REM          TOTAL: length of sequence
1130 REM          PAR1: control value 1
1140 REM          PAR2: control value 2
1150 REM        Exiting -
```

```
1160 REM        X(): array holding Logistic distribution
1170 REM     Local -
1180 REM        R9: uniform random number
1190 REM        K9: loop index, pointer to array X()
1200 REM ========================================================
1210    FOR K9 = 1 TO TOTAL
1220       R9 = RND
1230       X(K9) =(-PAR1 * -LOG(1 / R9 - 1)) / PAR2
1240    NEXT K9
1250 RETURN
```

RUN (Logistic)

.2444397	-.1863974	-.2409406	.2347128
7.638236E-02	-.3887807	2.201996E-02	-.3495008
-.1105958	.2638052	-.117558	.5738011
.3643674	-9.454778E-02	-.4969472	-.7498198
.1438304	.0594929	-9.527841E-02	-.2447326
-4.731763E-02	.3854163	-6.445607E-02	-.5390073
.3348468	.1629144	.1151333	-.4137757
-.1514502	-.3623395	-7.111392E-02	-.2720138
5.568125E-02	5.012304E-02	-9.667496E-02	-.1320908
.2483823	.3379697	6.416701E-02	-.1104716
7.707383E-02	-.0349204	-.1863644	-9.211429E-02
.4155534	-.2183071	9.904484E-02	.5903279
-.2664959	-.9240006		

Purpose

Generate a random-number data set exhibiting Poisson Probability Distribution characteristics.

Notes

This algorithm generates random-order, nonnegative integers. The control parameter SPREAD determines the distribution of values, which are unbounded at the upper end.

The mean of the distribution is the value of control parameter SPREAD (must be > 0).

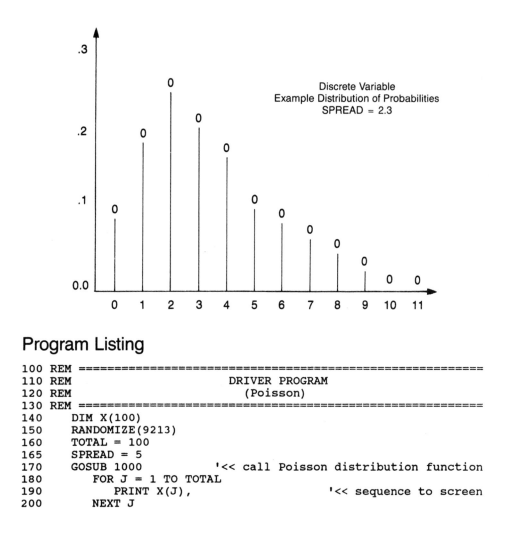

Discrete Variable
Example Distribution of Probabilities
SPREAD = 2.3

Program Listing

```
100 REM ========================================================
110 REM                    DRIVER PROGRAM
120 REM                      (Poisson)
130 REM ========================================================
140    DIM X(100)
150    RANDOMIZE(9213)
160    TOTAL = 100
165    SPREAD = 5
170    GOSUB 1000          '<< call Poisson distribution function
180       FOR J = 1 TO TOTAL
190          PRINT X(J),                   '<< sequence to screen
200       NEXT J
```

```
210 END
1000 REM ============================================== CTB3.10
1010 REM *******************>> POISSON <<*******************
1020 REM ==========================================================
1030 REM                Poisson Probability Distribution
1070 REM ==========================================================
1080 REM                      Variable Descriptions
1090 REM         Entering -
1100 REM           TOTAL: length of sequence
1110 REM           SPREAD: scaling parameter
1120 REM         Exiting -
1130 REM           X(): array holding poisson distribution
1140 REM         Local -
1150 REM           NUM: Poisson value
1160 REM           R9: uniform random number
1170 REM           T9: while loop limit
1180 REM           K9: loop index, pointer to array X()
1190 REM ==========================================================
1200     FOR K9 = 1 TO TOTAL
1210         NUM = 0
1220         R9 = RND
1230         T9 = EXP(-SPREAD)
1240           WHILE R9 > T9
1250               NUM = NUM + 1
1260               R9 = R9 * RND
1270           WEND
1280         X(K9) = NUM
1290     NEXT K9
1300 RETURN
```

RUN (Poisson)

7	4	7	10	4
3	6	2	6	9
3	5	3	4	2
4	3	8	5	5
3	9	10	7	5
3	4	2	3	8
3	4	4	4	7
4	6	4	5	3
2	0	8	7	3
2	2	6	8	7
6	3	4	6	7
6	3	9	5	7
7	5	6	3	0
7	5	6	8	7
6	3	6	5	9
2	7	5	3	9
1	7	3	4	11
8	5	2	4	6
3	3	3	6	4
3	10	5	3	4

Purpose

Generate a random-number data set exhibiting Rnd-Rnd Probability Distribution characteristics.

Notes

This subroutine uses a random decaying function to determine the distribution of discrete values. Occurrence frequency falls off with magnitude, similar to the Exponential Probability Distribution, but with more variability. To obtain the random-order integers, the random number generator is made to call itself recursively.

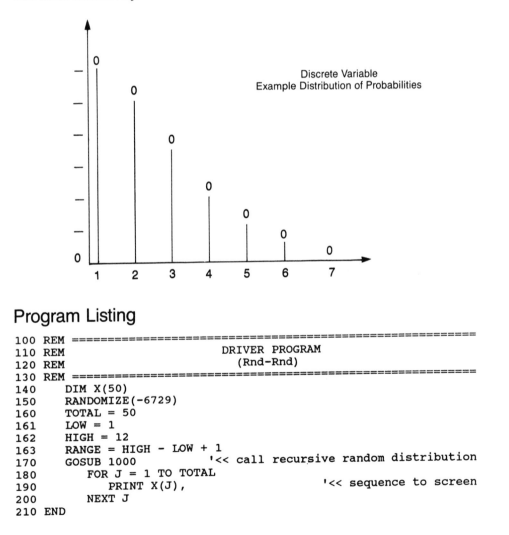

Discrete Variable
Example Distribution of Probabilities

Program Listing

```
100 REM ===============================================================
110 REM                         DRIVER PROGRAM
120 REM                           (Rnd-Rnd)
130 REM ===============================================================
140    DIM X(50)
150    RANDOMIZE(-6729)
160    TOTAL = 50
161    LOW = 1
162    HIGH = 12
163    RANGE = HIGH - LOW + 1
170    GOSUB 1000              '<< call recursive random distribution
180       FOR J = 1 TO TOTAL
190          PRINT X(J),                    '<< sequence to screen
200       NEXT J
210 END
```

```
1000 REM =================================================== CTB3.11
1010 REM *********************>> RND-RND <<********************
1020 REM ===================================================
1021 REM        RND-RND Probability Distribution Function
1029 REM ===================================================
1030 REM                 Variable Descriptions
1040 REM    Entering -
1050 REM      TOTAL: length pf sequence
1060 REM      RANGE: span of possible random numbers
1070 REM      LOW: lowest possible random number
1080 REM    Exiting -
1090 REM      X(): array holding number sequence
1100 REM    Local -
1110 REM      K9: loop index, pointer to array X()
1111 REM ===================================================
1120    FOR K9 = 1 TO TOTAL
1130       X(K9) = INT(RND * RND * (RANGE)) + LOW
1140    NEXT K9
1150 RETURN
```

RUN (Rnd-Rnd)

1	3	12	1	2
5	7	2	6	7
1	1	3	2	1
1	1	2	1	5
1	2	5	1	1
5	3	2	1	1
4	9	2	4	1
1	1	1	9	4
1	8	9	7	3
1	1	2	6	9

SUBROUTINE: Weibull

Purpose

Generate a random-number data set exhibiting Weibull Probability Distribution characteristics.

Notes

This function returns random-order, continuous real numbers larger than 0. Its curve can assume a variety of shapes in accordance with the value of its input parameter, DENSHAPE. The SPREAD parameter controls only the horizontal scale. There is no upper limit to values generated.

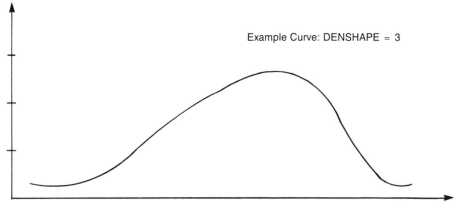

Example Curve: DENSHAPE = 3

Spread

Program Listing

```
100 REM ==========================================================
110 REM                      DRIVER PROGRAM
120 REM                        (Weibull)
130 REM ==========================================================
140     DIM X(50)
150     RANDOMIZE(-212)
160     TOTAL = 50
161     SPREAD = 20
162     DENSHAPE = 1
170     GOSUB 1000              '<< call Weibull distribution function
180        FOR J = 1 TO TOTAL
190           PRINT X(J);"  ";             '<< sequence to screen
195           IF J MOD 4 = 0 THEN PRINT
200        NEXT J
210 END
990 REM ================================================= CTB3.13
1000 REM *********************>> WEIBULL <<*********************
1010 REM ==========================================================
1020 REM          Weibull Probability Distribution Function
1080 REM ==========================================================
1090 REM                    Variable Descriptions
```

```
1100 REM      Entering -
1110 REM        TOTAL: length of sequence
1120 REM        SPREAD: horizontal scaling parameter
1130 REM        DENSHAPE : curve shaping parameter
1140 REM      Exiting -
1150 REM        X(): array holding Weibull distribution
1160 REM      Local -
1170 REM        R9: uniform random number
1180 REM        K9: loop index, pointer to array X()
1189 REM =======================================================
1190    FOR K9 = 1 TO TOTAL
1200       R9 = RND
1210       R9=1/(1-R9)
1220       X(K9) = SPREAD * LOG(R9)^(1/DENSHAPE)
1230    NEXT K9
1240 RETURN
```

RUN (Weibull)

40.04524	.4851622	4.304656	53.79547
10.61169	17.12798	4.832766	1.972481
13.93264	35.32088	2.844489	16.11783
26.49674	15.96843	67.06329	7.709352
44.64901	59.70074	9.911872	10.88667
24.85636	9.825422	20.45505	5.070353
44.1469	7.986445	20.25357	.5292715
8.91578	15.59778	9.748322	40.96782
32.06255	16.09293	19.19697	20.026
10.15478	8.690274	22.43852	8.365089
41.94628	8.466834	21.36433	28.97163
27.66084	16.13501	32.93699	5.288891
36.26468	1.497101		

Purpose

Generate a random-number data set exhibiting Triangular Probability Distribution characteristics.

Notes

This function returns continuous, random-order real numbers > 0 and < 1. Middle-value results are most likely to occur. The algorithm works by taking the average of two uniformly distributed random numbers.

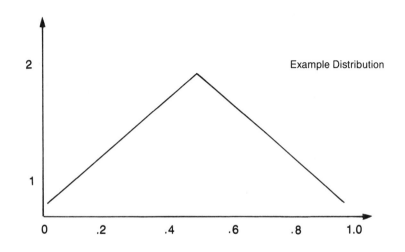

Example Distribution

Program Listing

```
100 REM ============================================================
110 REM                      DRIVER PROGRAM
120 REM                        (Triangle)
130 REM ============================================================
140    DIM X(50)
150    RANDOMIZE(62)
160    TOTAL = 50
170    GOSUB 1000        '<< call triangular distribution function
180      FOR J = 1 TO TOTAL
190        PRINT X(J);"  ";                '<< sequence to screen
195        IF J MOD 4 = 0 THEN PRINT
200      NEXT J
210 END
1000 REM ================================================== CTB3.14
1010 REM ********************>> TRIANGLE <<********************
1020 REM ============================================================
1030 REM        Triangular Probability Distribution Function
1060 REM ============================================================
1070 REM                    Variable Descriptions
1080 REM        Entering -
```

```
1090 REM         TOTAL: length of sequence
1100 REM      Exiting -
1110 REM        X(): array holding triangular distribution
1120 REM      Local -
1130 REM        R8: random number 1
1140 REM
1150 REM        R9: random number 2
1160 REM ========================================================
1170    FOR K9 = 1 TO TOTAL
1180       R8 = RND
1190       R9 = RND
1200       X(K9) = .5 * (R8+R9)
1210    NEXT K9
1220 RETURN
```

RUN (Triangle)

.5038861	.5351346	.6813608	.7823095
.2550567	.5876625	.7820417	.3398041
.1348132	.2662127	.2356735	.5426083
.5411047	.6523283	.2761432	.4957022
.9187554	.2494271	.4342123	.4759416
.7594646	.4828021	.5375177	.4320569
.6018065	.1996214	.2105709	.4846534
.5312303	.6689279	.3747588	.4262118
.6800603	.5816395	.7483431	.7210875
.7274956	.5505493	.8464605	.5055108
.3996104	.6103251	.4811226	.5875874
.469354	.21751	.7612163	.9472976
.2565506	.2505219		

4
Sorting and Searching

SUBROUTINE: Shellsrt   CTB4.1

Purpose

Arrange a table of values in ascending order.

Notes

The Shell sort algorithm is fast, compact, and easy to decipher. Although under certain conditions the common bubble sorting algorithm (not presented in this book) may be faster, musical sequences consisting of randomly generated data normally are so long and disjunct that the bubble sort is useless. However, when the list to be processed is 10 items or less and is "almost sorted," bubble sort is quicker.

An in-place binary sort, Shellsrt works by successively splitting the unordered list into smaller halves, rearranging contents along the way via a switching algorithm. If the original unsorted list must be preserved for future use by the calling program, it can be copied to array X( ) before entering the subroutine.

Shellsrt (and the other sorting subroutines in chapter 4) have interesting secondary applications. For example, if the internal "footsteps" of the sorting process are mapped to the pitch element table, patterns of the algorithm-in-motion will be engraved in sound. To observe the subroutine's internal function, modify Lines 1330-1340 as follows:

```
1330  X(K9) = X(COMPTR) : PRINT X(K9);
1340  X(COMPTR) = TEMP : PRINT X(COMPTR);
```

Programming Ideas

Map the sorting process (not the final sorted list) to the pitch parameter:

- Modify the DRIVER PROGRAM to generate integers instead of real numbers.
- Alter Lines 1330 and 1340 to store X(K9) and X(COMPTR) in an array to be used as a list of data pointers.
- Add Pitchtab (CTB1.3) to the program and use the array of pointers to select elements.

Program Listing

```
100 REM  ============================================================
110 REM                        DRIVER PROGRAM
120 REM                          (Shellsrt)
130 REM  ============================================================
140      DIM X(50)
150      TOTAL = 50
160      RANDOMIZE(907)
170      PRINT "ARRAY OF RANDOM-ORDER REAL NUMBERS (RANGE 0-1) --"
180        FOR J = 1 TO TOTAL
190           X(J) = RND
200           PRINT X(J);" ";            '<< unsorted list to screen
205           IF J MOD 4 = 0 THEN PRINT
210        NEXT J
220      PRINT
230      PRINT "ARRAY SORTED IN ASCENDING ORDER --"
240      GOSUB 1000                      '<< call Shell sort algorithm
250        FOR J = 1 TO TOTAL
260           PRINT X(J);" ";          ·'<< sorted list to screen
265           IF J MOD 4 = 0 THEN PRINT .
270        NEXT J
280 END
1000 REM  ============================================= CTB4.1
1010 REM  *********************>> SHELLSRT <<*********************
1020 REM  ============================================================
1030 REM                Shell Binary Sorting Routine
1070 REM  ============================================================
1080 REM                    Variable Descriptions
1090 REM      Entering -
1100 REM        X(): array of values to be sorted
1110 REM        TOTAL: length of list
1120 REM      Exiting -
1130 REM        X(): array sorted in ascending order
1140 REM      Local -
1150 REM        SUBDIV: list subdivision size
1160 REM        REMAINDER: original list size less SUBDIV
1170 REM        FLAG: 0 or 1 condition indicates switch or no
1180 REM              switch has occurred
1190 REM        TEMP: temporary storage
```

```
1200 REM        K9: loop index, first sublist pointer
1210 REM        COMPTR: second sublist pointer for comparison
1220 REM               and switch
1230 REM ==========================================================
1240     SUBDIV = TOTAL
1241     SUBDIV = INT(SUBDIV / 2)
1250        WHILE SUBDIV > 0
1270           REMAINDER = TOTAL - SUBDIV
1280           FLAG = 0
1290              FOR K9=1 TO REMAINDER
1300                 COMPTR = K9+SUBDIV
1310                 IF X(K9) <= X(COMPTR) THEN 1360
1320                 TEMP = X(K9)
1330                 X(K9) = X(COMPTR)
1340                 X(COMPTR) = TEMP
1350                 FLAG = 1
1360              NEXT K9
1370           IF FLAG > 0 THEN 1280
1371           SUBDIV = INT(SUBDIV / 2)
1372        WEND
1373 RETURN
```

RUN (Shellsrt)

ARRAY OF RANDOM-ORDER REAL NUMBERS (RANGE 0-1) --

4.812169E-02	.7713875	6.075752E-02	2.645075E-03
.1844897	.3039338	.8881675	.4952686
3.205848E-02	3.490919E-02	.1241964	.7503167
.6275101	.4167673	.7239834	.9648717
.1920969	.3482508	.3038005	.3526178
.8972669	.8775165	3.167737E-02	.4719656
.8802879	.15526	.7680267	.8041773
.5098734	.6378414	.4562689	.5814918
.9018071	.5404095	.7634572	.8652492
.6845679	.5400273	.9709026	.8740166
1.495528E-02	.7287969	.1147989	.5617123
.8437138	.8169844	.3768479	.4457315
.4311583	.5861449		

ARRAY SORTED IN ASCENDING ORDER --

2.645075E-03	1.495528E-02	3.167737E-02	3.205848E-02
3.490919E-02	4.812169E-02	6.075752E-02	.1147989
.1241964	.15526	.1844897	.1920969
.3038005	.3039338	.3482508	.3526178
.3768479	.4167673	.4311583	.4457315
.4562689	.4719656	.4952686	.5098734
.5400273	.5404095	.5617123	.5814918
.5861449	.6275101	.6378414	.6845679
.7239834	.7287969	.7503167	.7634572
.7680267	.7713875	.8041773	.8169844
.8437138	.8652492	.8740166	.8775165
.8802879	.8881675	.8972669	.9018071
.9648717	.9709026		

Purpose

Arrange a table of values in ascending order.

Notes

The Shell-Metzner sorting algorithm is a variation on Shellsrt. It is an in-place, binary sort; therefore, if the calling program must preserve the unsorted table for future reference, a copy can be placed in a separate array prior to entering the subroutine.

To observe the internal workings of S-Msort, modify Lines 1321 and 1330 as follows:

```
1321   X(PTR1) = X(COMPTR) : PRINT X(PTR1);
1330   X(COMPTR) = TEMP : PRINT X(COMPTR);
```

Programming Ideas

1) Alter—as explained in the comments for CTB4.1—the DRIVER PROGRAM and Subroutine S-Msort to place the internal steps of the sorting process in a new array of data pointers (store the values of X(PTR1) in Line 1321 and X(COMPTR) in Line 1330). Use the collection of pointers to sequence the elements of a volume parameter table.

2) Write a program which invokes a probability distribution function from chapter 3 to generate an array of 100 random-order integers, range 1 to 100. First, use the list items as pointers to the pitch parameter, then sort the list and use the items as pointers to a table of volume or articulation data. (The effect of the sorted list will be a variation on one of the curve-types introduced in Subroutine Group CURVES in chapter 1.)

Program Listing

```
100 REM  ==============================================================
110 REM                      DRIVER PROGRAM
120 REM                        (S-Msort)
130 REM  ==============================================================
140      DIM X(50)
150      TOTAL = 50
160      RANDOMIZE(-1192)
170      PRINT "ARRAY OF RANDOM-ORDER REAL NUMBERS (RANGE 0-1) --"
180         FOR J = 1 TO TOTAL
190            X(J) = RND
200            PRINT X(J);"  ";            '<< unsorted list to screen
205            IF J MOD 4 = 0 THEN PRINT
210         NEXT J
220      PRINT
230      PRINT "ARRAY SORTED IN ASCENDING ORDER --"
240      GOSUB 1010                        '<< call Shell-Metzner sort
250         FOR J = 1 TO TOTAL
```

```
260             PRINT X(J);" ";              '<< sorted list to screen
265            IF J MOD 4 = 0 THEN PRINT
270         NEXT J
280 END
1000 REM =================================================== CTB4.2
1010 REM *******************>> S-MSORT << *********************
1020 REM ===================================================
1030 REM             Shell-Metzner Binary Sorting Routine
1080 REM ===================================================
1090 REM                  Variable Descriptions
1100 REM      Entering -
1110 REM        X(): array of values to be sorted
1120 REM        TOTAL: length of array X()
1130 REM      Exiting -
1140 REM        X(): array sorted in ascending order
1150 REM      Local -
1160 REM        SUBDIV: list subdivision size
1170 REM        REMAINDER: original list size minus SUBDIV
1180 REM        PTR1: loop index, first sublist pointer
1190 REM        COMPTR: second sublist pointer for comparison
1200 REM                and switch
1210 REM        K9: loop index
1220 REM        TEMP: temporary storage
1230 REM ===================================================
1240     SUBDIV = TOTAL
1250     SUBDIV = INT(SUBDIV / 2)
1260        WHILE SUBDIV > 0
1270           REMAINDER =TOTAL - SUBDIV
1280              FOR K9 = 1 TO REMAINDER
1290                 PTR1 = K9
1300                 COMPTR = PTR1 + SUBDIV
1310                 IF X(PTR1) <= X(COMPTR) THEN 1350
1320                 TEMP = X(PTR1)
1321                 X(PTR1) = X(COMPTR)
1330                 X(COMPTR) = TEMP
1331                 PTR1 = PTR1 - SUBDIV
1340                 IF PTR1 >= 1 THEN 1300
1350              NEXT K9
1360           SUBDIV = INT(SUBDIV / 2)
1370        WEND
1380 RETURN
```

RUN (S-Msort)

```
ARRAY OF RANDOM-ORDER REAL NUMBERS (RANGE 0-1) --
 .5973313        .7643837        .1598939        .470861
 .4829669        .2991273        .2307121        .48326
 2.120948E-02    .2080812        .1828054        .8401147
 .5612412        6.199062E-03    .7838131        .3010076
 .6368144        .6547236        .4625071        .6421228
 .7318769        .2643115        .1994172        .984371
 .2961967        4.815859E-02    .667456         .3715144
 1.098728E-02    .5251247        .6225439        .5982917
 .3045323        .9728589        .5442342        .2885433
 .1178107        .1309239        .5263377        .223336
 .9201219        .153922         .4175485        .9190884
 .9747105        .8146192        .2120682        .4556955
 .8543913        .9570708
```

```
ARRAY SORTED IN ASCENDING ORDER --
  6.199062E-03      1.098728E-02      2.120948E-02      4.815859E-02
  .1178107          .1309239          .153922           .1598939
  .1828054          .1994172          .2080812          .2120682
  .223336           .2307121          .2643115          .2885433
  .2961967          .2991273          .3010076          .3045323
  .3715144          .4175485          .4556955          .4625071
  .470861           .4829669          .48326            .5251247
  .5263377          .5442342          .5612412          .5973313
  .5982917          .6225439          .6368144          .6421228
  .6547236          .667456           .7318769          .7643837
  .7838131          .8146192          .8401147          .8543913
  .9190884          .9201219          .9570708          .9728589
  .9747105          .984371
```

Purpose

Arrange a table of values in ascending order.

Notes

While the Quicksort subroutine is one of the fastest sorting algorithms, its drawbacks are that it is long, complex, and difficult to decipher. Moreover, when coded in BASIC—a language which doesn't offer a program-accessible stack—statements must be included to provide one. (In languages such as C or PASCAL, the stack code can be eliminated.)

To observe the internal workings of QUICKSRT, make the following code changes:

```
1420   IF COMPVAL < = A(SEGBOTTOM)
          THEN 1450
          ELSE X(SEGTOP) = X(SEGBOTTOM) : PRINT X(SEGTOP);

1440   IF SEGBOTTOM = SEGTOP
          THEN 1460
          ELSE IF COMPVAL > = X(SEGTOP)
             THEN 1430
             ELSE X(SEGBOTTOM) = X(SEGTOP):PRINT X(SEGBOTTOM);
```

Programming Ideas

1) Alter—as explained in the comments for CTB4.1—the DRIVER PROGRAM and subroutine Quicksrt to map the internal sorting process to an array of data table pointers. Use the pointer list to sequence the pitches of a melodic line.

2) Write a program which invokes CTB3.11 to fill an array with unsorted integers, range 1 to 64; sort the array using Quicksrt, then assign the table of pointers to the rhythm parameter. Build a file of durations using Subroutine Group MOTFORMS (chapter 2) to generate retrograde, inversion, retrograde-inversion and transposed forms of the duration values.

Program Listing

```
100 REM  ===========================================================
110 REM                         DRIVER PROGRAM
120 REM                           (Quicksrt)
130 REM  ===========================================================
140      DIM X(60),STACK(40)
150      TOTAL = 60
160      RANDOMIZE(-5249)
170      PRINT "ARRAY OF RANDOM-ORDER INTEGERS --"
180         FOR J= 1 TO TOTAL
190            X(J) = INT(RND*60)+1
```

```
200              PRINT X(J),              '<< unsorted list to screen
210          NEXT J
220      PRINT
230      PRINT "ARRAY SORTED IN ASCENDING ORDER --"
240      GOSUB 1000    '<< call Quicksort algorithm
250          FOR J = 1 TO TOTAL
260              PRINT X(J),              '<< sorted list to screen
270          NEXT J
280 END
1000 REM ================================================== CTB4.3
1010 REM ********************>> QUICKSRT <<********************
1020 REM ==========================================================
1030 REM                    Quicksort Subroutine
1110 REM ==========================================================
1120 REM                    Variable Descriptions
1130 REM     Entering -
1140 REM       X(): array of values to be sorted
1150 REM       STACK(): stack to hold array X() pointers
1160 REM       TOTAL: length of array X()
1170 REM     Exiting -
1180 REM       X(): array sorted in ascending order
1190 REM     Local -
1200 REM       FIN : indicator. When zero the sort is done
1210 REM       PTR: stack pointer. PTR+1 points to the top of the
segment, PTR+2 to bottom of segment
1220 REM       TOPVAL: value at top of segment
1230 REM       BOTTOMVAL: value at bottom of segment
1240 REM       SEGTOP: pointer to top of segment
1250 REM       SEGBOTTOM: pointer to bottom of segment
1260 REM       COMPVAL: value being compared against current X()
1270 REM ==========================================================
1280      FIN = 1
1290      PTR = 0
1300      STACK(PTR+1)=1
1310      STACK(PTR+2)=TOTAL
1320        WHILE FIN <> 0
1330          FIN=FIN-1
1340          PTR=FIN+FIN
1350          TOPVAL=STACK(PTR+1)
1360          BOTTOMVAL=STACK(PTR+2)
1370          COMPVAL=X(TOPVAL)
1380          SEGTOP=TOPVAL
1390          SEGBOTTOM=BOTTOMVAL+1
1400            WHILE SEGBOTTOM-1 <> SEGTOP
1410                SEGBOTTOM=SEGBOTTOM-1
1420                IF COMPVAL <=X(SEGBOTTOM) THEN 1450 ELSE
X(SEGTOP) = X(SEGBOTTOM)
1430                SEGTOP=SEGTOP+1
1440                IF SEGBOTTOM = SEGTOP THEN 1460 ELSE IF
COMPVAL  >= X(SEGTOP) THEN 1430 ELSE X(SEGBOTTOM) = X(SEGTOP)
1450            WEND
1460          X(SEGTOP)=COMPVAL
1470          IF BOTTOMVAL-SEGTOP < 2 THEN 1520
1480          PTR=FIN+FIN
1490          STACK(PTR+1)=SEGTOP+1
1500          STACK(PTR+2)=BOTTOMVAL
1510          FIN=FIN+1
1520          IF SEGBOTTOM - TOPVAL < 2 THEN 1570
1530          PTR=FIN+FIN
1540          STACK(PTR+1)=TOPVAL
```

```
1550          STACK(PTR+2)=SEGBOTTOM-1
1560          FIN=FIN+1
1570       WEND
1580 RETURN
```

RUN (Quicksrt)

```
ARRAY OF RANDOM-ORDER INTEGERS --
  9            4            33           39           5
 13           31            43           14           1
 32           36            55           10           49
 47           34            50           13           44
 38           17             9           13           29
 57           44            60           45           31
 10           34            48           28           21
 13           30            42           50           24
 16           35            53           22           17
  5           57            50            6           12
 14           15            15           46           39
 59           27            18           53           56

ARRAY SORTED IN ASCENDING ORDER --
  1            4             5            5            6
  9            9            10           10           12
 13           13            13           13           14
 14           15            15           16           17
 17           18            21           22           24
 27           28            29           30           31
 31           32            33           34           34
 35           36            38           39           39
 42           43            44           44           45
 46           47            48           49           50
 50           50            53           53           55
 56           57            57           59           60
```

Purpose

Arrange a table of values in ascending order.

Notes

This delayed replacement sort subroutine is an improved version of the standard replacement sort. In this case, the switch between two list items is delayed until the test item is confirmed to be the smallest, resulting in a 50% execution time savings.

The algorithm is compact and quite useful for lists of moderate length; however, as the number of items grows linearly, sorting time grows exponentially, so use Shellsrt or Quicksort for mammoth data tables.

A Print statement can be added to the algorithm after Line 1260 to observe internal subroutine operation:

```
1261   PRINT X(L9);
```

If your brand of BASIC has no SWAP statement, then rewrite Line 1290 as follows:

```
1290   IF K9 < > COMPVAL
            THEN TEMP = X(K9) :
                X(K9) = X(COMPVAL) :
                X(COMPVAL) = TEMP
```

As in the previously discussed sorting algorithms, the sorting is done in-place, so send a copy of the unsorted table to the subroutine if you wish to preserve it.

Programming Ideas

Write a program using Valratio (CTB2.25), Displace (CTB2.3), and Delrepl to:

- Fill an array with a random-order integer sequence that is redundancy-rate controlled.
- Sort the array, then process it through Subroutine Displace.
- Use the processed array as a list of pointers to a rhythm data table.

Program Listing

```
100  REM  =========================================================
110  REM                     DRIVER PROGRAM
120  REM                       (Delrepl)
130  REM  =========================================================
140       DIM X(50)
150       TOTAL = 50
160       RANDOMIZE(395)
```

```
170        PRINT "ARRAY OF RANDOM-ORDER REAL NUMBERS (RANGE 0-1) --"
180          FOR J = 1 TO TOTAL
190            X(J) = RND
200            PRINT X(J);"  ";          '<< unsorted list to screen
205            IF J MOD 4 = 0 THEN PRINT
210          NEXT J
220        PRINT
230        PRINT "ARRAY SORTED IN ASCENDING ORDER --"
240        GOSUB 1000                '<< call delayed replacement sort
250          FOR J = 1 TO TOTAL
260            PRINT X(J);"  ";           '<< sorted list to screen
265            IF J MOD 4 = 0 THEN PRINT
270          NEXT J
280 END
1000 REM ================================================= CTB4.4
1010 REM ********************>> DELREPL <<********************
1020 REM =====================================================
1030 REM            Delayed Replacement Sort Subroutine
1120 REM =====================================================
1130 REM                  Variable Descriptions
1140 REM      Entering -
1150 REM        X(): array of values to be sorted
1160 REM        TOTAL: length of array X()
1170 REM      Exiting -
1180 REM        X(): array sorted in ascending order
1190 REM      Local -
1200 REM        K9: loop index, pointer to X()
1210 REM        L9: loop index, pointer to X()
1220 REM        COMPVAL: indicator for switch of values
1230 REM =====================================================
1240     FOR K9=1 TO TOTAL - 1
1250        COMPVAL= K9
1260          FOR L9=K9+1 TO TOTAL
1270            IF X(L9) < X(COMPVAL) THEN COMPVAL=L9
1280          NEXT L9
1290        IF K9 <> COMPVAL THEN SWAP X(K9),X(COMPVAL)
1300     NEXT K9
1310 RETURN
```

RUN (Delrepl)

```
ARRAY OF RANDOM-ORDER REAL NUMBERS (RANGE 0-1) --
 7.155919E-02      .701075         .271695         .3698326
 8.292723E-02      .6086213        .974105         .2374561
 .805496           .7145967        8.513391E-02    .8675042
 .2759476          .4714548        .5599209        .4570592
 .7155345          .7779383        1.473796E-02    .2198053
 .2957044          .682204         .6176149        .7141531
 .1537254          .3349475        .2289642        .4213648
 .6583109          .1925289        .7922064        .5736793
 .9252446          .470097         .9743947        .2324367
 .5830054          .8447148        5.684006E-02    .6162041
 .7883928          .4084844        .0757364        .6788998
 .4921513          .8716719        .2127854        .937919
 .9545958          1.583236E-02

ARRAY SORTED IN ASCENDING ORDER --
 1.473796E-02      1.583236E-02    5.684006E-02    7.155919E-02
 .0757364          8.292723E-02    8.513391E-02    .1537254
```

```
.1925289       .2127854       .2198053       .2289642
.2324367       .2374561       .271695        .2759476
.2957044       .3349475       .3698326       .4084844
.4213648       .4570592       .470097        .4714548
.4921513       .5599209       .5736793       .5830054
.6086213       .6162041       .6176149       .6583109
.6788998       .682204        .701075        .7141531
.7145967       .7155345       .7779383       .7883928
.7922064       .805496        .8447148       .8675042
.8716719       .9252446       .937919        .9545958
.974105        .9743947
```

Purpose

Arrange a table of values in ascending order.

Notes

This insertion sort algorithm is surprisingly fast, yet simple to code and understand. It is also called the cardplayer's sort because during processing each unsorted item is inserted in its appropriate slot relative to already sorted values.

To follow the workings of the subroutine, alter Lines 1230 and 1240 as follows:

```
1230   IF FIRSTVAL > = X(L9) THEN PRINT FIRSTVAL;
                                  : GOTO 1270
1240   X(L9 + 1) = X(L9) : PRINT X(L9);
```

Programming Ideas

Write a program using Alterseq (CTB2.4) and Insort that:

- Sorts an array of random-order integers,
- Assigns the unsorted list to the pitch parameter.
- Assigns the original and retrograde forms of the sorted list to the volume parameter.
- And assigns the array created from mapping of the internal subroutine function to the rhythm parameter.

Program Listing

```
100 REM ============================================================
110 REM                      DRIVER PROGRAM
120 REM                        (Insort)
130 REM ============================================================
140     DIM X(50)
150     TOTAL = 50
160     RANDOMIZE(61)
170     PRINT "ARRAY OF RANDOM-ORDER REAL NUMBERS (RANGE 0-1) --"
180        FOR J = 1 TO TOTAL
190           X(J) = RND
200           PRINT X(J);"   ";          '<< unsorted list to screen
205           IF J MOD 4 = 0 THEN PRINT
210        NEXT J
220     PRINT
230     PRINT "ARRAY SORTED IN ASCENDING ORDER --"
240     GOSUB 1000                        '<< call insertion sort
250        FOR J = 1 TO TOTAL
260           PRINT X(J);"   ";          '<< sorted list to screen
265           IF J MOD 4 = 0 THEN PRINT
```

```
270          NEXT J
280 END
1000 REM ============================================== CTB4.5
1010 REM ********************>> INSORT <<************************
1020 REM ==============================================
1030 REM              Insertion Sorting Algorithm
1080 REM ==============================================
1090 REM              Variable Descriptions
1100 REM      Entering -
1110 REM        X(): array of values to be sorted
1120 REM        TOTAL: length of array X()
1130 REM      Exiting -
1140 REM        X(): array sorted in ascending order
1150 REM      Local -
1160 REM        K9: loop index, pointer to X()
1170 REM        L9: loop index, pointer to X()
1180 REM        FIRSTVAL: first value in unsorted list
1190 REM ==============================================
1200     FOR K9=1 TO TOTAL - 1
1210        FIRSTVAL = X(K9+1)
1220           FOR L9=K9 TO 1 STEP -1
1230              IF FIRSTVAL >= X(L9) THEN 1270
1240                 X(L9+1) = X(L9)
1250           NEXT L9
1260        L9=0
1270        X(L9+1) = FIRSTVAL
1280     NEXT K9
1290 RETURN
```

RUN (Insort)

ARRAY OF RANDOM-ORDER REAL NUMBERS (RANGE 0-1) --

.3680985	.9677071	3.048778E-03	.5820213
.2276111	.8308198	.3387595	4.974252E-02
.6498869	.3376741	.7471517	.2877007
.796608	.5657236	.3083645	.1179784
1.402688E-02	3.871101E-02	.7636699	.3792597
.5985913	.4297931	.4060975	.2549551
.8125694	.5146655	.2210602	.851327
.1496744	.3746883	.2769781	2.561408E-02
.8506901	.8500103	.3659047	.4641567
.6690955	.2426946	.8941509	1.052171E-02
.8866899	.269843	2.291048E-02	.2436276
.5792179	.2667219	5.888522E-02	.3058694
.1319945	.6398863		

ARRAY SORTED IN ASCENDING ORDER --

3.048778E-03	1.052171E-02	1.402688E-02	2.291048E-02
2.561408E-02	3.871101E-02	4.974252E-02	5.888522E-02
.1179784	.1319945	.1496744	.2210602
.2276111	.2426946	.2436276	.2549551
.2667219	.269843	.2769781	.2877007
.3058694	.3083645	.3376741	.3387595
.3659047	.3680985	.3746883	.3792597
.4060975	.4297931	.4641567	.5146655
.5657236	.5792179	.5820213	.5985913
.6398863	.6498869	.6690955	.7471517
.7636699	.796608	.8125694	.8308198
.8500103	.8506901	.851327	.8866899
.8941509	.9677071		

Purpose

Search an unsorted table for the locations of specific entries or keys (linear method).

Notes

The linear unsorted table search is the simplest and slowest of the four search algorithms included in this chapter. It scans the input array from front to back looking for occurrences of target items. In this DRIVER PROGRAM, the search is for array positions which store the lowest and highest values of the random number generator range—information which may be required by other parts of a long program, or which will be displayed to provide a run-time view of linear excursion. The position(s) and occurrence frequency of each item is returned to the main routine; if the search is unsuccessful, a message to that effect is printed.

In this implementation, the datum and key are treated interchangeably; however, some applications necessitate interpretation of the stored values as keys (pointers) to the addresses of a secondary array.

Programming Ideas

Write an interactive program that:

- Generates and displays an array of random-order integers (range 1 to 88) which will be converted to registrated pitches.
- Searches the array for the locations of a small group of pitch classes which, after viewing the sequence, the user designates to receive volume accents. (Use the MOD function to convert the array integers to octave-contained pitch classes.)
- Assigns 100% levels to corresponding addresses in the volume parameter array.
- Fills the remaining volume array addresses with low-level (20% to 60%) volume data.

Program Listing

```
100 REM ===================================================
110 REM                     DRIVER PROGRAM
120 REM                       (Tsearch1)
130 REM ===================================================
140     DIM X(200)
150     TOTAL = 200
160     LOW = 1
170     HIGH = 60
180     RANGE = HIGH - LOW + 1
190     RANDOMIZE(2937)
```

```
200        PRINT "ARRAY OF RANDOM-ORDER NUMBERS (RANGE 1-";RANGE;")"
210          FOR J = 1 TO TOTAL
220            X(J) = INT(RND * RANGE)+1
230            PRINT X(J),                '<< unsorted list to screen
240          NEXT J
250        PRINT
260        PRINT
270        TABLKEY = LOW
280        PRINT "LOWEST VALUE -";LOW
290        GOSUB 1000               '<< call linear unsorted table search
300        TABLKEY = HIGH
310        PRINT "HIGHEST VALUE -";HIGH
320        GOSUB 1000               '<< call linear unsorted table search
330 END
1000 REM ======================================================= CTB4.6
1010 REM *******************>> TSEARCH1 <<*********************
1020 REM =====================================================
1030 REM          Linear Unsorted Table Search Subroutine
1180 REM =====================================================
1190 REM                    Variable Descriptions
1200 REM     Entering -
1210 REM       X(): array of bounded random integers
1220 REM       TOTAL: length of sequence
1230 REM       TABLKEY: search argument (key to search for)
1240 REM     Exiting -
1250 REM       none  (subroutine is procedural)
1260 REM     Local -
1270 REM  .    ITEMCOUNT: occurrence frequency tabulator
1280 REM       K9: loop index, pointer to X(),
1290 REM           key position indicator
1300 REM =====================================================
1310    ITEMCOUNT = 0
1320      FOR K9 = 1 TO TOTAL
1330        IF TABLKEY = X(K9) THEN PRINT "FOUND AT POSITION
";K9 ELSE 1350
1340          ITEMCOUNT = ITEMCOUNT + 1
1350      NEXT K9
1360    PRINT "KEY ITEM OCCURRED";ITEMCOUNT;"TIME(S)"
1370    PRINT
1380 RETURN
```

RUN (Tsearch1)

ARRAY OF RANDOM-ORDER NUMBERS (RANGE 1- 60)

11	45	8	54	16
57	26	29	19	33
36	27	17	20	28
22	14	37	31	50
13	47	49	46	16
23	4	2	36	15
7	14	13	58	30
48	38	35	21	21
52	34	37	11	45
60	20	12	24	3
21	57	3	38	10
56	60	26	9	11
54	60	50	8	17
21	36	41	19	31
36	29	49	36	50

33	32	57	36	7
37	36	4	38	28
60	15	12	41	56
5	4	18	45	50
27	25	48	45	42
51	9	57	33	13
33	33	43	10	35
2	44	55	11	58
2	60	17	49	15
18	49	8	49	19
53	54	49	38	14
14	1	45	56	11
13	5	20	1	51
11	19	25	45	19
41	20	18	10	53
40	42	55	59	35
36	28	49	49	53
58	33	18	46	34
13	6	8	27	51
32	5	7	34	33
48	51	2	26	35
31	13	34	14	34
20	44	35	19	58
22	19	28	39	15
8	49	27	27	57

```
LOWEST VALUE - 1
FOUND AT POSITION   132
FOUND AT POSITION   139
KEY ITEM OCCURRED 2 TIME(S)

HIGHEST VALUE - 60
FOUND AT POSITION   46
FOUND AT POSITION   57
FOUND AT POSITION   62
FOUND AT POSITION   86
FOUND AT POSITION   117
KEY ITEM OCCURRED 5 TIME(S)
```

Purpose

Search a sorted table for the locations of specific entries or keys (binary method).

Notes

This binary search subroutine requires a sorted table of unique entries (keys). It is the fastest algorithm in common use, but may not be as appropriate as Tsearch1 (CTB4.6) in many musical situations because the sorting process significantly increases execution time. Moreover, since the algorithm functions by successively cutting its search in half until it finds the key, repeated items must be culled from the list, or the subroutine will simply report the first redundant item it locates and return to the main program.

This condition can be circumvented by treating the array entries as pointers to an array containing redundant items. For example, suppose we shuffle an array of unique (not necessarily consecutive) integers to serve as pointers—keys—to a second character-string array which stores several items of information in each address. The entries at a number of different array locations may be identical, but the keys to the addresses will be unique; furthermore, while the keys will be sorted in ascending order, they need not be continuous. In this manner, sorted data of one musical parameter can be searched for target items to be mapped onto another parameter having a completely different value range.

Programming Ideas

1) Write a program that sorts and searches the data of one musical parameter to obtain pointers to another parameter which is then altered in some manner.

2) Write a program that "filters" or zeros-out specific values at keyed locations in the volume parameter in accordance with a list provided by a sorted search of the pitch parameter for particular items.

Program Listing

```
100 REM  ==========================================================
110 REM                      DRIVER PROGRAM
120 REM                        (Tsearch2)
130 REM  ==========================================================
140      DIM X(50)
150      TOTAL = 50
160      PRINT "A SORTED ARRAY OF INTEGERS (RANGE 1-100) --"
170         FOR J = 1 TO TOTAL
180            X(J) = J  * 2
190            PRINT X(J),              '<< sorted list to screen
200         NEXT J
```

```
210      PRINT
220      PRINT
230      ARG = 58
240      PRINT "THE INTEGER";ARG;"WILL BE THE ITEM TO SEARCH FOR"
250      GOSUB 1000
260      IF KPOS = 0 THEN PRINT "NOT FOUND" ELSE PRINT "KEY ";ARG;
"= POS";KPOS;
270 END
1000 REM ==================================================== CTB4.7
1010 REM *****************>> TSEARCH2 <<*********************
1020 REM ====================================================
1030 REM             Binary Sorted Table Search Subroutine
1080 REM ====================================================
1090 REM                    Variable Descriptions
1100 REM       Entering -
1110 REM         X() array of sorted items (keys)
1120 REM         TOTAL: length of array X()
1130 REM         ARG: search argument (item to look for)
1140 REM       Exiting -
1150 REM         KPOS: location (address) of item if found,
1160 REM               0 if not found
1170 REM       Local -
1180 REM         LL: lower limit for current search portion
1190 REM         UL: upper limit for current search portion
1200 REM         KVAL: computed value of key
1210 REM         MP: computed halfway point
1220 REM ====================================================
1230     LL=0
1240     UL=TOTAL+1
1250     KPOS=0
1260     IF ARG < X(1) OR ARG > X(TOTAL) THEN RETURN
1270     IF UL >=LL THEN MP=INT((UL+LL)/2) : KV=X(MP) : IF KV <>
ARG THEN IF KV >= ARG THEN UL=MP-1 : GOTO 1270 ELSE LL=MP+1 :
GOTO 1270 ELSE KPOS=MP ELSE KPOS=UL
1280     IF ARG <> X(KPOS) THEN KPOS = 0
1290 RETURN
```

RUN (Tsearch2)

```
A SORTED ARRAY OF INTEGERS (RANGE 1-100) --
  2          4          6          8          10
 12         14         16         18          20
 22         24         26         28          30
 32         34         36         38          40
 42         44         46         48          50
 52         54         56         58          60
 62         64         66         68          70
 72         74         76         78          80
 82         84         86         88          90
 92         94         96         98         100


THE INTEGER 58 WILL BE THE ITEM TO SEARCH FOR
KEY  58 = POS 29
```

SUBROUTINE: Tsearch3

Purpose

Search a sorted array for targeted values (keys) using the interpolation method.

Notes

The interpolation search algorithm requires a sorted list of unique items or keys. It is faster than the binary search in some situations, particularly when list items are unevenly distributed (skewed). The key's value is used as an indicator of where to begin the search, much like the method people use to index an element in a sorted file.

Programming Ideas

Develop an interactive program that compares the data of two parameters for points of intersection, then alters values of a third parameter at array locations corresponding to the intersections. The outline for a hypothetical program follows:

Program Name: INTERSECTIONS

- Pitchtable Pointers (keys)—array X( ): Generate a random-order, nonredundant integer series consisting of 24 values, range 1 to 88.

- Rhythm Parameter Data—array Y( ): Generate a random-order, nonredundant integer series consisting of 24 values, range 20 to 60.

- Volume Parameter Data—array Z( ): Generate volume (in percentage) data by sorting and searching pitch pointer array X( ) for *each* of the integers contained in the rhythm data array Y( ); when the search confirms the presence of a specific value in both array X( ) and array Y( ), an indicator tells the program to put an accent (100% volume) for that pitch in the appropriate array Z( ) location; all other pitches receive 50% volume values. (Note that the idea of intersection is construed as the coexistence of values in arrays X( ) and Y( ); they need not be in identical locations.)

Program Listing

```
100 REM ============================================================
110 REM                       DRIVER PROGRAM
120 REM                         (Tsearch3)
130 REM ============================================================
140     DIM X(52)
150     TOTAL = 50
160     PRINT "A SORTED ARRAY OF INTEGERS (RANGE 1-100) --"
170        FOR J = 1 TO TOTAL
180           X(J) = J  * 2
190           PRINT X(J),                    '<< sorted list to screen
200        NEXT J
210     PRINT
220     PRINT
```

```
230     ARG = 96
240     PRINT "THE INTEGER";ARG;"WILL BE THE ITEM TO SEARCH FOR"
250     GOSUB 1000                    '<< call interpolation search
260     IF KPOS = 0 THEN PRINT "NOT FOUND" ELSE PRINT "KEY ";ARG;"
= POS";KPOS;
270 END
1000 REM ================================================ CTB4.8
1010 REM ****************>> TSEARCH3 <<***********************
1020 REM ================================================
1030 REM               Interpolation Search Subroutine
1140 REM ================================================
1150 REM                   Variable Descriptions
1160 REM     Entering -
1170 REM       X(): array of sorted items (keys)
1180 REM       TOTAL: length of array X()
1190 REM     Exiting -
1200 REM       KPOS: location (address) of item if found,
1210 REM             0 if not found
1220 REM     Local -
1230 REM       LL: lower search boundary
1240 REM       UL: upper search boundary
1250 REM       LOKEY: key at lower boundary
1260 REM       UPKEY: key at upper boundary
1270 REM       INTPOS: interpolated position in array for
1280 REM               next comparison
1290 REM       INTKEY: key at interpolated position
1300 REM ================================================
1310     LL = 0
1320     UL = TOTAL + 1
1330     X(LL) = X(1) - 1
1340     X(UL) = X(TOTAL) + 1
1350     LOKEY = X(1)
1360     UPKEY = X(TOTAL)
1370     KPOS = 0
1380     IF ARG < LOKEY OR ARG > UPKEY THEN RETURN
1390     IF UL < LL THEN RETURN
1400     INTPOS = LL + INT((UL - LL) * (ARG - LOKEY) / (UPKEY -
LOKEY))
1410     INTKEY = X(INTPOS)
1420     IF INTKEY <> ARG THEN IF INTKEY >= ARG THEN UL = INTPOS -
1: UPKEY = INTKEY: GOTO 1390 ELSE LL = INTPOS + 1: LOKEY = INTKEY:
GOTO 1390 ELSE KPOS = INTPOS
1430 RETURN
```

RUN (Tsearch3)

```
A SORTED ARRAY OF INTEGERS (RANGE 1-100) --
2            4            6            8            10
12           14           16           18           20
22           24           26           28           30
32           34           36           38           40
42           44           46           48           50
52           54           56           58           60
62           64           66           68           70
72           74           76           78           80
82           84           86           88           90
92           94           96           98           100

THE INTEGER 96 WILL BE THE ITEM TO SEARCH FOR
KEY  96 = POS 48
```

Purpose

Search a sorted list for targeted values using the proximity search method.

Notes

This algorithm requires a sorted list of unique items. More powerful than either the binary or interpolation search, it returns a subset of the array on either side of the value under search (even if the target item is missing).

This approach is applicable to musical situations in which a prioritized range of solutions to contextual requirements must be retrieved from a table of rules governing linear or vertical aggregates. For instance, melodic sequences might be generated by causing an input melodic interval class to trigger subsequent interval choices based upon generation rules stored in proximity to a target value. Also, random integers might dictate locations for random walks across a cluster of values.

Programming Ideas

1) Write an interactive program that:

- Fills a driver array with 20 random-order integers, range 1 to 76 (redundancy is all right).
- Fills a reference array with a 44-member, random-order series, range 1 to 88.
- Invokes a proximity search to locate values supplied by the driver array.
- Takes a random walk around the integers returned by the proximity search.
- Prints the random walk as registrated pitches.

2) Write an interactive program in which melodic interval succession is governed by a set of production rules stored in a reference array. Use values derived from a secondary parameter as search arguments for CTB4.8.

Program Listing

```
100 REM =================================================================
110 REM                         DRIVER PROGRAM
120 REM                           (Tsearch4)
130 REM =================================================================
140     DIM X(52)
150     TOTAL = 50
160     PRINT "A SORTED ARRAY OF INTEGERS (RANGE 1-100) --"
170       FOR J = 1 TO TOTAL
180         X(J) = J  * 2
190         PRINT X(J),              '<< sorted list to screen
200       NEXT J
210     PRINT
230     ARG = 42
240     SWIDTH = 5
```

```
250        PRINT "THE INTEGER";ARG;"WILL BE THE ITEM TO SEARCH FOR"
260        GOSUB 1000                      '<< call interpolation search
270        FOR J = LLL TO LUL
280            PRINT X(J)                   '<< send returned segment to screen
290        NEXT J
300 END
1000 REM =============================================== CTB4.8
1010 REM ******************>> TSEARCH4 <<*********************
1020 REM ================================================
1030 REM               Proximity Search Subroutine
1140 REM ================================================
1150 REM                  Variable Descriptions
1160 REM       Entering -
1170 REM         X(): array of sorted items (keys)
1180 REM         TOTAL: length of array X()
1190 REM         ARG: search argument (item to look for)
1200 REM         SWIDTH: width of search below & above item
1210 REM       Exiting -
1220 REM         LUL: upper limit of list of items returned
1230 REM         LLL: lower limit of list of items returned
1240 REM       Local -
1250 REM         K9: loop index, pointer to array X()
1260 REM ================================================
1270     FOR K9 = 1 TO TOTAL
1280         IF ARG <= X(K9) THEN 1310
1290     NEXT K9
1300     K9 = TOTAL + 1
1310     IF ARG = X(K9) THEN LUL = K9 + SWIDTH ELSE LUL = K9 +
SWIDTH - 1
1320     LLL = K9 - SWIDTH
1330     IF LUL > TOTAL THEN LUL = TOTAL
1340     IF LLL < 1 THEN LLL = 1
1350 RETURN
```

RUN (Tsearch4)

```
A SORTED ARRAY OF INTEGERS (RANGE 1-100) --
  2           4           6           8          10
 12          14          16          18          20
 22          24          26          28          30
 32          34          36          38          40
 42          44          46          48          50
 52          54          56          58          60
 62          64          66          68          70
 72          74          76          78          80
 82          84          86          88          90
 92          94          96          98         100

THE INTEGER 42 WILL BE THE ITEM TO SEARCH FOR
 32
 34
 36
 38
 40
 42
 44
 46
 48
 50
 52
```

5
Sound/Text Composition

SUBROUTINE GROUP: SNDTEXT

- Sndtext1   CTB5.1
- Sndtext2   CTB5.2

Purpose

Numeric-to-string and string-to-numeric conversion for correlating text and musical parameters.

Notes

Sndtext1 converts an array of integers to a single character string by using BASIC's CHR\$ function to interpret the values as ASCII codes. It also adds blanks randomly to simulate the appearance of articulated text. (Line 1290 causes any ASCII code larger than 122 to be interpreted as a blank space.) It may be adapted to a number of applications in which musical parameters and text are correlated in some fashion. For instance, a sequence of pitch parameter values—transposed to a suitable ASCII code range—will be converted to alphabetic characters whose codes represent the mapping of pitch onto text. The result, however, won't conform to human language because of the absence of syntactical rules.

Sndtext2 converts a text string to an array of integers by using BASIC's ASC function to retrieve the ASCII codes of the constituent characters. This array is then returned to the main routine for assignment as a list of pointers to any appropriately-scaled parameter table.

Programming Ideas

1) Write an interactive program that reads a text file and converts the characters to ASCII codes, then range-scales and assigns the sequence of integers to the pitch parameter of a melodic line.

2) Expand the above program to allow the user to process the output sequence in several ways (inversion, retrograde, etc.) for assignment to another musical parameter.

Program Listing

```
100 REM ============================================================
110 REM                         DRIVER PROGRAM
120 REM                          (Sndtext)
130 REM ============================================================
140    DIM X(51),Y(100)
150    TOTAL = 50
160    RANGE = 26                              '<< letters of alphabet
170    BLANKS = 10   '<< additional codes to be filtered as blanks
180    X(0) = TOTAL
190    RANDOMIZE(-4295)
200    PRINT "RANDOM INTEGERS TO INTERPRET AS ASCII CODES --"
210       FOR J = 1 TO TOTAL
220          X(J) = INT(RND * (RANGE+BLANKS)) + 97
230          PRINT X(J),               '<< integer array to screen
240       NEXT J
250    PRINT
260    PRINT "THE NUMBER-TO-CHARACTER CONVERTED TEXT --"
270    GOSUB 1000        '<< call numeric-to-character conversion
280    PRINT TEXT$          '<< text-converted sequence to screen
285    PRINT
290    PRINT "THE TEXT CONVERTED BACK TO INTEGERS "
300    PRINT "WITH NON ALPHABET-RANGE VALUES AS BLANKS --"
310    GOSUB 2000
320       FOR J = 1 TO TOTAL
330          PRINT Y(J),               '<< reconverted array to screen
340       NEXT J
350 END
1000 REM ==================================================== CTB5.1
1010 REM ******************>> SNDTEXT1 <<************************
1020 REM ============================================================
1030 REM          Integer-to-Character Conversion Subroutine
1150 REM ============================================================
1160 REM                     Variable Descriptions
1170 REM      Entering -
1180 REM        X(): sequence of integer values, to be interpreted
1190 REM             as ASCII codes
1200 REM        TOTAL: length of array X()
1210 REM      Exiting -
1220 REM        TEXT$: string of alphabet characters representing
1230 REM               mapping of numbers to text
1240 REM      Local -
1250 REM        K9: loop index, pointer to array X()
```

```
1260 REM ===========================================================
1270     TEXT$ = ""
1280        FOR K9 = 1 TO X(0)
1290           IF X(K9) > 122 THEN TEXT$ = TEXT$ + " " ELSE TEXT$ =
TEXT$ + CHR$(X(K9))
1300        NEXT K9
1310 RETURN
2000 REM =========================================== CTB5.2
2010 REM *******************>> SNDTEXT2 <<********************
2020 REM ===========================================================
2030 REM          Character-to-Integer Conversion Subroutine
2080 REM ===========================================================
2090 REM                Variable Descriptions
2100 REM      Entering -
2110 REM        TEXT$: character string
2120 REM      Exiting -
2130 REM        Y(): array holding integer-converted sequence
2140 REM      Local -
2150 REM        K9: loop index, pointer to array Y()
2160 REM ===========================================================
2170    Y(0) = LEN(TEXT$)
2180       FOR K9 = 1 TO Y(0)
2190          Y(K9) = ASC(MID$(TEXT$,K9,1))
2200       NEXT K9
2210 RETURN
```

RUN (Sndtext)

RANDOM INTEGERS TO INTERPRET AS ASCII CODES --

115	123	100	131	99
115	124	113	110	110
98	100	108	105	124
112	132	107	112	99
113	97	99	130	123
130	113	127	99	126
109	114	112	109	109
105	108	114	117	121
125	125	130	104	120
106	115	120	98	100

THE NUMBER-TO-CHARACTER CONVERTED TEXT --
s d cs qnnbdli p kpcqac   q c mrpmmilruy   hxjsxbd

THE TEXT CONVERTED BACK TO INTEGERS
WITH NON ALPHABET-RANGE VALUES AS BLANKS --

115	32	100	32	99
115	32	113	110	110
98	100	108	105	32
112	32	107	112	99
113	97	99	32	32
32	113	32	99	32
109	114	112	109	109
105	108	114	117	121
32	32	32	104	120
106	115	120	98	100

SUBROUTINE GROUP: WORDPLAY

○ Randline	CTB5.3
○ Nextword	CTB5.4
○ Strclean	CTB5.5
○ Average	CTB5.6
○ Randword	CTB5.7

Purpose

Provide common string handling procedures for use in sound/text programs.

Notes

Randline (CTB5.3) is an adaptation of the sampling-without-replacement algorithm Setflag (CTB2.5); it returns one copy of each text line in random order.

Nextword (CTB5.4) extracts the next word in line from a list of phrases supplied by the calling program, which also passes flags to signal processing status. The end-of-word is indicated by (" "), and the end-of-phrase by ("#").

Strclean (CTB5.5) uses BASIC's INSTR function to identify and remove all special characters from an array of text words. ("Cleaned" words produce a shorter string.)

Average (CTB5.6) computes the weighted average length of all words contained in the text, information which can be passed on to other parts of a long program.

Randword (CTB5.7) is similar in operation to Randline, except that it returns text words in random order. (Words may be repeated by virtue of their repetition in the text, but each address of array WORD$ is selected only once.)

Programming Idea

Write a program that reads prepared text from a data file and derives integers (pointers) for several musical parameters from the word letters. Include subroutines to generate any number of randomizations of the text words and lines for conversion to pitch, rhythm, and articulation parameter sequences.

Program Listing

```
100 REM =================================================================
110 REM                         DRIVER PROGRAM
120 REM                           (Wordplay)
130 REM =================================================================
140     DIM WORD$(200),TEXT$(13)
150     DIM TXTLN(12),TXTWD(200),X(20),WTABL(20)
```

```
160          FOR J = 1 TO 20
170             X(J) = J
180          NEXT J
190       READ TOTAL
200       PRINT "THE ORIGINAL TEXT --"
210          FOR J = 1 TO TOTAL
220             READ TEXT$(J)
230             PRINT TEXT$(J)
240          NEXT J
250       PRINT
260       RANDOMIZE(10312)
270       PRINT "A RANDOM ORDERING OF THE TEXT LINES --"
280       GOSUB 1000                    '<< call random-order lines
290       TEXT$(TOTAL) = TEXT$(TOTAL) + "   #"
300       PRINT "WORDS IN TEXT" : PRINT
310       CHARSET$ =" abcdefghijklmnopqrstuvwxyz0123456789"
320       CHARSET$ = CHARSET$ + "ABCDEFGHIJKLMNOPQRSTUVWXYZ"
330       ENDFLAG = 0 : PHRPTR = 1 : POSIT = 1 : COUNT = 0
340          WHILE ENDFLAG <> 1
350             GOSUB 2000                       '<< call next word
360             CLNWORD$ = NXTWORD$
370             GOSUB 3000          '<< call string clean-up & compress
380             WRDCNT = WRDCNT + 1
390             NXTWORD$ = CLNWORD$
400             PRINT NXTWORD$,
410             WORD$(WRDCNT) = NXTWORD$
420             SIZE = LEN(NXTWORD$)
430             WTABL(SIZE) = WTABL(SIZE) + 1
440          WEND
450       PRINT
460       P$="  ##       ###                  ##       ###"
470       PRINT "length  frequency           length  frequency"
480          FOR J = 1 TO 20 STEP 2
490             PRINT USING P$;J,WTABL(J),J+1,WTABL(J+1)
500          NEXT J
510       GOSUB 4000                      '<< call weighted average
520       PRINT
530       PRINT "AVERAGE WORD LENGTH = ";AVERAGE
540       PRINT "A RANDOM ORDERING OF THE TEXT WORDS --"
550       GOSUB 5000                      '<< call random word-walk
560       PRINT
570 END
580 REM +++++++++++++++++++++++++++++++++++++++++++++++++++++++++++
590             DATA 12
600             DATA "At morn -at noon -at twilight dim-"
610             DATA "Maria! thou hast heard my hymn!"
620             DATA "In joy and woe -in good and ill-"
630             DATA "Mother of God, be with me still!"
640             DATA "When the hours flew brightly by,"
650             DATA "And not a cloud obscured the sky,"
660             DATA "My soul, lest it should truant be,"
670             DATA "Thy grace did guide to thine and thee;"
680             DATA "Now, when storms of Fate o'rcast"
690             DATA "Darkly my Present and my Past,"
700             DATA "Let my Future radiant shine"
710             DATA "With sweet hopes of thee and thine!"
720 REM +++++++++++++++++++++++++++++++++++++++++++++++++++++++++++
1000 REM ===================================================== CTB5.3
1010 REM ******************>> RANDLINE <<************************
1020 REM =====================================================
```

```
1030 REM                    Line-order Randomization Subroutine
1070 REM  ==========================================================
1080 REM                         Variable Descriptions
1090 REM      Entering -
1100 REM        TEXT$(): array holding lines of text
1110 REM        TOTAL: number of lines in TEXT$()
1120 REM      Exiting -
1130 REM        none  (subroutine is procedural)
1140 REM      Local -
1150 REM        LINSTEP: random number
1160 REM        TXTLN(): array to store occurrence flags
1170 REM        K9: loop index
1180 REM  ==========================================================
1190      FOR K9 = 1 TO TOTAL
1200          LINSTEP = INT(RND * TOTAL)+1
1210          IF TXTLN(LINSTEP)= 1 THEN 1200
1220          PRINT TEXT$(LINSTEP)
1230          TXTLN(LINSTEP) = 1
1240      NEXT K9
1250   RETURN
2000 REM  ================================================ CTB5.4
2010 REM  *******************>> NEXTWORD <<********************
2020 REM  ==========================================================
2030 REM                    Substring Extraction Subroutine
2080 REM  ==========================================================
2090 REM                         Variable Descriptions
2100 REM      Entering -
2110 REM        TEXT$(): list of phrases to be broken into words
2120 REM        PHRPTR: phrase pointer
2130 REM        POSIT: position in phrase being analyzed
2140 REM      Exiting -
2150 REM        ENDFLAG: signal for end of processing (if = 1)
2160 REM        NXTWORD$: next word (extracted)
2170 REM      Local -
2180 REM        SCANCHAR$: character being scanned
2190 REM        K9: phrase loop index
2200 REM        L9: word loop index
2210 REM  ==========================================================
2220      NXTWORD$ = ""
2230          FOR K9 = POSIT TO LEN(TEXT$(PHRPTR))
2240              SCANCHAR$ = MID$(TEXT$(PHRPTR),K9,1)
2250              IF SCANCHAR$ = "#" THEN ENDFLAG = 1 : RETURN
2260              IF SCANCHAR$ <> " " THEN 2300
2270          NEXT K9
2280      PHRPTR = PHRPTR + 1 : POSIT = 1
2290      IF NXTWORD$ = "" THEN 2230 ELSE ENDFLAG = 0 : RETURN
2300      NXTWORD$ = NXTWORD$ + SCANCHAR$
2310      IF K9 = LEN(TEXT$(PHRPTR)) THEN PHRPTR = PHRPTR + 1 :
POSIT = 1 : ENDFLAG = 0 : RETURN
2320          FOR L9 = K9 + 1 TO LEN(TEXT$(PHRPTR))
2330              SCANCHAR$ = MID$(TEXT$(PHRPTR),L9,1)
2340              IF SCANCHAR$ = " " THEN POSIT = L9 : GOTO 2380
2350              NXTWORD$ = NXTWORD$ + SCANCHAR$
2360          NEXT L9
2370      PHRPTR = PHRPTR + 1 : POSIT = 1
2380      ENDFLAG = 0
2390   RETURN
3000 REM  ================================================ CTB5.5
3010 REM  *******************>> STRCLEAN <<********************
3020 REM  ==========================================================
```

```
3030 REM     This subroutine strips all special characters from
3040 REM     a string, then compresses it.
3050 REM ========================================================
3060 REM                     Variable Descriptions
3070 REM     Entering -
3080 REM        CLNWORD$: string to be cleaned
3090 REM        CHARSET$: string of legal characters to be kept
3100 REM     Exiting -
3110 REM        CLNWORD$: cleaned string
3120 REM     Local -
3130 REM        TBUFF$: temporary string buffer
3140 REM        K9: loop index, pointer to CLNWORD$ characters
3150 REM ========================================================
3160     TBUFF$ = ""
3170        FOR K9 = 1 TO LEN(CLNWORD$)
3180     IF INSTR(CHARSET$,MID$(CLNWORD$,K9,1)) <> 0 THEN TBUFF$ =
TBUFF$+MID$(CLNWORD$,K9,1)
3190        NEXT K9
3200     CLNWORD$ = TBUFF$
3210 RETURN
4000 REM ================================================ CTB5.6
4010 REM ******************>> AVERAGE <<**********************
4020 REM ========================================================
4030 REM     This subroutine computes the weighted average length
4040 REM     of all words contained in the text.
4050 REM ========================================================
4060 REM                     Variable Descriptions
4070 REM     Entering -
4080 REM        X(): array of values to be averaged
4090 REM        WTABL(): array of weights corresponding to each X()
4100 REM        TOTAL: number of values in X() and WTABL()
4110 REM     Exiting -
4120 REM        AVERAGE: weighted average length of words
4130 REM     Local -
4140 REM        PRODSUM: sum of products of value and weight
4150 REM        WEIGHTSUM: sum of weights
4160 REM        K9: loop index, pointer to WTABLE()
4170 REM ========================================================
4180     PRODSUM = 0 : WEIGHTSUM = 0
4190        FOR K9 = 1 TO TOTAL
4200           PRODSUM = PRODSUM + WTABL(K9) * X(K9)
4210           WEIGHTSUM = WEIGHTSUM + WTABL(K9)
4220        NEXT K9
4230     AVERAGE = PRODSUM / WEIGHTSUM
4240 RETURN
5000 REM ================================================ CTB5.7
5010 REM ******************>> RANDWORD <<*********************
5020 REM ========================================================
5030 REM              Word-order Randomization Subroutine
5050 REM ========================================================
5060 REM                     Variable Descriptions
5070 REM     Entering -
5080 REM        WORD$(): array holding words of text
5090 REM        WRDCNT: number of words in array WORD$()
5100 REM     Exiting -
5110 REM        none    (subroutine is procedural)
5120 REM     Local -
5130 REM        TXTWD(): array to store occurrence flags
5140 REM        WRDSTEP: random number
5150 REM        K9: loop index
```

```
5160 REM ========================================================
5170    FOR K9 = 1 TO WRDCNT
5180       WRDSTEP = INT(RND * WRDCNT)+1
5190       IF TXTWD(WRDSTEP) = 1 THEN 5180
5200       PRINT WORD$(WRDSTEP);" ";
5210       TXTWD(WRDSTEP) = 1
5220       IF K9 MOD 10 = 0 THEN PRINT
5230    NEXT K9
5240 RETURN
```

RUN (Wordplay)

```
THE ORIGINAL TEXT --
At morn -at noon -at twilight dim-
Maria! thou hast heard my hymn!
In joy and woe -in good and ill-
Mother of God, be with me still!
When the hours flew brightly by,
And not a cloud obscured the sky,
My soul, lest it should truant be,
Thy grace did guide to thine and thee;
Now, when storms of Fate o'rcast
Darkly my Present and my Past,
Let my Future radiant shine
With sweet hopes of thee and thine!

A RANDOM ORDERING OF THE TEXT LINES --
Darkly my Present and my Past,
Let my Future radiant shine
Now, when storms of Fate o'rcast
My soul, lest it should truant be,
In joy and woe -in good and ill-
With sweet hopes of thee and thine!
And not a cloud obscured the sky,
At morn -at noon -at twilight dim-
When the hours flew brightly by,
Mother of God, be with me still!
Thy grace did guide to thine and thee;
Maria! thou hast heard my hymn!
```

WORDS IN TEXT

At	morn	at	noon	at
twilight	dim	Maria	thou	hast
heard	my	hymn	In	joy
and	woe	in	good	and
ill	Mother	of	God	be
with	me	still	When	the
hours	flew	brightly	by	And
not	a	cloud	obscured	the
sky	My	soul	lest	it
should	truant	be	Thy	grace
did	guide	to	thine	and
thee	Now	when	storms	of
Fate	orcast	Darkly	my	Present
and	my	Past	Let	my
Future	radiant	shine	With	sweet
hopes	of	thee	and	thine

length	frequency		length	frequency
1	1		2	19
3	19		4	17
5	12		6	7
7	2		8	3
9	0		10	0
11	0		12	0
13	0		14	0
15	0		16	0
17	0		18	0
19	0		20	0

AVERAGE WORD LENGTH = 3.8

A RANDOM ORDERING OF THE TEXT WORDS --
did twilight a my radiant and When joy still sweet
and Present brightly with be my sky storms With obscured
Future heard Maria thine good and hymn lest Darkly the
hours hopes Thy soul of guide Mother God Now orcast
woe morn at should In ill me in it thee
and thou shine At my flew and of when of
hast grace thee And My Let by at Fate
Past the truant my not be dim cloud to thine
noon

SUBROUTINE GROUP: GEN-CON

○ Genpoem	CTB5.8
○ Artcheck	CTB5.9
○ Sndtext2	CTB5.2
○ Pitchtab	CTB1.3

Purpose

Compose three-line poems by the random selection of words within predetermined vocabulary categories; convert to musical pitches.

Notes

Genpoem is a low-intelligence poem composition subroutine which simply randomizes word selections for poem structures dictated by the data statements in Lines 5570-5600. The four poem forms are reminiscent of Haiku in their brevity and syntax; however, the resulting verse may not be to everyone's taste due to the frequent juxtaposition of remote imagery and unusual linkage of various parts of speech. To control the "nonsense factor," reduce the number of words in the adjective, noun, verb, and preposition categories to include only those which produce minimal ambiguity in any possible combination. You must also correspondingly alter word-total variables in Lines 200 and 230 or complete mayhem will result. Conversely, increased ambiguity and metaphorical madness is achieved by the imaginative augmentation of program vocabulary.

Programming Ideas

Write an interactive program that:

- Reads in vocabulary from a file.
- Allows the user to control the poem ambiguity level via a variable which gradually increases or decreases vocabulary size.
- Converts the returned poems to data for the pitch, rhythm, and articulation parameters of a melodic line for soprano voice.
- Outputs the completed notelist to a disk file (see Scoreform, CTB6.21).

Program Listing

```
100 REM ============================================================
110 REM                      DRIVER PROGRAM
120 REM                        (Gen-Con)
130 REM ============================================================
140 REM     This group of subroutines composes 4 poems (somewhat
150 REM     resembling Haiku), then maps the ASCII values of the
160 REM     constituent letters onto the pitch domain.
170 REM +++++++++++++++++++++++++++++++++++++++++++++++++++++++++++++
```

```
180      DIM P$(84),VOCAB$(300),W(15),SET(300)
190 REM >>> assign parts of speech totals (see DATA categories)
200      AR = 2
210      AD = 72
220      NO = 103
230      VE = 55
240      PR = 15
250      WORDTOT = AR + AD + NO + VE + PR
260      GOSUB 4000                      '<< initialize pitch data table
270      RANDOMIZE(667)
280      PRINT "EACH LINE OF EACH POEM WILL BE PRINTED, THEN " :
PRINT "CONVERTED TO CORRESPONDING PITCH SEQUENCE"
290         FOR J = 1 TO 4
300            PRINT "POEM ";J
310            GOSUB 1000                   '<< call poem generator
320            PRINT:PRINT
330         NEXT J
340 END
1000 REM ================================================= CTB5.8
1010 REM ****************>> GENPOEM <<************************
1020 REM =========================================================
1030 REM      This subroutine generates 3-line poems which bear
1040 REM      a resemblance to Haiku.  It consults 1 of four
1050 REM      poem form schemes to provide proper syntax.
1100 REM =========================================================
1110 REM                    Variable Descriptions
1120 REM      Entering -
1130 REM        J: flag from DRIVER to load program vocabulary
1140 REM        WORDTOT: vocabulary size
1150 REM        AR: number of articles in vocabulary
1160 REM        AD: number of adjectives in vocabulary
1170 REM        NO: number of nouns in vocabulary
1180 REM        VE: number of verbs in vocabulary
1190 REM        PR: number of prepositions in vocabulary
1200 REM      Exiting -
1210 REM        LIN$: full poem line
1220 REM      Local -
1230 REM        VOCAB$(): array of program vocabulary
1240 REM        SET(): flag array to prevent word repetition
1250 REM        W(): array storing current poem formal structure
1260 REM        W: current part of speech, or blank space
1270 REM        L: low end vocabulary delimiter
1280 REM        S: range span for parts of speech categories
1290 REM        RNDWRD: randomly selected word
1300 REM        K9: loop index, pointer to W()
1310 REM =========================================================
1320      LIN$ = ""
1330      IF J > 1 THEN 1370
1340         FOR K9 = 1 TO WORDTOT
1350            READ VOCAB$(K9)                    '<< load vocabulary
1360         NEXT K9
1370         FOR K9 = 1 TO 15
1380            READ W(K9)          '<< load 1 of 4 unique poem forms
1390         NEXT K9
1400         FOR K9 = 1 TO 15
1410            W = W(K9)
1420 REM << if end-of-text (W=-1) or end-of-line (W=0), call  >>
1430 REM << article-checking subroutine, print line of text,  >>
1440 REM << call text-to-pitch conversion subroutine to print >>
1450 REM << resulting pitch sequence.                         >>
```

```
1460          IF W = -1 THEN GOSUB 2000 : PRINT LIN$ : GOSUB 3000 :
RETURN
1470          IF W =  0 THEN GOSUB 2000 : PRINT LIN$ : GOSUB 3000 :
LIN$= "" : GOTO 1550
1480 REM >>>  locate vocab range for selected part of speech
1490      IF W=1 THEN L=1:S=AR ELSE IF W=2 THEN L=AR+1:S=AD
ELSE IF  W=3   THEN L=AR+AD+1:S=NO ELSE IF W=4   THEN  L=AR+AD+NO+1
:S=VE ELSE L=AR+AD+NO+VE+1:S=PR
1500          RNDWRD = INT(RND * S) + L
1510          IF RNDWRD <= AR THEN 1540 '<<permit article repet.
1520          IF SET(RNDWRD) = 1 THEN 1500 '<<prevent word repet.
1530          SET(RNDWRD) = 1
1540          LIN$ = LIN$ + " " + VOCAB$(RNDWRD) '<< build a line
1550      NEXT K9
1560 RETURN
2000 REM ============================================= CTB5.9
2010 REM ******************>> ARTCHECK <<************************
2020 REM =============================================
2030 REM  This subroutine checks for article-adjective agreement.
2040 REM  It scans the line of poetry most recently created by
2050 REM  subroutine GENPOEM.  If it finds the article A before
2060 REM  a vowel, it changes it to the article AN.
2070 REM =============================================
2080 REM                    Variable Descriptions
2090 REM     Entering -
2100 REM       LIN$: uncorrected line of text
2110 REM     Exiting -
2120 REM       LIN$: text line after article checking/correction
2130 REM     Local -
2140 REM       B$: stores indicator to add letter N to article
2150 REM       I: loop index, pointer to LIN$ substring
2160 REM =============================================
2170    FOR I = 1 TO LEN(LIN$) - 2
2180          IF MID$(LIN$,I,3) = " A " THEN B$ = MID$(LIN$,I+3,1)
ELSE 2200
2190          IF B$="A" OR B$="E" OR B$="I" OR B$="O" OR B$="U"
THEN LIN$ = LEFT$(LIN$,I+1) + "N" + MID$(LIN$,I+2)
2200      NEXT I
2210 RETURN
3000 REM ============================================= CTB5.2
3010 REM ******************>> SNDTEXT2 <<************************
3020 REM                 (Adapted to program specs)
3030 REM =============================================
3040    LINELENGTH = LEN(LIN$)
3050      FOR M9 = 1 TO LINELENGTH
3060          NOTENUM = ASC(MID$(LIN$,M9,1))-32 '<<convert to int
3070          PRINT P$(NOTENUM);" ";        '<< convert to pitch
3080      NEXT M9
3090      PRINT
3100 RETURN
4000 REM ============================================= CTB1.3
4010 REM ******************>> PITCHTAB <<************************
4020 REM                 (Adapted to program specs)
4030 REM =============================================
4040    P$(0) = " R "        '<< blank spaces will print as rests
4050    NOTE$ = " CC# DD# E FF# GG# AA# B"
4060    OCTAVE$ = "1234567"
4070      FOR K9 = 1 TO 7
4080          FOR L9 = 1 TO 12
4090              P$(L9+(K9-1) * 12) = MID$(NOTE$,(L9*2-1),2) +
```

```
                MID$(OCTAVE$,K9,1)
4100               NEXT L9
4110             NEXT K9
4120 RETURN
4130 REM ===========================================================
5000 REM ++++++++++++++++++++++++++++++++++++++++++++++++++++++++++++
5010 REM                     PROGRAM VOCABULARY
5020 REM                     ++++++++++++++++++
5030 REM
5040 REM                         ARTICLES
5050 REM ++++++++++++++++++
5060 DATA A,THE
5070 REM ++++++++++++++++++
5080 REM                        ADJECTIVES
5090 REM ++++++++++++++++++
5100 DATA AUTUMN,HIDDEN,BITTER, MISTY,SILENT,EMPTY,VERDANT
5110 DATA DRY,DARK,SUMMER,ICY,DELICATE,QUIET,BEMUSED,DIMPLED
5120 DATA WHITE,COOL,SPRING,WINTER,DAPPLED,MOLTEN,FLORAL,DAMP
5130 DATA TWILIGHT,DAWN,CRIMSON,WISPY,AZURE,FRIGID,ASHEN,WHITE
5140 DATA BLUE,BILLOWING,BROKEN,COLD,DAMP,FALLING,INDIGO,SILKEN
5150 DATA FROSTY,GREEN,LONG,LATE,LINGERING,LIMPID,DUSTY,MIDNIGHT
5160 DATA LITTLE,EVENING,MUDDY,OLD,RED,ROUGH,TRANQUILL,WISTFUL
5170 DATA STILL,SMALL,SPARKLING,THROBBING,VERMILION,SOUR,LEMON
5180 DATA WANDERING,WITHERED,WILD,BLACK,YOUNG,STRICKEN,FLEECY
5190 DATA RADIANT,TENDER,DARK
5200 REM ++++++++++++++++++
5210 REM                          NOUNS
5220 REM ++++++++++++++++++
5230 DATA WATERFALL,RIVER,BREEZE,MOON,CAVE,MOON,DREAMSCAPE,DEER
5240 DATA RAIN,WIND,SEA,TABLEAU,SNOWFLAKE,LAKE,SUNSET,SAND-GRAIN
5250 DATA PINE,SHADOW,LEAF,DAWN,GROTTO,FOREST,TROUT,POOL,WIND,ASH
5260 DATA HILL,CLOUD,MEADOW,SUN,GLADE,BIRD,BROOK,MILKWEED,WILLOW
5270 DATA BUTTERFLY,BUSH,DEW,STORMCLOUD,FIELD,FIR,BRANCH,FLAME
5280 DATA FLOWER,FIREFLY,FEATHER,GRASSBED,HAZE,MOUNTAIN,HONEYDEW
5290 DATA NIGHT,POND,SHADE,SNOWFLAKE,DRAGONFLY,LAUREL,COMET,STAR
5300 DATA SILENCE,SOUND,SKY,SHAPE,SURF,THUNDERCLAP,MEADOW,GLOW
5310 DATA VIOLET,PLUME,WILDFLOWER,WAVE,SPIRIT,TWILIGHT,HALO,OWL
5320 DATA SPIDER WEB,LONLINESS,MIST,IVY,DREAM,LIGHT,WOOD,SEASHELL
5330 DATA SWAN,CEDAR,ICE,ROSE,THORN,SUNBEAM,BLOSSOM,GULL,PETAL
5340 DATA STONE,BEE,LEAF,HORIZON,SHOWER,AIR,ROOT,LILAC,HEART
5350 DATA WHISPER,BREATH,SCENT
5360 REM ++++++++++++++++++
5370 REM                          VERBS
5380 REM ++++++++++++++++++
5390 DATA SHAKES,DRIFTS,HAS STOPPED,STRUGGLES,IS DEPARTING
5400 DATA HAS FALLEN,HAS PASSED,SLEEPS,CREEPS,RECLINES,SIGHS
5410 DATA FLUTTERS,HAS RISEN,IS FALLING,IS TRICKLING,DAMPENS
5420 DATA DRINKS IN,TREMBLES,SWALLOWS,TRANSCENDS,MOCKS,LINGERS
5430 DATA MURMURS,IS FLOATING,DREAMS,RETURNS,WAS GLEAMING,RESTS
5440 DATA IS SWEETENING,FLICKERS,SHIVERS,VANISHES,SPARKS,WEAVES
5450 DATA IS GLOWING,HAS EMBARKED,IS PLUNGING,SHINES,IS PRAYING
5460 DATA HAS HIDDEN,DROWNS,BEAMS DOWN,TWITTERS,HAS DANCED,GLIDES
5470 DATA IS WHISPERING,HAS BURNT,BREATHES,EMBRACES,DRONES
5480 DATA DESCENDS,LIFTS,CREEPS,DWELLS,FLICKERS
5490 REM ++++++++++++++++++
5500 REM                       PREPOSITIONS
5510 REM ++++++++++++++++++
5520 DATA ON,IN,FROM,UNDER,OVER,NEAR,BENEATH,ATOP,WITH,ACROSS
5530 DATA BESIDE,ASTRIDE,IMMERSED IN,INSIDE,THROUGH
5540 REM ++++++++++++++++++
```

```
5550 REM                    FORMAL STRUCTURES
5560 REM ++++++++++++++++++
5570 DATA 1,2,3,0,1,3,4,5,1,3,0,2,2,3,-1
5580 DATA 3,5,1,3,0,1,2,3,5,1,3,0,2,3,-1
5590 DATA 1,2,3,0,5,1,2,3,0,1,3,4,-1,-1,-1
5600 DATA 1,2,3,4,0,1,2,2,3,0,5,1,2,3,-1
```

RUN (Gen-Con)

EACH LINE OF EACH POEM WILL BE PRINTED, THEN
CONVERTED TO CORRESPONDING PITCH SEQUENCE

POEM 1
 THE INDIGO SNOWFLAKE
 R D#5 D#4 C4   R   E4 A4 B3 E4 D4 A#4   R   D5 A4 A#4
F#5 C#4 G4 G#3 F#4 C4
 THE WILLOW MURMURS INSIDE THE WILDFLOWER
 R D#5 D#4 C4   R F#5 E4 G4 G4 A#4 F#5   R   G#4 E5 C#5
G#4 E5 C#5 D5   R
E4 A4 D5 E4 B3 C4   R D#5 D#4 C4   R F#5 E4 G4 B3
C#4 G4 A#4 F#5 C4 C#5
 MUDDY BILLOWING CEDAR
 R G#4 E5 B3 B3 G#5   R   A3 E4 G4 G4 A#4 F#5 E4 A4
D4   R A#3 C4 B3 G#3 C#5

POEM 2
 HILL IN A SEA
 R D#4 E4 G4 G4   R   E4 A4   R G#3   R   D5 C4 G#3
 THE ROUGH HONEYDEW UNDER A WIND
 R D#5 D#4 C4   R C#5 A#4 E5 D4 D#4   R   D#4 A#4 A4 C4
G#5 B3 C4 F#5   R E5 A4 B3 C4 C#5   R G#3   R F#5 E4
A4 B3
 SILENT BUTTERFLY
 R   D5 E4 G4 C4 A4 D#5   R   A3 E5 D#5 D#5 C4 C#5 C#4
G4 G#5

POEM 3
 A MOLTEN GULL
 R G#3   R G#4 A#4 G4 D#5 C4 A4   R   D4 E5 G4 G4
 ON THE AUTUMN SWAN
 R A#4 A4   R D#5 D#4 C4   R G#3 E5 D#5 E5 G#4 A4   R
D5 F#5 G#3 A4
 A MILKWEED HAS PASSED
 R G#3   R G#4 E4 G4 F#4 F#5 C4 C4 B3   R D#4 G#3 D5   R
B4 G#3 D5 D5 C4 B3

POEM 4
 THE LONG LAKE STRUGGLES
 R D#5 D#4 C4   R   G4 A#4 A4 D4   R   G4 G#3 F#4 C4   R   D5
D#5 C#5 E5 D4 D4   G4 C4 D5
 A QUIET BLUE RIVER
 R G#3   R   C5 E5 E4 C4 D#5   R   A3 G4 E5 C4   R C#5 E4
F5 C4 C#5
 WITH A DAMP WHISPER
 R F#5 E4 D#5 D#4   R G#3   R   B3 G#3 G#4 B4   R F#5 D#4 E4
D5 B4 C4 C#5

Purpose

Shift the positions of letters (and blanks) of an input text via prime numbers.

Notes

Sound/text composition often requires a number of patterned transformations of an original text. Of course, subroutines from chapter 2 can be adapted to accomplish serial and random-order variations, but when more gradual transformations are needed, a procedure such as Cycltext is appropriate.

Originally a cryptographic subroutine, Cycltext uses two variables—PNUM and NUM2—to rearrange the characters of an input text; it is nondisruptive, leaving the original copy intact for further use by the calling program. Reiterative invocation of the subroutine (with cyclically incremented/decremented values for the control variables) produces gradual, noticeably related changes to the input text. Random selection of a range of control variable values produces less recognizable results.

Programming Ideas

1) Modify the DRIVER PROGRAM to include two nested loops which cycle ascending PNUM values with consecutive integer values of NUM2 in every combination; observe the effect on output.

2) Write a program that produces systematic, patterned reductions (gradually remove letters or words) of an input text while shifting the letters.

3) Write a program that gradually replaces targeted consonants with vowels. (Hint: Strclean, CTB5.5 uses BASIC's INSTR function to search one string for occurrences of letters contained in a reference string.) After replacement, invoke Cycltext to generate further transformations.

Program Listing

```
100  REM  ============================================================
110  REM                    DRIVER PROGRAM
120  REM                     (Cycltext)
130  REM  ============================================================
140       PRINT "ORIGINAL LINE OF TEXT:"
150       LIN$ = "apples sound beautiful"
160       PRINT LIN$
170       PRINT
180       PNUM = 13   '<< a prime number smaller than length of LIN$
190       NUM2 = 8       '<< an integer between 1 and length of LIN$
200          GOSUB 1000            '<< call cyclical text shifter
210       PRINT "PRIME-SHIFTED TEXT:"
220       PRINT NEWLIN$
230  END
1000 REM  ================================================= CTB5.10
```

```
1010 REM *********************>> CYCLTEXT <<*********************
1020 REM ============================================================
1030 REM         Cyclical (prime number) Text Shift Subroutine
1040 REM ============================================================
1050 REM                     Variable Desciptions
1060 REM     Entering -
1070 REM       LIN$: line of text to be shifted
1080 REM       PNUM: prime number smaller than length of LIN$
1090 REM       NUM2: an integer between 1 and length of LIN$
1100 REM     Exiting:
1110 REM       NEWLINE$: shifted line of text
1120 REM     Local -
1130 REM       SHIFTCHAR: LINE$ substring pointer
1140 REM       NUMCHARS: length of LIN$
1150 REM       POSNUM: loop index, NEWLINE$ substring pointer
1160 REM ============================================================
1170     SHIFTCHAR = NUM2 - PNUM
1180     NUMCHARS = LEN(LIN$)
1190     IF NUMCHARS-INT(NUMCHARS/PNUM)*PNUM = 0 THEN NUMCHARS=
NUMCHARS+1
1200     NEWLIN$ = STRING$(NUMCHARS," ")
1210       FOR POSNUM = 1 TO NUMCHARS
1220           SHIFTCHAR = SHIFTCHAR + PNUM
1230           IF SHIFTCHAR > NUMCHARS THEN SHIFTCHAR = SHIFTCHAR
- NUMCHARS
1240           MID$(NEWLIN$,POSNUM,1) = MID$(LIN$,SHIFTCHAR,1)
1250       NEXT POSNUM
1260 RETURN
```

RUN (Cycltext)

```
ORIGINAL LINE OF TEXT:
apples sound beautiful

PRIME-SHIFTED TEXT:
sudpa fnpesiuabetol lu
```

6
General Composition

SUBROUTINE: Loopgen1   CTB6.1

Purpose

Provide two modes—additive and subtractive—of note loop alteration over a number of copies.

Notes

This procedural subroutine is oriented toward music in which repeated patterns are subjected to gradual change. It generates a given number of copies (loops) of a source integer sequence while altering loop length. In the additive alteration mode, the loop copies begin with a predetermined melodic nucleus and grow longer over successive iterations. In the subtractive mode, the first loop copy begins with the entire source sequence and subsequent copies grow shorter with each iteration. The variable STARTNUM determines the initial loop nucleus size, the variable FACTOR controls the number of values added to the nucleus or subtracted from the entire sequence, and the variable PERIOD tells the subroutine when to advance to the next loop-size. Loop copies are printed out within the subroutine and are not passed back to the calling program.

Programming Ideas

Include Loopgen1 in a program that:

- Generates a sequence of random-order, registered 12-tone pitch series.
- Derives integers for the rhythm duration parameter from the first 12-tone series generated in the first step.
- Provides duration values to match the pitches by making length-altered copies of the rhythm integers in the additive or subtractive mode.
- Maps the rhythm duration sequence, in retrograde order and properly scaled, to the volume parameter.

Program Listing

```
100  REM  ============================================================
200  REM                      DRIVER PROGRAM
202  REM                        (Loopgen1)
205  REM  ============================================================
220     DIM NUM(15)
230     PERIOD = 2
240     FACTOR = 3
250     STARTNUM = 15
260     NOTES = 15
270     MANY = 10
280     MODE$ = "S"
290        FOR J = 1 TO NOTES
300           NUM(J) = J                    '<< fill array with values
310        NEXT J
320     GOSUB 1000      '<< call loop generator (subtractive mode)
330     MODE$ = "A"
340     STARTNUM = 1
350     PRINT:PRINT
360     GOSUB 1000           '<< call loop generator (additive mode)
370  END
1000 REM  ==================================================== CTB6.1
1010 REM  ******************>> LOOPGEN1 <<***********************
1020 REM  ============================================================
1030 REM     Additive/Subtractive Loop Alteration Subroutine
1160 REM  ============================================================
1170 REM                  Variable Descriptions
1180 REM     Entering -
1190 REM       NUM(): array containing numeric sequence
1200 REM       PERIOD: number of cycles between loop change
1210 REM       FACTOR: number of values to add/subtr
1220 REM       STARTNUM: sequence nucleus in additive mode
1230 REM       NOTES: number of values in original sequence
1240 REM       MANY: number of loop iterations
1250 REM       MODE$: holds flag for additive/subtractive mode
1260 REM
1270 REM     Exiting -
1280 REM       none
1290 REM
1300 REM     Local -
1310 REM       ALTER: stores current sequence length
1320 REM       SHORT: holds number of values to add/subtract
1330 REM       ITER: counts cycles, controls loop growth/trunc.
```

```
1340 REM        COPIES: loop index
1350 REM =================================================================
1360    SHORT = FACTOR
1370    ITER = PERIOD
1380    IF MODE$ = "A" THEN ALTER = STARTNUM ELSE ALTER = NOTES
1390    IF MODE$ = "S" THEN PRINT "SUBTRACTIVE MODE -" ELSE PRINT
"ADDITIVE MODE -"
1400        FOR COPIES = 0 TO MANY-1
1410            IF COPIES < ITER THEN 1440
1420            IF MODE$ = "A" THEN ALTER = STARTNUM + SHORT ELSE
ALTER = NOTES - SHORT
1430                IF ALTER > NOTES THEN ALTER = NOTES
1440                FOR DUP = 1 TO ALTER
1450                    PRINT NUM(DUP);
1460                NEXT DUP
1470            PRINT
1480            IF COPIES = MANY THEN 1530
1490            IF COPIES < ITER THEN 1520
1500            SHORT = SHORT + FACTOR
1510            ITER = ITER + PERIOD
1520        NEXT COPIES
1530 RETURN
```

RUN (Loopgen1)

```
SUBTRACTIVE MODE -
 1   2   3   4   5   6   7   8   9  10  11  12  13  14  15
 1   2   3   4   5   6   7   8   9  10  11  12  13  14  15
 1   2   3   4   5   6   7   8   9  10  11  12
 1   2   3   4   5   6   7   8   9  10  11  12
 1   2   3   4   5   6   7   8   9
 1   2   3   4   5   6   7   8   9
 1   2   3   4   5   6
 1   2   3   4   5   6
 1   2   3
 1   2   3


ADDITIVE MODE -
 1
 1
 1   2   3   4
 1   2   3   4
 1   2   3   4   5   6   7
 1   2   3   4   5   6   7
 1   2   3   4   5   6   7   8   9  10
 1   2   3   4   5   6   7   8   9  10
 1   2   3   4   5   6   7   8   9  10  11  12  13
 1   2   3   4   5   6   7   8   9  10  11  12  13
```

SUBROUTINE: Loopgen2

Purpose

Provide a systematic rotation of loop elements over a given number of copies; shifted elements may be placed in reverse order.

Notes

This procedure is pattern/phase-music oriented. It generates a given number of copies (loops) of an integer sequence while rotating (in forward or reverse order) a predetermined number of loop elements. Control variables are MANY—the number of altered loop copies to return, FACTOR—the number of loop elements to shift from end-of-loop to front-of-loop, and REVERSE$—a signal to place the shifted elements in reverse order.

When the procedure is used to produce music which emphasizes phasing several layers of pitch loops, it is helpful to add another control variable (as in Loopgen1, CTB6.1) to govern rotation frequency over the total number of returned copies. For example, suppose you wish to subject each parameter of a melodic sequence to independent element rotation. The pitch parameter might shift two elements every other copy while the rhythm parameter shifts three elements with each copy, and so on.

Programming Ideas

Write an interactive program using Loopgen2 that:

- Allows the user to input values for all control variables.
- Provides options to independently rotate pitch, rhythm, articulation, and volume parameter elements of a melodic sequence.
- Formats and files a score consisting of multiple notelists to be played concurrently.

Program Listing

```
100 REM  ============================================================
110 REM                        DRIVER PROGRAM
115 REM                          (Loopgen2)
120 REM  ============================================================
130      DIM X(20),TEMP(20)
140      NUMVALS = 15
150      FACTOR = 4
160      MANY = 6
170      REVERSE$ = "Y"
180      PRINT "ORIGINAL SEQUENCE -"
190        FOR J = 1 TO NUMVALS
200           PRINT J;
210           X(J) = J          '<< load array with number sequence
220        NEXT J
230      PRINT
```

```
240        PRINT MANY;"COPIES TO BE MADE. DURING EACH CYCLE"
250        PRINT FACTOR;"VALUES WILL BE SHIFTED, REVERSE ORDER -"
260        GOSUB 1000                          '<< call loop generator
270 END
1000 REM ================================================== CTB6.2
1010 REM *******************>> LOOPGEN2 <<**********************
1020 REM ======================================================
1030 REM              Loop Element Rotation Subroutine
1070 REM ======================================================
1080 REM                    Variable Descriptions
1090 REM     Entering -
1100 REM        X(): holds original number sequence
1110 REM        NUMVALS: total in sequence
1120 REM        FACTOR: number of values to shift
1130 REM        MANY: number of loops to return
1140 REM        REVERSE$: flag to reverse shifted values
1150 REM     Exiting -
1160 REM        none (original X() array contents are destroyed)
1170 REM
1180 REM     Local -
1190 REM        TEMP(): stores values to be shifted
1200 REM        X(): stores loops, rearranged each cycle
1210 REM        COPIES: loop index
1212 REM        HOLD: loop index, pointer to array TEMP()
1220 REM        GROUP: loop index
1230 REM        SHIFT: loop index, pointer to array X()
1240 REM        REPLACE: loop index, pointer to array X()
1250 REM        CURRLOOP: loop index, pointer to array X()
1260 REM ======================================================
1270       FOR COPIES = 1 TO MANY
1280 REM >>> remove array values to be shifted
1290          FOR HOLD = 0 TO FACTOR - 1
1300             TEMP(HOLD + 1) = X(NUMVALS - HOLD)
1310          NEXT HOLD
1320 REM >>> slide remaining values to end of array
1330          FOR GROUP = 1 TO FACTOR
1340             FOR SHIFT = NUMVALS TO 1 STEP - 1
1350                X(SHIFT) = X(SHIFT - 1)
1360             NEXT SHIFT
1370          NEXT GROUP
1380 REM >>> place values to be moved at head of array
1390 REM >>> if flagged, reverse them
1400          FOR REPLACE = 1 TO FACTOR
1410          IF REVERSE$ = "Y" THEN X(REPLACE) = TEMP(REPLACE ELSE
X(REPLACE) = TEMP(FACTOR + 1 - REPLACE)
1420          NEXT REPLACE
1430          PRINT
1440          FOR CURRLOOP = 1 TO NUMVALS
1450          PRINT X(CURRLOOP);
1460          NEXT CURRLOOP
1470          PRINT
1480       NEXT COPIES
1490 RETURN
```

RUN (Loopgen2)

```
ORIGINAL SEQUENCE -
 1  2  3  4  5  6  7  8  9  10  11  12  13  14  15
 6 COPIES TO BE MADE. DURING EACH CYCLE
```

4 VALUES WILL BE SHIFTED, REVERSE ORDER -

```
15   14   13   12    1    2    3    4    5    6    7    8    9   10   11

11   10    9    8   15   14   13   12    1    2    3    4    5    6    7

 7    6    5    4   11   10    9    8   15   14   13   12    1    2    3

 3    2    1   12    7    6    5    4   11   10    9    8   15   14   13

13   14   15    8    3    2    1   12    7    6    5    4   11   10    9

 9   10   11    4   13   14   15    8    3    2    1   12    7    6    5
```

SUBROUTINE GROUP: PRIMOPS

- ○ Primintv   CTB6.3
- ○ Primenum   CTB6.4

Purpose

Generate two arrays:

- A range-limited prime number list and
- A list of numeric intervals between the prime numbers.

Notes

Subroutine Primintv invokes Subroutine Primenum to check each ascending consecutive integer within a predetermined range to see if it is prime; if so, array X( ) receives it. Primintv then subtracts the previous prime number from the current one and places the remainder in array Y( ).

Interestingly, shifting the prime number testing range upward increases the interval size range at the high end while preserving the smallest interval size. In rhythmic applications, you can harness this characteristic to create a gradual expansion or contraction of duration patterns by generating prime interval sequences derived from contiguous integer ranges.

Programming Ideas

1) Modify the DRIVER PROGRAM to sequentially generate prime number intervals in the following ranges: 1 to 300, 300 to 600, 600 to 900, 900 to 1200, 1200 to 1500. Observe the relative occurrence frequency shift of various numeric interval sizes.

2) Write an interactive program which:
   - Allows the user to input values for the variables LOW and HIGH.
   - Offers options to scale the returned prime interval array to the range requirements of any musical parameter.
   - Prepares a set of pointers to the requested element table.

Program Listing

```
100 REM =============================================================
110 REM                        DRIVER PROGRAM
120 REM                          (Primops)
130 REM =============================================================
140     DIM X(100), Y(100)
150     LOW = 500
160     HIGH = 800
170     PRINT "PRIME NUMBERS WITHIN RANGE ";LOW;"TO";HIGH;" --"
180     GOSUB 1000              '<< call prime interval generator
190        FOR J = 1 TO PCNT
```

```
200            PRINT X(J),          '<< prime number array to screen
210         NEXT J
220      PRINT : PRINT
230      PRINT "NUMERIC INTERVALS BETWEEN PRIMES --"
240         FOR J = 1 TO PCNT-1
250            PRINT Y(J),          '<< prime interval array to screen
260         NEXT J
270 END
1000 REM =================================================== CTB6.3
1010 REM *****************>> PRIMINTV <<*********************
1020 REM ===================================================
1030 REM    This subroutine invokes the prime number indicator
1040 REM    subroutine to locate primes, then creates two
1050 REM    array sequences: 1) a list of the primes, and
1060 REM    2) a list of numeric intervals separating primes.
1070 REM    The list can be mapped to various musical parameters,
1080 REM    and can be modified in scale by addition or
1090 REM    subtraction of a numerical constant.
1100 REM ===================================================
1110 REM                 Variable Descriptions
1120 REM    Entering -
1130 REM      LOW: smallest integer within test range
1140 REM      HIGH: largest integer within test range
1150 REM      PRIM: (from SR 2000) prime flag
1160 REM    Exiting -
1170 REM      NUM: (to SR 2000) current integer to be tested
1180 REM      X(): list of prime numbers
1190 REM      Y(): list of numeric intervals between primes
1200 REM    Local -
1210 REM      PCNT: prime number counter, pointer to X(),Y()
1220 REM ===================================================
1230    PCNT = 0
1240       FOR NUM = LOW TO HIGH
1250          GOSUB 2000          '<< call prime number indicator
1260          IF PRIM <> 1 THEN 1300
1270          PCNT = PCNT + 1
1280          X(PCNT) = NUM
1290          IF PCNT >= 2 THEN Y(PCNT-1) = X(PCNT)-X(PCNT-1)
1300       NEXT NUM
1310 RETURN
2000 REM =================================================== CTB6.4
2010 REM *****************>> PRIMENUM <<*********************
2020 REM ===================================================
2030 REM    This subroutine locates and returns prime numbers
2040 REM    from a stream of consecutive numbers within a
2050 REM    specified range. (Prime numbers are integers
2060 REM    which have only themselves or the number 1
2070 REM    as a factor.)
2080 REM ===================================================
2090 REM                 Variable Descriptions
2100 REM    Entering -
2110 REM      NUM: number to be tested for prime
2120 REM    Exiting -
2130 REM      PRIM: flag indicating a  prime number
2140 REM    Local -
2150 REM      DIVISOR: loop index, divisor for prime test
2160 REM ===================================================
2170    PRIM = 1
2180       IF NUM = 1 THEN PRIM = 0 : RETURN ELSE IF NUM = 2 OR
NUM = 3 THEN RETURN
```

```
2190          IF NUM = INT(NUM/2) * 2 THEN PRIM = 0 : RETURN
2200           FOR DIVISOR = 3 TO INT(SQR(NUM)) STEP 2
2210            IF NUM = INT(NUM/DIVISOR) * DIVISOR THEN PRIM = 0 :
RETURN
2220           NEXT DIVISOR
2230 RETURN
```

RUN (Primops)

```
PRIME NUMBERS WITHIN RANGE  500 TO 800  --
 503           509           521           523           541
 547           557           563           569           571
 577           587           593           599           601
 607           613           617           619           631
 641           643           647           653           659
 661           673           677           683           691
 701           709           719           727           733
 739           743           751           757           761
 769           773           787           797

NUMERIC INTERVALS BETWEEN PRIMES --
 6             12            2             18            6
 10            6             6             2             6
 10            6             6             2             6
 6             4             2             12            10
 2             4             6             6             2
 12            4             6             8             10
 8             10            8             6             6
 4             8             6             4             8
 4             14            10
```

Purpose

Prepare a first-order table of transitional probabilities to determine a melodic pitch class order.

Notes

A two-dimensional matrix holds occurrence frequency probabilities which make the current note choice conditional on the previous choice. The appropriate probabilities are entered in the matrix P( ), either as program DATA statements or via user INPUT statements.

For output data to be accurate, it is important that the sum of each column be 1.0. The data table should be well-thought-out to prevent situations with no exit. For instance, if, in the following table, the probability that C follows F is changed to 0.0, the probability that F follows F is changed to 1.0, and the probability that G follows F is changed to 0.0, nothing but pitch F will be generated once F is selected.

		LAST PITCH			
		C	F	G	B
	C	0.0	0.5	0.1	0.0
NEXT	F	0.1	0.2	0.5	0.1
PITCH	G	0.6	0.3	0.1	0.5
	B	0.3	0.0	0.3	0.4

Example of Concept.

Read the columns for the last pitch and the rows for the next pitch. For instance, if the last pitch returned was B (column 4), then the probability of the next pitch being B (row 4) is 0.4. This principle can be extended to three, four or more dimensions, but quickly becomes difficult to comprehend.

Programming Idea

Write an interactive program based on Trantabl that allows the user to input data for the matrix and apply it to any musical parameter.

Program Listing

```
100 REM  ================================================================
110 REM                          DRIVER PROGRAM
115 REM                            (Trantabl)
120 REM  ================================================================
130 REM     To change the probabilities in this program, edit
140 REM     the DATA statements which are read into the table.
150 REM  ================================================================
160      DIM P(4,4),P$(4)
170 REM >> load pitch character set
180      P$(1)="C"
190      P$(2)="F"
200      P$(3)="G"
210      P$(4)="B"
220      TOTAL = 25
230      LASTPITCH = 3
240      PRINT
250      PRINT "CURRENT PROBABILITY TABLE --"
260         FOR J1 = 1 TO 4
270            FOR J2 = 1 TO 4
280               READ P(J1,J2)          '<< load probability table
290               PRINT P(J1,J2),             '<< send to screen
300            NEXT J2
310            PRINT
320         NEXT J1
330 REM  +++++++++++++++++++++++++++++++++++++++++++++++++++++++++++++
340      DATA .0,.5,.1,.0
350      DATA .1,.2,.5,.1
360      DATA .6,.3,.1,.5
370      DATA .3,.0,.3,.4
380 REM  +++++++++++++++++++++++++++++++++++++++++++++++++++++++++++++
390      RANDOMIZE(14111)
395      PRINT : PRINT "PITCH SEQUENCE --"
400      PRINT P$(LASTPITCH);" ";
410         FOR J = 1 TO TOTAL-1
420            GOSUB 1000           '<< call transition probability
430            PRINT P$(NEXTPITCH);" "; '<< send choice to screen
440            LASTPITCH = NEXTPITCH
450         NEXT J
460 END
1000 REM  ============================================== CTB6.5
1010 REM  *******************>> TRANTABL <<*******************
1020 REM  ================================================================
1030 REM     First-order Transition Probabilities Subroutine
1240 REM  ================================================================
1450 REM                     Variable Descriptions
1460 REM     Entering -
1470 REM        LASTPITCH: holds last note choice
1480 REM     Exiting -
1490 REM        NEXTPITCH: holds the current note choice
1500 REM     Local -
1510 REM        U: uniform random number
1520 REM        T9: threshold test value
1530 REM        K9: loop index, pointer to data table
1540 REM  ================================================================
1550      U = RND
1560      T9 = 0
1570         FOR K9 = 1 TO 4
1580            T9 = P(K9,LASTPITCH) + T9
```

```
1590          IF U <= T9 THEN 1610
1600      NEXT K9
1610    NEXTPITCH = K9
1620 RETURN
```

RUN (Trantabl)

```
CURRENT PROBABILITY TABLE --
0               .5          .1          0
.1              .2          .5          .1
.6              .3          .1          .5
.3              0           .3          .4

PITCH SEQUENCE --
G B B F F G F G B G G C G F G F C G C G F G G F F
```

SUBROUTINE GROUP: VALUPROB

○ Probtabl   CTB6.6
○ Probcalc   CTB6.7

Purpose

Generate an array of random-order integers distributed in accordance with weights contained in a cumulative probability table.

Notes

Subroutine Probtabl establishes a table of occurrence frequency probabilities from weights contained in the Line 1220 DATA statement. Since the weights are relative, the program user need not be concerned with their sum. (Subroutine Probcalc reconciles them with the random-number generator range.)

Subroutine Probcalc returns random-order integers $1 - n$ over a run of n values in relative proportion to probability weights contained in WTABLE( ). The output array X( ) serves as a set of pointers to any musical parameter.

Programming Ideas

1) Write a program that:

  • Allows the user to enter values for variables PROBS, TOTAL, and array WTABLE( ).

  • Offers an option to read a probability weight disk file to fill WTABLE( ).

  • Assigns the output set of pointers to any selected parameter element table.

2) Adapt Freqtabl (CTB1.27) to record the occurrence frequencies of alphabet letters in a source text. Enter a short poem in English, and use the occurrence frequencies as probability weights to generate an array of pitches. Repeat the frequency analysis and pitch generation for poems in French, Italian, and German; observe the respective effects on tonal characteristics.

Program Listing

```
100 REM ==============================================================
110 REM                      DRIVER PROGRAM
115 REM                       (Valuprob)
120 REM ==============================================================
130     DIM WTABLE(5), X(40)
140     RANDOMIZE(111)
150     PROBS = 5
160     TOTAL = 40
170     GOSUB 1000                    '<< call probability table subr.
```

```
180     GOSUB 2000                    '<< call table look-up & test
190         FOR J = 1 TO TOTAL
200             PRINT X(J),               '<< send choices to screen
210         NEXT J
220 END
1000 REM ================================================== CTB6.6
1010 REM *****************>> PROBTABL  <<*********************
1020 REM ==================================================
1030 REM     This subroutine reads relative weights into a
1040 REM     cumulative probability table (array).
1050 REM ==================================================
1060 REM                   Variable Descriptions
1070 REM     Entering -
1080 REM       PROBS: number of relative probability weights
1090 REM     Exiting -
1100 REM       WTABLE(): data table containing relative weights
1110 REM     Local -
1120 REM       WSUM: holds current sum of probability weights
1130 REM       K9: loop index, pointer to array WTABLE()
1140 REM ==================================================
1150     WSUM = 0
1160         FOR K9 = 1 TO PROBS
1170             READ WTABLE(K9)
1180             WTABLE(K9)=WTABLE(K9)+WSUM
1190             WSUM=WTABLE(K9)
1200         NEXT K9
1210 REM ++++++++++++++++++++++++++++++++++++++++++++++++++++
1220 DATA 1,2,3,4,5
1230 REM ++++++++++++++++++++++++++++++++++++++++++++++++++++
1240 RETURN
2000 REM ================================================== CTB6.7
2010 REM *****************>> PROBCALC  <<*********************
2020 REM ==================================================
2030 REM     This subroutine generates random-order integers
2040 REM     whose occurrence frequencies are distributed
2050 REM     in proportion to weights contained in a cumulative
2060 REM     probability table.
2100 REM ==================================================
2110 REM                   Variable Descriptions
2120 REM     Entering -
2130 REM       TOTAL: number of values to be returned
2140 REM       WTABLE(): array containing relative weights
2150 REM       PROBS: number of relative probability weights
2160 REM       WSUM: holds current sum of probability weights
2170 REM     Exiting -
2180 REM       X(): array containing selected values
2190 REM     Local -
2200 REM       WSUM: stores current sum of probability weights
2210 REM       R: random number, scaled to sum of weights
2220 REM       L9: loop index, pointer to WTABLE()
2230 REM       K9: loop index, pointer to array X()
2240 REM ==================================================
2250         FOR K9 = 1 TO TOTAL
2260             R = RND * WSUM
2270             FOR L9 = 1 TO PROBS
2280                 IF R <= WTABLE(L9) THEN 2300
2290             NEXT L9
2300             X(K9) = L9
2310         NEXT K9
2320 RETURN
```

RUN (Valuprob)

4	3	4	3	5
3	5	3	2	5
4	4	4	5	4
4	5	3	5	5
5	3	5	2	4
4	4	2	3	4
4	3	4	1	3
5	2	4	5	4

SUBROUTINE: Randwalk

Purpose

Simulate a simple, bi-directional random walk which is restricted at the upper and lower boundaries.

Notes

This subroutine "tosses a coin" to determine each step up or down the consecutive integer series from an input start point. It cannot step-in-place because each decision in Line 1200 forces a move of one position. Repeated values can be obtained by filling an array with integers distributed according to a compositional plan and then walking through the array using the output of Randwalk as pointers.

Programming Ideas

1) Write a program that:

   - Reads a composed pitch sequence from a disk file.

   - Assigns the sequence to a program array.

   - Allows the user to select the random walk start location.

   - Generates an output array consisting of a random walk of n values through the composed pitches.

   - Uses the integers in the output array as literal probability weights to generate other musical parameters (use Subroutine Group VALUPROB).

2) Adapt the above program to read a disk text file (add appropriate string-handling subroutines from chapter 5); allow the user to create an output disk file consisting of random walks through the words of the input file. How does the output of Randwalk (CTB6.8) differ from the output of subroutines Randline (CTB5.3) and Randword (CTB5.7)?

Program Listing

```
100 REM  ================================================================
110 REM                         DRIVER PROGRAM
115 REM                           (Randwalk)
120 REM  ================================================================
130     RANDOMIZE(4873)
140     LASTLOC = 7
150     PRINT "START POSITION = ";LASTLOC
160        FOR J = 1 TO 40
170        GOSUB 1000                              '<< call random walk
180        PRINT CURRLOC,            '<< send current step to screen
190        LASTLOC = CURRLOC
200     NEXT J
210 END
1000 REM  =========================================== CTB6.8
```

```
1010 REM ******************>> RANDWALK <<********************
1020 REM ==========================================================
1030 REM    This subroutine simulates a simple, bi-directional
1040 REM    random walk which is restricted at both ends.
1050 REM ==========================================================
1060 REM                   Variable Descriptions
1070 REM
1080 REM    Entering -
1090 REM      LASTLOC: previous location of walker
1100 REM    Exiting -
1110 REM      CURRLOC: present location of walker
1120 REM    Local -
1130 REM      D: step direction storage
1140 REM      U: random number determining step direction
1150 REM      S: next step value after computation
1160 REM
1170 REM ==========================================================
1180      D=1
1190      U=RND
1200      IF U < .5 THEN D = -1
1210      S = LASTLOC + D
1220      IF S > 15 THEN S = 14     '<< upper boundary test & reset
1230      IF S < 1 THEN S = 2       '<< lower boundary test & reset
1240      CURRLOC = S
1250 RETURN
```

RUN (Randwalk)

```
START POSITION =  7
  6            7            6            5            4
  5            6            5            4            3
  2            3            4            5            6
  5            6            7            6            5
  4            5            6            7            6
  5            6            7            6            7
  8            9            8            9           10
  9            8            7            6            7
```

SUBROUTINE: Matwalk

Purpose

Simulate a multidirectional random walk within the boundaries of a two-dimensional matrix.

Notes

This procedure differs from Randwalk (CTB6.8) in that the walker is free to step up, down, sideways, diagonally, or in-place around a rectangular plane. Vertical/horizontal proportions of the matrix are determined in Line 160 and the walker's start position coordinates are set in Line 170 of the DRIVER PROGRAM. By reshaping the matrix in various proportions, the program user can influence the character of the number sequence produced by a random walk. For example, when the values generated by the walk are to be interpreted as pointers to a registrated pitch element table, the consequences of matrix reconfiguration are significant:

15 × 6 matrix

```
 1  2  3  4  5  6  7  8  9 10 11 12 13 14 15
16 17 18 19 20 21 22 23 24 25 26 27 28 29 30
31 32 33 34 35 36 37 38 39 40 41 42 43 44 45
46 47 48 49 50 51 52 53 54 55 56 57 58 59 60
61 62 63 64 65 66 67 68 69 70 71 72 73 74 75
76 77 78 79 80 81 82 83 84 85 86 87 88 89 90
```

The 15 × 6 matrix produces melodic interval-sizes of the magnitude (+ or −) 1, 14, 15, and 16 exclusively.

4 × 9 matrix

```
 1  2  3  4
 5  6  7  8
 9 10 11 12
13 14 15 16
17 18 19 20
21 22 23 24
25 26 27 28
29 30 31 32
33 34 35 36
```

The 4 × 9 matrix produces melodic interval-sizes of the magnitude (+ or −) 1, 3, 4, and 5 exclusively.

Programming Ideas

1) Modify the DRIVER PROGRAM to read the contents of an integer data file into the two-dimensional matrix.

2) Assign the output resulting from variously configured matrices as pointers to rhythm, volume, and articulation element tables.

Program Listing

```
100 REM =============================================================
110 REM                         DRIVER PROGRAM
115 REM                           (Matwalk)
120 REM =============================================================
130    DIM W(10,10)
140    COUNT = 0
150    TOTAL = 40
160    XLOC = 5 : YLOC = 5                  '<< matrix start coordinates
170    ROWS = 10 : COLS = 10
180    PRINT "THE MATRIX FOR THIS RANDOM WALK -"
190       FOR J1 = 1 TO ROWS
200          FOR J2 = 1 TO COLS
210             W(J1,J2)=((J1-1) * COLS) + J2
220             COUNT = COUNT + 1
230             IF (COUNT/COLS) = J1 THEN PRINT W(J1,J2) ELSE
PRINT W(J1,J2);
240                IF COUNT < 9 THEN PRINT " ";
250          NEXT J2
260       NEXT J1
270    PRINT "START COORDINATES ARE: ROW ";XLOC;"COLUMN ";YLOC
275    PRINT : RANDOMIZE(6568)
290    GOSUB 1000                                '<< call matrix walk
300 END
1000 REM ========================================== CTB6.9
1010 REM ********************>> MATWALK <<********************
1020 REM =============================================================
1030 REM             Two-Dimensional Random Walk Subroutine
1110 REM =============================================================
1120 REM                    Variable Descriptions
1130 REM       Entering -
1140 REM         W(n,n): random walk matrix
1150 REM         TOTAL: number of random steps to be taken
1160 REM         XLOC: stores current location on horizontal
1170 REM         YLOC: stores current location on vertical
1180 REM         ROWS: length of matrix
1190 REM         COLS: width of matrix
1200 REM       Exiting -
1210 REM         none (subroutine is procedural)
1220 REM       Local -
1230 REM         XSTEP: random number -1, 0, or + 1
1240 REM         YSTEP: random number -1. 0, or + 1
1250 REM         K9: loop index
1260 REM =============================================================
1270       FOR K9 = 1 TO TOTAL
1280          PRINT W(XLOC,YLOC),
1290          XSTEP = INT(RND * 3) - 1
1300          YSTEP = INT(RND * 3) - 1
1310          XLOC = XLOC + XSTEP
1320          YLOC = YLOC + YSTEP
1330          IF XLOC <= 0 THEN XLOC = 2 ELSE IF XLOC > ROWS THEN
XLOC = ROWS - 1
1340          IF YLOC <= 0 THEN YLOC = 2 ELSE IF YLOC > COLS THEN
YLOC = COLS - 1
1350       NEXT K9
1360 RETURN
```

RUN (Matwalk)

```
THE MATRIX FOR THIS RANDOM WALK -
 1   2   3   4   5   6   7   8   9  10
11  12  13  14  15  16  17  18  19  20
21  22  23  24  25  26  27  28  29  30
31  32  33  34  35  36  37  38  39  40
41  42  43  44  45  46  47  48  49  50
51  52  53  54  55  56  57  58  59  60
61  62  63  64  65  66  67  68  69  70
71  72  73  74  75  76  77  78  79  80
81  82  83  84  85  86  87  88  89  90
91  92  93  94  95  96  97  98  99 100

START COORDINATES ARE: ROW  5 COLUMN  5
45              44              53              62              52
52              43              52              41              32
31              22              21              12              13
23              12              11              22              21
21              32              23              13              24
33              22              22              32              22
31              21              32              31              21
11              22              23              13              13
```

SUBROUTINE: Voss CTB6.10

Purpose

Generate an integer array which exhibits fractal ($1/f$ fractional noise) characteristics.

Notes

This function generates sequential integer patterns which are self-similar in nature. Many composers consider Fractal patterns to be more useful than other types of randomly generated sequences because they seem to closely resemble the patterns found in traditional music. Subroutine output consistently reflects a high degree of microformal/macroformal relatedness in that patterns on the large scale are similar to internal patterns. Moreover, a group of values selected from the end of a sequence will seem to be close variants of a group of integers selected from the beginning of the same sequence. (To test this, compare the number and type of melodic interval-sizes between the internal values of each sequence chunk.) Each $1/f$ value returned by the function is conditional on the one previously generated, and all constituent values correlate logarithmically with the past, which is why the process is said to have long-term memory.

Programming Ideas

1) Write an interactive program that allows the user to enter element tables and control variables and which provides options to generate and file the pitch, rhythm, volume, and articulation parameters of a fractal melodic line. Transcribe the melody for a solo instrument, such as a clarinet.

2) Write an interactive program that builds and files a polyphonic musical texture using the fractal algorithm. Perform the score on a digital synthesizer.

3) Run the above programs using carefully thought-out input to provide material for a composition for a solo instrument and synthesizer.

Program Listing

```
100 REM  =========================================================
110 REM                      DRIVER PROGRAM
120 REM                         (Voss)
130 REM  =========================================================
140     DIM X(50)
150     RANDOMIZE(4906)
160     TOTAL = 50
170     LAST = 24
180     GOSUB 1000        '<< call one-over-f distribution function
190        FOR J = 1 TO TOTAL
200           PRINT X(J),                '<< sequence to screen
210        NEXT J
```

```
220 END
1000 REM ================================================= CTB6.10
1010 REM *******************>> VOSS <<************************
1020 REM =================================================
1080 REM                      Fractals Subroutine
1090 REM =================================================
1100 REM                      Variable Descriptions
1110 REM        Entering -
1120 REM          TOTAL: length of sequence
1130 REM          LAST: last value generated
1140 REM        Exiting -
1150 REM          X(): array holding one-over-f distribution
1160 REM        Local -
1170 REM          FRACT: current one-over-f value
1180 REM          HALFVALS: 1/2 the number of possible values
1190 REM          PROB: 1 / number of possible values
1200 REM          R9: uniform random number
1210 REM          S9: stores in-progress computation
1220 REM          K9: loop index, pointer to array X()
1230 REM =================================================
1240 REM
1260     FOR K9 = 1 TO TOTAL
1270        FRACT = 0
1280        HALFVALS = 16   ' = 1/2 number of poss values
1290        PROB = .03125 ' = 1/num poss values
1300           WHILE HALFVALS > = 1
1310              S9 = INT(LAST/HALFVALS)
1320              IF S9 = 1 THEN LAST = LAST-HALFVALS
1330              R9 = RND
1340              IF R9 < PROB THEN S9 = 1-S9
1350              FRACT= FRACT + S9 * HALFVALS
1360              HALFVALS = HALFVALS/2
1370              PROB = PROB * 2
1380           WEND
1390        X(K9) = FRACT
1400        LAST = FRACT
1410     NEXT K9
1420 RETURN
```

RUN (Voss)

25	24	25	24	25
25	26	26	26	26
26	30	23	20	28
30	29	25	25	25
24	25	29	29	28
28	29	28	29	28
28	29	30	30	30
30	20	23	20	21
23	23	21	21	21
23	18	19	19	19

SUBROUTINE GROUP: RDINTCHD

- Rdintchd   CTB6.11
- Pitchtab   CTB1.3

Purpose

Generate a group of variable-density chords built from constrained, random-order interval sizes.

Notes

Designed to provide a background chordfile from which melodic lines will be extracted, Rdintchd builds varying-length vertical structures from low pitch to high pitch via random-interval selection from a circumscribed, continuous interval-size range. The chord root (C to B), starting octave (1 to 3), number of chord members (3 to 9), and interval-range limits (1 to 12) are randomly chosen within the DRIVER PROGRAM. The final selection of each upward interval is made in Line 1230 in conformity to values passed from the main routine. To illustrate, if variable SMALL is set to 4 and variable LARGE is set to 7, then the resultant chords will be composed entirely of random-order major 3rd, perfect 4th, augmented 4th, and perfect 5th intervals.

Programming Ideas

1) Modify the DRIVER PROGRAM to accept user-input values for the primary control variables; don't forget to add prompts and error-detection statements to alert the user when he/she has entered values which will cause program failure (too many wide intervals over a large number of chord tones will quickly go out of the pitch table range).

2) Add a program subroutine to file the chords on disk; place flags in the file after each chord to signal chord articulation.

3) Add a program subroutine to randomly extract the chords from a file, display them on the CRT, and generate random-order melodic pitches based on the chord sequence.

4) Apply the integer values of the chordfile as pointers to other musical parameter tables.

Program Listing

```
100 REM  ============================================================
110 REM                    DRIVER PROGRAM
115 REM                     (Rdintchd)
120 REM  ============================================================
130    DIM P$(96)
140    RANDOMIZE(-9416)
150    TOTAL = 5                    '<< number of discrete chords
160    GOSUB 2000                         '<< call pitch table
```

```
170          FOR J = 1 TO TOTAL
180              PRINT "CHORD";J
190              ROOT = INT(RND * 12)+1     '<< chord start pitch (C-B)
200              OCTAVE = INT(RND * 3)+1 '<< chord start octave (1-3)
210              CHORDMEMS = INT(RND * 7)+3  '<< number of chordtones
220              SMALL = INT(RND * 5)+1      '<< smallest rnd interval
230              LARGE = INT(RND * 8)+5      '<< largest rnd interval
240              INTVALRANGE = LARGE - SMALL + 1
250              GOSUB 1000  '<< call random-interval chord generator
260              PRINT
270          NEXT J
280 END
1000 REM ================================================= CTB6.11
1010 REM *******************>> RDINTCHD <<*********************
1020 REM =====================================================
1030 REM        Constrained Random-Interval Chord/Scale Generator
1050 REM =====================================================
1060 REM                  Variable Descriptions
1070 REM     Entering -
1080 REM       ROOT: lowest chordmember
1090 REM       OCTAVE: octave register for chord initiation
1100 REM       CHORDMEMS: number of tones contained in chord
1110 REM       SMALL: smallest interval size selected
1120 REM       INTVALRANGE: overall range for interval choice
1130 REM     Exiting -
1140 REM       none (subroutine is procedural)
1150 REM     Local -
1160 REM       INTVAL: selected interval size for next chordmem
1170 REM       CHORDTONE: next chordmember
1180 REM       K9: loop index
1190 REM =====================================================
1200     CHORDTONE = ROOT
1210     FOR K9 = 1 TO CHORDMEMS
1220         PRINT P$(CHORDTONE + ((OCTAVE-1) * 12));" ";
1230         INTVAL = INT(RND * (INTVALRANGE))+SMALL
1240         CHORDTONE = CHORDTONE + INTVAL
1250     NEXT K9
1260 PRINT
1270 RETURN
2000 REM ================================================= CTB1.3
2010 REM *******************>> PITCHTAB <<*********************
2020 REM =====================================================
2030 REM     This subroutine initializes a pitch data table
2040 REM     corresponding to integer values 1-n.
2050 REM =====================================================
2060     NOTE$ = " CC# DD# E FF# GG# AA# B"
2070     OCTAVE$ = "1234567"
2080     FOR K9 = 1 TO 7
2090         FOR L9 = 1 TO 12
2100             P$(L9+(K9-1)*12) = MID$(NOTE$,(L9*2-1),2)+MID$
(OCTAVE$,K9,1)
2110         NEXT L9
2120     NEXT K9
2130 RETURN
```

SUBROUTINE GROUP: RDINTCHD   203

RUN (Rdintchd)

```
CHORD 1
 F2   C3  D#3

CHORD 2
F#1   C2   C3   E3 G#3   D4

CHORD 3
 C3  F#3   E4

CHORD 4
 E2   C3   G3 C#4   G4

CHORD 5
 E2   D3  A#3
```

SUBROUTINE GROUP: OCTSCALE

- ○ Octscale   CTB6.12
- ○ Pitchtab   CTB1.3

Purpose

Generate registrated, octave-repeating, scale/gamut segments derived from an input interval array.

Notes

OCTSCALE is similar to RDINTCHD (CTB6.11) in that it returns varying-length pitch sequences arranged in low to high order. However, the intent here is to prepare scales/gamuts identical in interval content from octave to octave as a resource for an external melody generation procedure.

The subroutine first selects the scale-start pitch (tonic) and start octave, then determines the scale-segment length before computing the gamut pitches (dictated by the interval array GAMINTS ( )). The process continues until the number of segments required by SEGTOTAL is reached, whereupon the process repeats for each of the unique interval sets called for by GAMUTS.

You can easily convert this subroutine group to interactive use, but statements must be added to prevent the user from requesting scales/gamuts which exceed pitch-element table boundaries.

Programming Ideas

1) Modify the DRIVER PROGRAM to prompt user input for the array GAMINTS( ) and the variables GAMUTS, SEGTOTAL, and INTOTAL.

2) Modify Octscale (CTB6.12) to prompt user input for variables TONIC, STARTOCTAVE, and SCALEMEMS.

3) Write an interactive program which includes Rdintchd (CTB6.11) and Octscale (CTB6.12); provide code to file the output on disk.

Program Listing

```
100 REM ============================================================
110 REM                       DRIVER PROGRAM
115 REM                         (Octscale)
120 REM ============================================================
130     DIM GAMINTS(12),P$(96)
140     GAMUTS = 3                         '<< number of unique gamuts
150     RANDOMIZE(882)
160     SEGTOTAL = 3     '<< # of scale segments to return per gamut
170     INTOTAL = 6                   '<< number of intervals in scale
180     GOSUB 2000                             '<< call pitch table
190        FOR J1 = 1 TO GAMUTS
200           PRINT "SCALE GAMUT";J1;"INTERVAL SET ---";
210           HIGHOCTAVE = 7
220           EXCEED = 0
```

```
230 REM >>> select an octave-containable (scale) interval set
240         FOR J2 = 1 TO INTOTAL
250             GAMINTS(J2) = INT(RND * 3) + 1
260             EXCEED = EXCEED + GAMINTS(J2)
270             IF EXCEED > 11 THEN 220        '<< within octave?
280         NEXT J2
290         FOR J = 1 TO INTOTAL
300             PRINT  GAMINTS(J);
310         NEXT J
320       PRINT
330       GOSUB 1000                          '<< call scale generator
340     NEXT J1
350 END
1000 REM ================================================== CTB6.12
1010 REM ******************>> OCTSCALE <<**********************
1020 REM ==================================================
1030 REM     This subroutine generates octave-repeating
1040 REM     scales from a set of intervals.
1050 REM ==================================================
1060 REM                    Variable Descriptions
1070 REM     Entering -
1080 REM       P$(): pitch name table
1090 REM       GAMINTS(): array of interval sizes
1100 REM       TONIC: lowest scale/gamut member
1110 REM       HIGHOCTAVE: upper register octave limit
1120 REM       INTOTAL: number of intervals in GAMINTS()
1130 REM       SEGTOTAL: numeric length of scale segment
1140 REM     Exiting -
1150 REM       none (subroutine is procedural)
1160 REM     Local -
1170 REM       COUNT: tabulates chordtone generation
1180 REM       SCALETONE: next chord/gamut member
1190 REM       STARTOCTAVE: scale segment beginning register
1200 REM       SCALEMEMS: number of tones in scale segment
1210 REM       K9: loop index
1220 REM       L9: loop index, pointer to array GAMINTS()
1230 REM       M9: loop index, pointer to array P$()
1240 REM ==================================================
1250     FOR K9 = 1 TO SEGTOTAL
1260         TONIC= INT(RND * 12)+1
1270         STARTOCTAVE = INT(RND * 3)+1
1280         SCALEMEMS = INT(RND * 17)+4
1290         PRINT "scale segment";K9;"=";SCALEMEMS;"notes"
1300         COUNT = 0
1310         FOR L9 = STARTOCTAVE TO HIGHOCTAVE
1320             SCALETONE = TONIC
1330             FOR M9 = 1 TO INTOTAL+1
1340                 PRINT P$(SCALETONE + ((L9-1) * 12));" ";
1350                 COUNT = COUNT + 1
1360                 IF COUNT = SCALEMEMS THEN 1410
1370                 IF M9 > INTOTAL THEN 1400
1380                 SCALETONE = SCALETONE + GAMINTS(M9)
1390             NEXT M9
1400         NEXT L9
1410         PRINT
1420     NEXT K9
1430     PRINT
1440   RETURN
2000 REM ================================================== CTB1.3
2010 REM ******************>> PITCHTAB <<**********************
```

```
2020 REM ============================================================
2030 REM     This subroutine initializes a pitch data table
2040 REM     corresponding to integer values 1-n.
2050 REM ============================================================
2060     NOTE$ = " CC# DD# E FF# GG# AA# B"
2070     OCTAVE$ = "1234567"
2080        FOR K9 = 1 TO 7
2090           FOR L9 = 1 TO 12
2100              P$(L9+(K9-1)*12) = MID$(NOTE$,(L9*2-1),2)+MID$
(OCTAVE$,K9,1)
2110           NEXT L9
2120        NEXT K9
2130 RETURN
```

RUN (Octscale)

```
SCALE GAMUT 1 INTERVAL SET --- 1  2  1  2  2  2
scale segment 1 = 5 notes
F#2   G2   A2  A#2   C3
scale segment 2 = 4 notes
G#2   A2   B2   C3
scale segment 3 = 5 notes
A#3   B3  C#4   D4   E4


SCALE GAMUT 2 INTERVAL SET --- 3  1  1  1  3  2
scale segment 1 = 11 notes
 D1  F1 F#1   G1 G#1   B1 C#2   D2   F2 F#2   G2
scale segment 2 = 12 notes
F#3  A3 A#3   B3   C4 D#4   F4 F#4   A4 A#4   B4   C5
scale segment 3 = 15 notes
F#2  A2 A#2   B2   C3 D#3   F3 F#3   A3 A#3   B3   C4 D#4   F4 F#4


SCALE GAMUT 3 INTERVAL SET --- 1  2  2  2  1  1
scale segment 1 = 12 notes
 C2 C#2 D#2   F2   G2 G#2   A2   C3 C#3 D#3   F3   G3
scale segment 2 = 17 notes
A#2  B2 C#3 D#3   F3 F#3   G3 A#3   B3 C#4 D#4   F4 F#4   G4 A#4
B4 C#5
scale segment 3 = 17 notes
F#1   G1   A1   B1 C#2   D2 D#2 F#2   G2   A2   B2 C#3   D3 D#3 F#3
G3   A3
```

SUBROUTINE GROUP: INTGAM

  ○ Intgam   CTB6.13
  ○ Pitchtab   CTB1.3

Purpose

Generate a group of variable-density gamuts/chords from an input interval array.

Notes

This subroutine group is a hybrid version of Rdintchd (CTB6.11) and Octscale (CTB6.12). It returns gamuts based on a fixed set of random-order intervals, but the group of intervals need not be octave-constrained. (The interval sequence will simply be reiteratively applied to measure the current pitch outcome against the previous pitch.)

Although the DRIVER PROGRAM generates random values for variables GAMINTS( ), ROOT, OCTAVE, and CHORDMEMS, an interactive version of the subroutine would optionally allow the user to determine these values.

Programming Ideas

1) Write an interactive program that:

   • Includes subroutines Rdintchd (CTB6.11), Octscale (CTB6.12), and Intgam (CTB6.13).

   • Offers the program user three methods of generating scale/gamut/chord sequences, plus a fourth option to manually enter the individual pitches of each sequence.

   • Places end-of-segment flags in the output array.

   • Files on disk the complete set of scales/chords produced by a single program run.

2) Write a program that individually extracts the sequences from a file and passes them to a melody-generation subroutine.

Program Listing

```
100 REM ==========================================================
110 REM                      DRIVER PROGRAM
115 REM                        (Intgam)
120 REM ==========================================================
130     DIM GAMINTS(12),P$(96)
140     RANDOMIZE(1301)
150     TOTAL = 5               '<< number of chords/scales to return
160     INTOTAL = 6                  '<< number of intervals in set
170     GOSUB 2000                        '<< call pitch table
180        FOR J = 1 TO INTOTAL
190           GAMINTS(J) = INT(RND * 3)+1  '<< select interval set
```

```
200          NEXT J
210          FOR J = 1 TO TOTAL
220             PRINT "CHORD";J
230             ROOT = INT(RND * 12)+1
240             OCTAVE = INT(RND * 3)+1
250             CHORDMEMS = INT(RND * 14)+6
260             GOSUB 1000          '<< call interval gamut generator
270             PRINT
280          NEXT J
290 END
1000 REM =================================================== CTB6.13
1010 REM ******************>> INTGAM <<************************
1020 REM ====================================================
1030 REM    This subroutine generates non octave-repeating
1040 REM    chords/gamuts from a set of intervals.
1050 REM ====================================================
1060 REM                 Variable Descriptions
1070 REM    Entering -
1080 REM       P$(): pitch name table
1090 REM       GAMINTS(): array of interval sizes
1100 REM       ROOT: lowest chord/gamut member
1110 REM       OCTAVE: octave register for chord initiation
1120 REM       CHORDMEMS: number of tones contained in gamut
1130 REM       INTOTAL: number of intervals in GAMINTS()
1140 REM    Exiting -
1150 REM       none (subroutine is procedural)
1160 REM    Local -
1170 REM       COUNT: tabulates chordtone generation
1180 REM       CHORDTONE: next chord/gamut member
1190 REM       K9: loop index
1200 REM       L9: loop index, pointer to array GAMINTS()
1210 REM ====================================================
1220    COUNT = 0
1230    CHORDTONE = ROOT + ((OCTAVE - 1) * 12)
1240       FOR K9 = 1 TO 100
1250          FOR L9 = 1 TO INTOTAL
1260             PRINT P$(CHORDTONE);" ";
1270             COUNT = COUNT + 1
1280             IF COUNT = CHORDMEMS THEN RETURN
1290             CHORDTONE = CHORDTONE + GAMINTS(L9)
1300          NEXT L9
1310       NEXT K9
1320 RETURN
2000 REM =================================================== CTB1.3
2010 REM ******************>> PITCHTAB <<**********************
2020 REM ====================================================
2030 REM    This subroutine initializes a pitch data table
2040 REM    corresponding to integer values 1-n.
2050 REM ====================================================
2070    NOTE$ = " CC# DD# E FF# GG# AA# B"
2080    OCTAVE$ = "1234567"
2090       FOR K9 = 1 TO 7
2100          FOR L9 = 1 TO 12
2110             P$(L9+(K9-1)*12) = MID$(NOTE$,(L9*2-1),2)+MID$
(OCTAVE$,K9,1)
2120          NEXT L9
2130       NEXT K9
2140 RETURN
```

RUN (Intgam)

```
CHORD 1
 G1 A#1 C#2 D#2  F2  G2 A#2 C#3  E3 F#3 G#3 A#3 C#4  E4
CHORD 2
 E1  G1 A#1  C2  D2  E2  G2
CHORD 3
 G3 A#3 C#4 D#4  F4  G4 A#4 C#5  E5 F#5 G#5 A#5 C#6  E6  G6  A6
CHORD 4
 A2  C3 D#3  F3  G3  A3  C4 D#4 F#4 G#4 A#4  C5 D#5
CHORD 5
G#2  B2  D3  E3 F#3 G#3  B3  D4  F4  G4  A4  B4  D5  F5 G#5 A#5
 C6  D6
```

SUBROUTINE GROUP: RHYPROPS

○ Parstore	CTB1.4
○ Parxtrct	CTB1.5
○ Rhyprops	CTB6.14

Purpose

Convert rhythmic proportions into time durations.

Notes

One important method of dealing with time articulation within a composition is to conceive a sequence of proportional rhythmic relationships to be translated into attack points or note durations. While the serial timepoint system derives its values from details within a set of integers, the proportional method takes a more global approach; it first describes what the relationships will be among the rhythmic details, then computes the final note durations. Since serial procedures act upon proportional rhythmic flow, results are produced which differ from those of the timepoint system. (Refer to output that follows the program listing.)

Proportional information consists of three parts; for example, 1:4:8 means that there will be one duration that will occupy the amount of time taken by four one-eighth note durations. Inversely, 4:1:8 means that four notes will equally divide the amount of time taken by a one-eighth note. The output is expressed as fractions of a whole note. For example, 4/1 represents a duration equal to four whole notes; 1/4 means a duration equal to one-quarter of a whole note.

To illustrate this concept, the DRIVER PROGRAM dictates three rhythmic proportions for conversion to rhythm values; you can adapt it to accept a proportional series from the keyboard by adding an array to hold the input.

To prevent the return of overly complex fractions, the following guidelines should be observed:

- When value 1 is larger than value 2 (e.g., 9:8), value 2 should conform to one of the following numbers:

    1, 2, 4, 8, 16.

- When value 2 is larger than value 1 (e.g., 4:9), value 1 should conform to one of the above numbers.

Programming Ideas

1) Modify the DRIVER PROGRAM to accept keyboard input of all control variables.

2) Add a file-writing subroutine to store the output.

Program Listing

```
100 REM =============================================================
110 REM                        DRIVER PROGRAM
120 REM                         (Rhyprops)
130 REM =============================================================
510     DIM C#(3)
520     TOTAL = 3'<< nmbr of information items for each proportion
530     GOSUB 1010                    '<< call multiple value storage
540     E = 0: I = 1: F = TOTAL: G = 1
550     PRINT "ORIGINAL FORM --"
560     GOSUB 2000                         '<< call value extraction
570     PRINT
580     PRINT"RETROGRADE FORM -- "
590     E = 0: I = TOTAL: F = 1: G = -1
600     GOSUB 2000                         '<< call value extraction
610     PRINT
620     PRINT "INVERTED FORM -- "
630     E = 1: I = 1: F = TOTAL: G = 1
640     GOSUB 2000                         '<< call value extraction
650     PRINT
660     PRINT "RETROGRADE INVERSION FORM -- "
670     E= 1: I = TOTAL: F = 1: G = -1
680     GOSUB 2000                         '<< call value extraction
690     PRINT
700 END
1000 REM ======================================================= CTB1.4
1010 REM ****************>> PARSTORE <<************************
1020 REM                  (adapted to program specs)
1030 REM =============================================================
1040 PRINT "+++++++ VALUE 1, VALUE 2, METRICAL BASE +++++ "
1050     FOR K9 = 1 TO TOTAL
1060         R1# = K9 * K9
1070         R2# = K9 + 3
1080         B# = 8
1090         PRINT "SELECTED PROPORTION";K9;"-->";R1#;":";R2#;", ";
"BASE";B#
1100         R1#= R1# * 1000000!
1110         R2#=R2# * 1000
1120         C#(K9) = R1#+ R2#+ B#
1130     NEXT K9
1140 RETURN
2000 REM ======================================================= CTB1.5
2010 REM ****************>> PARXTRCT <<************************
2020 REM                 (adapted to program specs)
2030 REM =============================================================
2040     FOR K9 = I TO F STEP G
2050         D# = C#(K9)
2060         D# = D#/1000000!
2070         R1 = INT(D#)
2080         R2 = INT((D# - INT(D#)) * 1000)
2090         D# = D# * 1000
2100         B  = INT((D# - INT(D#)) * 1000+.5)
2110         GOSUB 3000         '<< call proportion/rhythm conversion
2120     NEXT K9
2130 RETURN
3000 REM ====================================================== CTB6.14
3010 REM ****************>> RHYPROPS <<************************
3020 REM =============================================================
3030 REM     This subroutine converts numeric proportions
```

```
3040 REM     into rhythm duration values.
3050 REM ========================================================
3060 REM                 Variable Descriptions
3070 REM    Entering -
3080 REM      R1: proportion value #1
3090 REM      R2: proportion value #2
3100 REM      B: rhythm median value
3110 REM      E: flag to invert proportion
3120 REM    Exiting -
3130 REM      none (subroutine is procedural)
3140 REM    Local -
3150 REM      CUM: converted duration numerator
3160 REM      DUR: converted duration denominator
3170 REM      L9: loop index
3180 REM ========================================================
3190    IF E = 1 THEN SWAP R1,R2
3200    IF R1 < R2 THEN 3280
3210    CUM = 1
3220    DUR = R1 * B / R2
3230    IF DUR <> INT(DUR) THEN CUM = CUM * 2 : DUR = DUR * 2 :
GOTO 3230
3240         FOR L9 = 1 TO R1
3250            PRINT CUM;"/";DUR,
3260         NEXT L9
3270    RETURN
3280    DUR = R2/R1
3290    IF INT(DUR) <> DUR THEN DUR = DUR * 2 : B = B * 2 :
GOTO 3290
3300         FOR L9 = 1 TO R1
3310            PRINT DUR;"/";B,
3320         NEXT L9
3330 RETURN
```

RUN (Rhyprops)

```
+++++++ VALUE 1, VALUE 2, METRICAL BASE ++++++
SELECTED PROPORTION 1 --> 1 : 4 , BASE 8
SELECTED PROPORTION 2 --> 4 : 5 , BASE 8
SELECTED PROPORTION 3 --> 9 : 6 , BASE 8
ORIGINAL FORM --
   4 / 8        5 / 32        5 / 32        5 / 32        5 / 32
   1 / 12       1 / 12        1 / 12        1 / 12        1 / 12
   1 / 12       1 / 12        1 / 12        1 / 12
RETROGRADE FORM --
   1 / 12       1 / 12        1 / 12        1 / 12        1 / 12
   1 / 12       1 / 12        1 / 12        1 / 12        5 / 32
   5 / 32       5 / 32        5 / 32        4 / 8
INVERTED FORM --
   1 / 32       1 / 32        1 / 32        1 / 32        1 / 10
   1 / 10       1 / 10        1 / 10        1 / 10        3 / 16
   3 / 16       3 / 16        3 / 16        3 / 16        3 / 16

RETROGRADE INVERSION FORM --
   3 / 16       3 / 16        3 / 16        3 / 16        3 / 16
   3 / 16       1 / 10        1 / 10        1 / 10        1 / 10
   1 / 10       1 / 32        1 / 32        1 / 32        1 / 32
```

SUBROUTINE GROUP: POLYRHY

　　　　　○ Polyrhy　　　　　CTB6.15
　　　　　○ Durred　　　　　CTB1.16

Purpose

Generate multiple, polyrhythmic/metric, random-order, synchronously terminating, rhythm duration sequences on four selectable complexity levels.

Notes

The operation of Polyrhy is inversely similar to the method musicians use to figure out how to count a particular rhythm pattern. It computes the requested number of durations by subdividing and randomly regrouping the number of metrical pulse values required to fill the specific number of whole notes indicated by the variable TIMESCALE. The variable LEVEL selects the pulse subdivision degree required to produce a particular complexity level. (Smaller pulse subdivisions and subsequent random micropulse regroupings produce patterns which are more aperiodic in nature.) The variable M1 is the median—the metric/rhythmic base value of the duration sequence; for example:

4 = one-quarter whole note
5 = one-fifth whole note
7 = one-seventh whole note, etc.

Computed rhythm durations are reduced to lowest terms (consistent with the metrical base) by Subroutine Durred and are stored in array FRACTION$.

The DRIVER PROGRAM is set up to output four layers of rhythm durations, each of a different meter, length, and complexity level. Variables TOTAL, MEDIAN, and LEVEL grow larger with each loop iteration, but variable TIMESCALE remains constant to ensure that diverse-length duration sequences will end synchronously.

Programming Ideas

1) Modify the DRIVER PROGRAM to be interactive and add a subroutine to file the output sequences on disk.

2) Write a program that invokes Polyrhy (CTB6.15) and Loopgen2 (CTB6.2) to process duration sequences, and which then assigns them to pitch sequences generated by another subroutine, such as Trantabl (CTB6.5).

Program Listing

```
100 REM ==========================================================
110 REM                 DRIVER PROGRAM
120 REM                   (Polyrhy)
130 REM ==========================================================
```

```
140     DIM DUR(100), FRACTION$(100)
150     RANDOMIZE(19388)
160     TOTAL = 10
170     M1= 3
180     LEVEL = 1
190     TIMESCALE = 10
200         FOR J = 1 TO 4
210             PRINT "PASS ";J
220             PRINT "LENGTH OF RHYTHM SEQUENCE = ";TOTAL
230             PRINT "MEDIAN =";M1
240             PRINT "TIMESCALE = ";TIMESCALE;"(scale = 1-10)"
250             PRINT "LEVEL = ";LEVEL;
260             PRINT "(from a choice of 1-2-4-8)"
270             GOSUB 1000
280                 FOR J1 = 1 TO TOTAL
290                     PRINT FRACTION$(J1),
300                 NEXT J1
310             PRINT:PRINT
320             LEVEL = LEVEL + LEVEL
330             TOTAL = TOTAL + 10
340             M1 = M1 + 1
350         NEXT J
360 END
1000 REM ================================================= CTB6.15
1010 REM *******************>> POLYRHY <<***********************
1020 REM =================================================
1030 REM     This subroutine computes random-order rhythm
1040 REM     duration sequences on 4 selectable levels of
1050 REM     complexity.  It produces polyrhythmic/metric
1060 REM     output layers which occupy identical time frames;
1070 REM     That is, as long as the timescale remains
1080 REM     constant, all independent output layers will
1090 REM     end synchronously, regardless of metrical
1100 REM     orientation (3/4,4/4,5/4,7/4,9/4,etc.).
1110 REM =================================================
1120 REM                     Variable Descriptions
1130 REM     Entering -
1140 REM       TOTAL: length of rhythm sequence
1150 REM       TIMESCALE: arbitrary time reference
1160 REM       M1: basic metrical unit
1170 REM       LEVEL: degree of complexity (1-2-4-8)
1180 REM     Exiting -  (to DRIVER)
1190 REM       FRACTION$(): array storing duration fractions
1200 REM     Exiting -  (to DURRED subroutine)
1210 REM       DUR(): array storing fraction numerators
1220 REM       NEWMED: reduced fraction denominator
1230 REM       K9:loop index, pointer to DUR()
1240 REM     Local -
1250 REM       ODD: holds flag for odd number of values
1260 REM       SUM: total of micropulses in raw sequence
1270 REM       MBASE: number of micropulses to distribute
1270 REM       MBASE: number of micropulses to distribute
1280 REM       MEDIAN: metrical base value (3,4,5,7,9,etc)
1290 REM       FACTOR: determinant of rnd generator range
1300 REM       RANGE: span of rnd generator
1310 REM       WEDGE: low bias of rnd generator
1320 REM       RCOMP: rnd generator overrun or underrun
1330 REM       U,R0,F0: random values for duration numerators
1340 REM       K9: loop index, pointer to DUR(), FRACTION$()
1350 REM       L9: loop index, pointer to DUR()
```

```
1360 REM ==============================================================
1370    ODD = 0
1380    SUM = 0
1390    MEDIAN = M1
1400 REM +++++++++++++++++++++++++++++++++++++++++++++++++++++++++++++
1410 REM     Lines 1440-1530 reconcile sequence length with
1420 REM     metrical base value and timescale.
1430 REM +++++++++++++++++++++++++++++++++++++++++++++++++++++++++++++
1440    MBASE = MEDIAN * TIMESCALE
1450    IF TOTAL = 1 THEN DUR(1) = TIMESCALE : GOTO 1840 ELSE IF
TIMESCALE - TOTAL > 0 THEN 1490
1460       FOR K9 = 1 TO 30
1470          IF TOTAL > MBASE THEN MEDIAN = MEDIAN * 2 : MBASE =
MBASE * 2 ELSE 1580
1480       NEXT K9
1490    IF MBASE/2 <> INT(MBASE/2) THEN MBASE = MBASE - 1 : ODD
= M1
1500       FOR K9 = 1 TO 100
1510          IF MBASE/2 <> INT(MBASE/2) OR MEDIAN/2 <>
INT(MEDIAN/2) THEN 1580
1520          IF TOTAL <= MBASE / 2 THEN MEDIAN = MEDIAN / 2 :
MBASE = MBASE / 2 ELSE 1580
1530       NEXT K9
1540 REM +++++++++++++++++++++++++++++++++++++++++++++++++++++++++++++
1550 REM     Lines 1580-1790 compute micropulse (subdivision)
1560 REM     level and generate random-order durations.
1570 REM +++++++++++++++++++++++++++++++++++++++++++++++++++++++++++++
1580    MBASE = MBASE * LEVEL
1590    MEDIAN = MEDIAN * LEVEL
1600    IF LEVEL = 4 THEN FACTOR = 3 ELSE IF LEVEL = 8 THEN
FACTOR = 4 ELSE FACTOR = LEVEL
1610    WEDGE = FACTOR
1620    RANGE = (FACTOR + LEVEL) + INT(MBASE/TOTAL)
1630       FOR K9 = 1 TO TOTAL
1640          U = INT(RND * RANGE) + WEDGE
1650          DUR(K9) = U
1660          SUM = SUM + U
1670       NEXT K9
1680    RCOMP = MBASE - SUM
1690       FOR K9 = 1 TO 10000
1700          FOR L9 = 1 TO TOTAL
1710             IF RCOMP < 0 THEN 1730
1720             IF RCOMP = 0 THEN 1760 ELSE DUR(L9) = DUR(L9) + 1 :
RCOMP = RCOMP - 1 : GOTO 1740
1730             IF DUR(L9) < 2 THEN 1740 ELSE DUR(L9) = DUR(L9) - 1
: RCOMP = RCOMP + 1
1740          NEXT L9
1750       NEXT K9
1760    IF ODD < 1 THEN 1840
1770    R0 = INT(RND * TOTAL) + 1
1780    F0 = INT(RND * TOTAL) + 1
1790    IF TOTAL > 1 AND F0 = R0 THEN 1780 ELSE DUR(R0) = DUR(R0)
+ DUR(F0) : DUR(F0) = -1
1800 REM +++++++++++++++++++++++++++++++++++++++++++++++++++++++++++++
1810 REM     Lines 1140-1880 reduce duration fraction and
1820 REM     load the sequence into a character string array
1830 REM +++++++++++++++++++++++++++++++++++++++++++++++++++++++++++++
1840    FOR K9 = 1 TO TOTAL
1850       NEWMED = MEDIAN
1860       IF DUR(K9)/2 = INT(DUR(K9)/2) AND NEWMED/2 = INT
```

```
(NEWMED/2) THEN GOSUB 2000        '<< call fraction reduction
1870      IF DUR(K9) < 0 THEN FRACTION$(K9) = STR$(1)+"/"+MID$
(STR$(ODD),2) ELSE FRACTION$(K9) = STR$(DUR(K9)) + "/" + MID$(STR
$(NEWMED),2)
1880     NEXT K9
1890 RETURN
2000 REM ================================================= CTB1.16
2010 REM ****************>> DURRED <<**************************
2020 REM                   (modified form)
2030 REM =================================================
2040     DUR(K9) = DUR(K9)/2
2050     NEWMED = NEWMED/2
2060     IF DUR(K9)/2 = INT(DUR(K9)/2) AND NEWMED/2 = INT(NEWMED/2)
THEN 2040
2070 RETURN
```

RUN (Polyrhy)

```
PASS  1
LENGTH OF RHYTHM SEQUENCE =  10
MEDIAN = 3
TIMESCALE =  10 (scale = 1-10)
LEVEL =  1 (from a choice of 1-2-4-8)
  3/3            3/3          6/3          2/3          5/3
  1/3            5/3          2/3          1/3          2/3

PASS  2
LENGTH OF RHYTHM SEQUENCE =  20
MEDIAN = 4
TIMESCALE =  10 (scale = 1-10)
LEVEL =  2 (from a choice of 1-2-4-8)
  1/8            3/4          1/8          3/8          1/2
  5/8            1/8          3/4          7/8          7/8
  1/4            3/4          3/8          1/8          7/8
  1/1            1/8          1/8          3/8          7/8

PASS  3
LENGTH OF RHYTHM SEQUENCE =  30
MEDIAN = 5
TIMESCALE =  10 (scale = 1-10)
LEVEL =  4 (from a choice of 1-2-4-8)
  9/20           5/20         9/20         1/10         1/20
  7/20           1/20        11/20         9/20         5/10
  1/20           3/20         3/10         9/20         1/5
  5/20           5/10         5/10         7/20         5/20
  7/20          13/20         9/20         3/20         2/5
  3/20          11/20         5/20         5/20         3/5

PASS  4
LENGTH OF RHYTHM SEQUENCE =  40
MEDIAN = 6
TIMESCALE =  10 (scale = 1-10)
LEVEL =  8 (from a choice of 1-2-4-8)
  1/48           1/12         5/24        19/48        21/48
 11/24          17/48        13/48         1/48        11/48
  9/48           3/48         1/24         5/12         1/3
 11/24           1/6         3/24        23/48        15/48
  9/24           9/24         1/3          1/12         1/6
  1/3            1/48         1/48         9/48        19/48
  1/24          11/24         1/3          1/6          9/48
  3/12          23/48         1/3          3/24        13/48
```

SUBROUTINE GROUP: MELINE
- Rest   CTB6.16
- Rdmelint   CTB6.17
- Pitchtab   CTB1.3

Purpose

Generate a random-order, interval-constrained melodic pitch sequence containing a percentage of rest values.

Notes

The core of this group is Rdmelint, similar in concept to Rdintchd but differing in two respects. Firstly, it returns a bi-directional melodic line rather than a unidirectional harmonic chord sequence. Secondly, the probability that the overall line direction will drift upward or downward is influenced by the value entered for variable UP.

Subroutine Rest allows the user to provide a rest occurrence probability (in percentage) to articulate the melodic line; uniform random integers smaller than a threshold value trigger the insertion of rests.

Programming Ideas

Write a program based on Subroutine Group MELINE that:

- Contains control variables for increasing or decreasing the interval-size range over the course of program execution.

- Allows the user to generate a number of disparate-range melodic sequences within a single run.

- Files the melodies on disk along with keys to facilitate the extraction of individual sequences (see Subroutine Group SEQFILE for help).

- Individually retrieves melodic sequences for the application of variation procedures.

- Prints out the original melodies in alternation with their variations in ABACADAE form (rondo).

Program Listing

```
100 REM ==========================================================
110 REM                      PROGRAM DRIVER
120 REM                        (Meline)
130 REM ==========================================================
140    DIM NOTE$(100),P$(84)
150    RANDOMIZE(-3192)
160    TOTAL = 10                        '<< length of sequence
170    SMALL = 1               '<< smallest allowable interval
180    LARGE = 3               '<< largest allowable interval
```

Help Us Help You!

So that we can better fill your reading needs, please take a moment to complete and return this card. We appreciate your comments and suggestions.

1. I am interested in books on the following subjects:
- ☐ automotive
- ☐ aviation
- ☐ business
- ☐ computer, hobby
- ☐ computer, professional
- ☐ engineering (specify): _____
- ☐ other (specify) _____
- ☐ other (specify) _____

- ☐ electronics, hobby
- ☐ electronics, professional
- ☐ finance
- ☐ how to, do-it-yourself

2. I own/use a computer:
- ☐ IBM
- ☐ Apple
- ☐ Commodore
- ☐ Other (specify)

- ☐ Macintosh
- ☐ ATARI
- ☐ Amiga

3. This card came from TAB book (specify title and/or number): _____

4. I purchase books:
- ☐ from general bookstores
- ☐ from technical bookstores
- ☐ from college bookstores
- ☐ other (specify)

- ☐ through the mail
- ☐ by telephone
- ☐ by electronic mail

Comments _____

Name _____
Address _____
City _____
State _____ Zip _____

TAB BOOKS Inc.

See page 249 for a Special Companion Disk Offer

Yes, I'm interested. Send me:

_____ copies 5¼″ disk requiring 360K (#6698S), $24.95 .... $ _____

_____ copies 3½″ disk requiring 360K (#6699S), $24.95 .... $ _____

_____ TAB BOOKS catalog (free with purchase; otherwise send $1.00 in check or money order (credited to your first purchase) .... $ _____

Shipping & Handling: $2.50 per disk in U.S.
($5.00 per disk outside U.S.) $ _____

PA, NY and ME add applicable sales tax $ _____

TOTAL $ _____

☐ Check or money order enclosed made payable to TAB BOOKS Inc.

Charge my ☐ VISA ☐ MasterCard ☐ American Express

Acct No. _____ Exp. Date _____

Signature _____

Name _____

Address _____

City _____ State _____ Zip _____

TOLL-FREE ORDERING: 1-800-822-8158
(in PA and AK call 1-717-794-2191)

or write to TAB BOOKS Inc., Blue Ridge Summit, PA, 17294-0840

Prices subject to change. Orders outside the U.S. must be paid in international money order in U.S. dollars.

TAB 3384

BUSINESS REPLY MAIL

FIRST CLASS   PERMIT NO. 9   BLUE RIDGE SUMMIT, PA 17214

POSTAGE WILL BE PAID BY ADDRESSEE

TAB BOOKS Inc.
Blue Ridge Summit, PA 17214-9988

BUSINESS REPLY MAIL

FIRST CLASS   PERMIT NO. 9   BLUE RIDGE SUMMIT, PA 17214

POSTAGE WILL BE PAID BY ADDRESSEE

TAB BOOKS Inc.
Blue Ridge Summit, PA 17214-9988

```
190      UP = 80          '<< probability (in %) of ascending interval
200      REST = 0             '<< probability (in %) of rest occurrence
210      START = 48                 '<< sequence starting value
220      GOSUB 3010                      '<< call pitch table
230        FOR J = 1 TO 4
240           NOTE$(1) = P$(START)
250           NOTE = START
260           PRINT "PASS";J
270           PRINT "TOTAL =";TOTAL;";SMALL=";SMALL;";LARGE =";
LARGE;";UP =";UP;";REST=";REST;";START =";START
280           PRINT NOTE$(1),
290             FOR J1 = 2 TO TOTAL
300                GOSUB 1000              '<<call rest probability
310                IF FLAG = 0 THEN GOSUB 2000 '<< call interval
generator
320                PRINT NOTE$(J1),        '<< send array to screen
330             NEXT J1
340           PRINT : PRINT
350           TOTAL = TOTAL + 10
360           SMALL = SMALL + 1
370           LARGE = LARGE + 2
380           INTVALRANGE = LARGE-SMALL+1
390           UP = UP - 20
400           REST = REST + 10
410        NEXT J
420 END
1000 REM =================================================== CTB6.16
1010 REM ******************>> REST <<************************
1020 REM ===================================================
1030 REM     This subroutine is similar to ADDORN, in that
1040 REM     it checks a rest percentage threshold value
1050 REM     before deciding whether to insert a rest note
1060 REM ===================================================
1070 REM                 Variable Descriptions
1080 REM     Entering -
1090 REM       REST: threshold test value (% of rest)
1100 REM       NOTE$(): array to receive rest string (if selected)
1110 REM       P$(0): pitchtable array address holding rest string
1120 REM       J1: pointer to NOTE$() array
1130 REM     Exiting -
1140 REM       FLAG: signal to DRIVER not to call pitch generator
1150 REM       NOTE$():
1160 REM     Local - none
1170 REM ===================================================
1180     FLAG = 0
1190     IF RND * 100 <= REST  THEN NOTE$(J1) = P$(0) : FLAG = 1
1200 RETURN
2000 REM =================================================== CTB6.17
2010 REM ******************>> RDMELINT <<********************
2020 REM ===================================================
2030 REM     This subroutine resembles RDINTCHD in concept.
2040 REM     However, it generates an interval-contained
2050 REM     melodic sequence which is bi-directional
2060 REM     as opposed to RDINTCHD's harmonic, unidirectional
2070 REM     orientation.
2080 REM ===================================================
2090 REM                 Variable Descriptions
2100 REM     Entering -
2110 REM       SMALL: smallest allowable interval-size
```

```
2120 REM        INTVALRANGE: span of allowable interval-sizes
2130 REM        NOTE: most recent note generated
2140 REM        UP: probability of upward interval motion
2150 REM        NOTE$(): array to be filled with notes/rests
2160 REM        P$(): pitch table array
2170 REM        J1: pointer to NOTE$() array
2180 REM     Exiting -
2190 REM        NOTE$():
2200 REM     Local -
2210 REM        U: range-controlled random integer
2220 REM ==============================================================
2230     U = INT(RND * INTVALRANGE) + SMALL
2240     IF RND * 100 <= UP THEN NOTE = NOTE + U ELSE NOTE = NOTE
- U
2250     IF NOTE > 84 THEN NOTE = NOTE - 12 ELSE IF NOTE < 1 THEN
NOTE = NOTE + 12      '<< in bounds?
2260     NOTE$(J1) = P$(NOTE)
2270 RETURN
3000 REM =========================================== CTB1.3
3010 REM *****************>> PITCHTAB <<*********************
3020 REM ==============================================================
3030     NOTES$ = " CC# DD# E FF# GG# AA# B"
3040     OCTAVE$ = "1234567"
3050     P$(0) = " R "
3060         FOR K9 = 1 TO 7
3070             FOR L9 = 1 TO 12
3080                 P$(L9+(K9-1)*12) = MID$(NOTES$,(L9*2-1),2)+MID$
(OCTAVE$,K9,1)
3090             NEXT L9
3100         NEXT K9
3110 RETURN
```

RUN (Meline)

PASS 1
TOTAL = 10 ;SMALL= 1 ;LARGE = 3 ;UP = 80 ;REST= 0 ;START = 48

B4	C5	C#5	D5	D#5
D5	D#5	E5	F5	E5

PASS 2
TOTAL = 20 ;SMALL= 2 ;LARGE = 5 ;UP = 60 ;REST= 10 ;START = 48

B4	F#4	D#4	F4	D4
E4	B3	D4	A3	C4
D#4	F4	A4	C5	G4
A4	R	B4	D5	F5

PASS 3
TOTAL = 30 ;SMALL= 3 ;LARGE = 7 ;UP = 40 ;REST= 20 ;START = 48

B4	R	F#4	R	B4
G4	R	E4	A3	D4
F4	R	C#4	A3	E3
A3	F#3	D#3	A#2	F3
R	R	C#3	G#2	D2
R	G2	R	D3	G2

PASS 4
TOTAL = 40 ;SMALL= 4 ;LARGE = 9 ;UP = 20 ;REST= 30 ;START = 48

B4	E4	G3	R	R

B3	F#3	D3	R	F#3
A#2	F2	R	A1	F1
B1	R	G1	C2	G1
B1	F2	C2	G#1	R
E1	A1	C1	F1	C2
F1	R	R	C1	G1
C1	R	R	F1	R

SUBROUTINE GROUP: PARTSPAN

- Partspan   CTB6.18
- Pitchtab   CTB1.3

Purpose

Compute instrumental voice ranges from a common pitch aggregate in one of three modes: stratified, interlocking, or common.

Notes

In circumstances requiring the coordinated generation of melodic lines from a source element table (such as ascendingly sorted scale or chord-pitch gamuts), control over the range/register segment occupied by each voice may be desirable. Partspan accomplishes this task by dividing the total pitch gamut into equal subranges, or by distributing overlapping range/register assignments to all parts, or by making the entire gamut range available to each part.

The DRIVER PROGRAM is configured to generate random pitches selected from within the range of each part; simple modification (Line 360) will allow the substitution of subroutine calls to other melody-generation algorithms.

By extension, CTB6.18 can be applied to any sequence of values—ascending, descending, or random-order—to determine the details of selected parameters by interpreting subroutine output as a set of pointer ranges for the extraction of element-table segments.

Programming Idea

Write an interactive program that generates a chord file using Intgam (CTB6.13), extracts part ranges for four instruments, serializes pitch-parameter note selections for each voice, and then generates durations for the rhythm parameter of each voice using Subroutine Group POLYRHY. Transcribe the output to conventional musical form for performance by four acoustical instruments.

Program Listing

```
100 REM  ==========================================================
110 REM                   DRIVER PROGRAM
120 REM                     (Partspan)
130 REM  ==========================================================
140    DIM P$(84),NOTE(48),PART(4),ADJUST(4)
150    CHORDLENGTH = 48                           '<< pitchbank
160    VOICES = 4                              '<< nmbr of parts
170    MELENGTH = 30              '<< notes in each derived part
180    RANDOMIZE(9019)
190       FOR J = 1 TO CHORDLENGTH
200          NOTE(J) = J                  '<< load pitchbank pointers
```

```
210         NEXT J
220       GOSUB 2000                              '<< call pitch table
230       PRINT "PITCHBANK UPON WHICH MELODIES WILL BE BASED --"
240         FOR J = 1 TO CHORDLENGTH
250           PRINT P$(J),              '<< send pitchbank to screen
260         NEXT J
270       PRINT : PRINT
280       GOSUB 1000                      '<< call part range computation
290         FOR J1 = 1 TO 2
300           IF J1 = 2 THEN PRINT "PASS 2, INTERLOCKING -" : D$ =
"I" ELSE PRINT "PASS 1, STRATIFIED  -" : D$ = "S"
310             FOR J2 = 1 TO VOICES
320               PRINT "VOICE";J2;"MELODY"
330               PRINT "RANGE =";P$(ADJUST(J2));" TO ";
340               PRINT P$(ADJUST(J2) + PART(J2) - 1)
350             FOR J3 = 1 TO MELENGTH
360               R = INT(RND * PART(J2)) + ADJUST(J2)
370               PRINT P$(NOTE(R)),
380             NEXT J3
390               PRINT
400             NEXT J2
410               PRINT
420         NEXT J1
430 END
1000 REM ==================================================== CTB6.18
1010 REM *******************>> PARTSPAN <<*********************
1020 REM ========================================================
1030 REM     This subroutine computes stratified or interlocking
1040 REM     instrumental part ranges in reference to a pitch
1050 REM     bank which will be used to generate melodic lines.
1060 REM ========================================================
1070 REM                 Variable Descriptions
1080 REM     Entering -
1090 REM       VOICES: number of part ranges
1100 REM       CHORDLENGTH: number of notes in source pitch bank
1110 REM       D$: flag to indicate stratified or interlocking
1120 REM     Exiting -
1130 REM       ADJUST(): array of part low pitches
1140 REM       PART(): array of part ranges
1150 REM     Local -
1160 REM       SPAN: subdivision of total pitch bank range
1170 REM       EXTRA: any remainder from subdivision
1180 REM       COMP: compensatory value added to part(s)
1190 REM       K9: loop index, pointer to arrays PART(),ADJUST()
1200 REM ========================================================
1210     SPAN = INT(CHORDLENGTH / VOICES)
1220     EXTRA = CHORDLENGTH-(VOICES*SPAN)
1230       FOR K9 = 1 TO VOICES
1240           IF EXTRA <= 0 THEN COMP = 0 ELSE COMP = 1
1250           PART(K9) = SPAN + COMP
1260           EXTRA = EXTRA - 1
1270           ADJUST(1) = 1
1280           IF K9 < VOICES THEN ADJUST(K9+1) = ADJUST(K9) +
PART(K9)
1290       NEXT K9
1300     IF D$ = "S" THEN 1350
1310 REM >>> interlock part pitch ranges
1320       FOR K9 = 1 TO VOICES-1
1330           PART(K9) = PART(K9) + INT(PART(K9) * .5)
1340       NEXT K9
```

```
1350 RETURN
2000 REM ================================================ CTB1.3
2010 REM ******************>> PITCHTAB <<********************
2020 REM ================================================
2030 REM    This subroutine initializes a pitch data table
2040 REM    corresponding to integer values 1-n.
2050 REM ================================================
2060     NOTE$ = " CC# DD# E FF# GG# AA# B"
2070     OCTAVE$ = "1234567"
2080      FOR K9 = 1 TO 7
2090         FOR L9 = 1 TO 12
2100            P$(L9+(K9-1)*12) = MID$(NOTE$,(L9*2-1),2)+MID$
(OCTAVE$,K9,1)
2110            NEXT L9
2120         NEXT K9
2130 RETURN
```

RUN (Partspan)

PITCHBANK UPON WHICH MELODIES WILL BE BASED --

C1	C#1	D1	D#1	E1
F1	F#1	G1	G#1	A1
A#1	B1	C2	C#2	D2
D#2	E2	F2	F#2	G2
G#2	A2	A#2	B2	C3
C#3	D3	D#3	E3	F3
F#3	G3	G#3	A3	A#3
B3	C4	C#4	D4	D#4
E4	F4	F#4	G4	G#4
A4	A#4	B4		

PASS 1, STRATIFIED -
VOICE 1 MELODY
RANGE = C1 TO   F2

G1	F#1	F2	C1	D#2
C1	G1	B1	G1	A#1
E1	D1	D#1	G#1	F#1
D2	F#1	A#1	F#1	D#2
D1	F2	G#1	D2	A#1
D2	A#1	D#1	D1	A1

VOICE 2 MELODY
RANGE = C2 TO   F3

A2	D#2	D#3	F#2	C2
D#3	G2	F3	F#2	G#2
C2	G#2	A#2	E3	A2
A#2	D#3	C#3	D#2	C2
D2	D2	G2	G2	D2
E2	A#2	F3	D#2	B2

VOICE 3 MELODY
RANGE = C3 TO   F4

A3	F4	C#3	G#3	D#4
C3	F3	D#3	D#4	C#4
C#3	C#3	G#3	E4	B3
D#4	B3	G#3	E3	F3
A#3	C#3	F3	A3	D4
D#4	E4	E3	C#3	D3

VOICE 4 MELODY
RANGE = C4 TO B4

D4	D#4	F#4	B4	F4
G4	E4	D4	C#4	C#4
G4	G#4	F4	C#4	B4
A4	G4	C4	C#4	F#4
D#4	C4	F#4	G#4	C#4
C#4	A4	G#4	A4	F#4

PASS 2, INTERLOCKING -
VOICE 1 MELODY
RANGE = C1 TO F2

F2	D#1	D2	F#1	B1
D2	G1	F#1	A1	F2
D2	D#2	E1	F#1	D#1
F1	F#1	F2	E2	C#2
G#1	E1	D2	B1	C#1
C#2	F2	C1	F2	G1

VOICE 2 MELODY
RANGE = C2 TO F3

F#2	C3	F#2	F3	F#2
F3	G2	E3	C#3	F2
E2	C2	A#2	A2	E2
F3	D2	D#2	C#3	F#2
C#3	C2	E2	F3	A#2
D3	F2	C#2	F3	A2

VOICE 3 MELODY
RANGE = C3 TO F4

C#4	F3	A3	G#3	F3
G#3	C3	E3	F3	D4
D3	C#3	B3	G3	C#4
F3	E3	C3	F4	A3
D#3	E4	G3	C#3	C3
C#3	F#3	D#3	D3	C4

VOICE 4 MELODY
RANGE = C4 TO B4

F#4	G4	A4	A#4	C4
F4	A4	F#4	D4	E4
B4	A4	F4	E4	A4
B4	F#4	E4	G#4	B4
F#4	A#4	G#4	F#4	D4
C4	D4	C4	B4	E4

SUBROUTINE GROUP: ORNAMENT
  ○ Ornselec   CTB6.19
  ○ Addorn   CTB6.20

Purpose

Generate a random-order pitch sequence, then add embellishments to selected notes in accordance with probability weights for four ornament types.

Notes

The DRIVER PROGRAM spins-up a temporary array of random-order pitches. The array is then passed to Subroutine Ornselec, which loads a probability table with weights for each of four ornament patterns, then calls Subroutine Addorn to expand the pitch array by inserting the selected embellishments.

The four standard ornament types (_ –, – _, _ – _, – _ –,) may be augmented to include any number and type of pattern desired by the program user; simply dimension larger arrays EMBTABLE( ), DEC( ), and ORN( ) and enter the appropriate patterns.

Programming Ideas

1) Modify the DRIVER PROGRAM to allow user-input melodic sequences for embellishment.

2) Modify the DRIVER PROGRAM to read a pitch data file for the embellishment of melodies.

3) Add a subroutine to the program to introduce and apply rest note probabilities.

4) Write an interactive program that:

   • Generates melodies using Trantabl (CTB6.5).

   • Includes Subroutine Group Ornament.

   • Includes Loopgen2 (CTB6.2).

   • Writes multiple, processed loop melodies to disk.

Program Listing

```
100 REM ======================================================
110 REM                    DRIVER PROGRAM
120 REM                      (Ornament)
130 REM ======================================================
140    DIM P$(84),TEMP(200),NOTE$(500)
150    DIM DEC(6),ORN(4),EMBTABLE(4)
160    ORN(1) = 1002 : ORN(2) = 2003
170    ORN(3) = 2004 : ORN(4) = 4006
180    DEC(1) = -1 : DEC(2) = 0 : DEC(3) = -1
```

```
190     DEC(4) = 0  : DEC(5) = 1 : DEC(6) = 0
200     DECO =  100              '<< % of sequence notes to decorate
210     RANDOMIZE(-11001)
220     GOSUB 3000                       '<< call pitch table
230     MELENGTH = 20
240     PRINT "UNEMBELLISHED PITCH SEQUENCE =";MELENGTH;"NOTES --"
250        FOR J = 1 TO MELENGTH
260           TEMP(J) = INT(RND * 81) + 2
270           PRINT P$(TEMP(J)),      '<< random sequence to screen
280        NEXT J
290     PRINT : PRINT
300     GOSUB 1000                       '<< call ornament selection
310     PRINT "EMBELLISHED PITCH SEQUENCE =";T3;"NOTES ---"
320        FOR J = 0 TO T3
330           PRINT NOTE$(J),        '<< embellished seq. to screen
340        NEXT J
350 END
1000 REM ============================================== CTB6.19
1010 REM ******************>> ORNSELEC <<************************
1020 REM ******** (variation of PROBTABL  subroutine) **********
1030 REM ======================================================
1040 REM     This subroutine loads a probability table
1050 REM     with weights for each of 4 ornament patterns,
1060 REM     then calls ADDORN subroutine to interpolate
1070 REM     the selected embellishments.
1080 REM ======================================================
1090 REM                    Variable Descriptions
1100 REM     Entering -
1110 REM       P$(): pitch table array
1120 REM       TEMP(): stores sequence prior to decoration
1130 REM       MELENGTH: number of notes in original sequence
1140 REM       DECO: percentage of sequence notes to decorate
1150 REM     Exiting -
1160 REM       NOTE$(): stores final, embellished sequence
1170 REM       T3: final number of notes in sequence
1180 REM     Local -
1190 REM       EMBTABLE(): stores ornament pattern probabilities
1200 REM       WSUM: sum of ornament probability weights
1210 REM       K9: loop index, pointer to array TEMP()
1220 REM ======================================================
1230    T3 = 0
1240    IF DECO = 0 THEN 1360
1250    PRINT "ORNAMENTS BEING ADDED (PROB. WEIGHTS 4,3,2,1) ---"
1260    PRINT "1) _ - 2) - _ 3) - _ - 4) _ - _"
1270    WSUM = 0
1280       FOR K9 = 1 TO 4
1290          READ  EMBTABLE(K9)
1300          EMBTABLE(K9) = EMBTABLE(K9) + WSUM
1310          WSUM = EMBTABLE(K9)
1320       NEXT K9
1330 REM +++++++++++++++++++
1340 DATA 4,3,2,1
1350 REM +++++++++++++++++++
1360    FOR K9 = 1 TO MELENGTH
1370       IF RND * 100 > DECO THEN NOTE$(T3) = P$(TEMP(K9)) ELSE
GOSUB 2000
1380       T3 = T3 + 1
1390    NEXT K9
1400    PRINT
1410 RETURN
```

```
2000 REM =================================================== CTB6.20
2010 REM ********************>> ADDORN <<************************
2020 REM ===================================================
2030 REM      This subroutine adds selected embellishment
2040 REM      patterns to a pre-existent melodic sequence.
2050 REM      In the process, the sequence is transferred
2060 REM      to a pitch character string array.
2070 REM ===================================================
2080 REM                 Variable Descriptions
2090 REM      Entering -
2100 REM        P$(): pitch table array
2110 REM        TEMP(): stores sequence prior to decoration
2120 REM        EMBTABLE():
2130 REM        ORN(): array of ornament patterns
2140 REM        DEC(): array of values for pattern reference
2150 REM        NOTE$(): stores final, embellished sequence
2160 REM        WSUM: sum of ornament probability weights
2170 REM       K9: pointer to array TEMP()
2180 REM      Exiting -
2190 REM        NOTE$(): (above)
2200 REM        T3: pointer to array NOTE$()
2210 REM      Local -
2220 REM        I8: loop index, pointer to array DEC()
2230 REM        I9: loop index, pointer to array DEC()
2240 REM        M9: loop index, pointer to array ORN()
2250 REM        N9: loop index, pointer to array DEC()
2260 REM ===================================================
2270      FOR M9 = 1 TO 4
2280          IF RND * WSUM > EMBTABLE(M9) THEN 2350
2290          I8 = INT(ORN(M9) / 1000) : I9 = CINT((ORN(M9) / 1000
- INT(ORN(M9) / 1000)) * 1000)
2300          FOR N9 = I8 TO I9
2310             NOTE$(T3) = P$(TEMP(K9) + DEC(N9))
2320             T3 = T3 + 1
2330          NEXT N9
2340          RETURN 1390
2350      NEXT M9
2360 RETURN 1390
3000 REM =================================================== CTB1.3
3010 REM ********************>> PITCHTAB <<********************
3020 REM ===================================================
3030 REM      This subroutine initializes a pitch data table
3040 REM      corresponding to integer values 1-n.
3050 REM ===================================================
3060      NOTE$ = " CC# DD# E FF# GG# AA# B"
3070      OCTAVE$ = "1234567"
3080        FOR K9 = 1 TO 7
3090          FOR L9 = 1 TO 12
3100             P$(L9+(K9-1)*12) = MID$(NOTE$,(L9*2-1),2)+MID$
(OCTAVE$,K9,1)
3110          NEXT L9
3120        NEXT K9
3130 RETURN
```

RUN (Ornament)

```
UNEMBELLISHED PITCH SEQUENCE = 20 NOTES --
    G4          F#4            B2            D#1          D#1
    G7          D#3            A6            D7           D5
    A6          C3             F#7           E5           F#4
    C3          C2             A5            A#5          G#6

ORNAMENTS BEING ADDED (PROB. WEIGHTS 4,3,2,1) ---
1) _ - 2) - _ 3) - _ - 4) _ - _

EMBELLISHED PITCH SEQUENCE = 45 NOTES ---
    G4          F#4            F#4            F4           B2
    A#2         B2             D1             D#1          D1
    D#1         G7             F#7            D#3          D3
    D#3         A6             G#6            D7           C#7
    D5          C#5            G#6            A6           C3
    B2          F#7            F7             D#5          E5
    F#4         F4             F#4            C3           B2
    C2          B1             C2             A5           G#5
    A5          A#5            A5             G6           G#6
```

SUBROUTINE GROUP: SEQFILE

     ○ Seqstore   CTB6.21

     ○ Seqxtrct   CTB6.22

Purpose

Provide a means for filing and retrieving an articulated group of integer sequences.

Notes

Sometimes a long program must be broken up into more manageable sections and called or "chained" one segment at a time. Moreover, microcomputer memory limitations may prevent passing arrays from one program segment to the next, thus necessitating disk storage of data in one subprogram for retrieval in another. When this is the case, data generated at the beginning of a series of routines must be made available for reference by chained program components.

Subroutine Seqstore generates and files an array of integer sequences, together with keys to the length of each constituent sequence. (Subroutine calls to other data-generating algorithms may be substituted for Line 1200 code.) Array X( ) is then passed back to the calling program where it is available for further processing.

Subroutine Seqxtrct reads a sequence data file that contains sequence-length keys. It places each value in array Y( ) which is passed back to the main routine after printout. (The length keys are left in the array, but they can be stripped by simple subroutine modification.)

Programming Ideas

Write an interactive program using Subroutine Group SEQFILE that:

- Invokes Rdintchd (CTB6.11) in Line 1200 of Seqstore (CTB6.21) to generate an extensive chordfile.

- Retrieves the chordfile from disk and makes the chords individually available to a melody generation subroutine.

- Derives interval-constrained random-order melodic sequences from the chordfile.

Program Listing

```
100 REM ===============================================================
110 REM                     DRIVER PROGRAM
120 REM                      (Seqfile)
130 REM ===============================================================
140     DIM X(200)
150     SEQTOTAL = 4                        '<< number of sequences
160     OPEN "O",#1,"SEQ.DAT"              '<< open file for writing
```

```
170     PRINT "FILE LOOKS LIKE THIS ---"
180     GOSUB 1000                      '<< call sequence filing routine
190     CLOSE #1
200     OPEN "I",#1,"SEQ.DAT"              '<< open file for reading
210     PRINT "EXTRACTED SEQUENCES LOOK LIKE THIS --"
220     GOSUB 2000          '<< call sequence extraction routine
230     CLOSE #1
240 END
1000 REM ================================================= CTB6.21
1010 REM *******************>> SEQSTORE <<*********************
1020 REM =======================================================
1030 REM                 Sequence-Group Filing Subroutine
1040 REM =======================================================
1050 REM                     Variable Descriptions
1060 REM     Entering -
1070 REM       SEQTOTAL: number of sequences to store
1080 REM     Exiting -
1090 REM       X(): array containing sequence and keys
1100 REM     Local -
1110 REM       SEQLEN: random-length number sequence
1120 REM       FILEVAL: integer for array storage & filing
1130 REM       K9: loop index
1140 REM       L9: loop index, pointer to array X()
1150 REM       T8: counter, pointer to array X()
1160 REM =======================================================
1170       FOR K9 = 1 TO SEQTOTAL
1180           SEQLEN = INT(RND * 20)+5
1190           FOR L9 =  1 TO SEQLEN
1200               FILEVAL = L9 * K9
1210               IF L9 = 1 THEN X(L9+T8) = FILEVAL * 1000 + SEQLEN
ELSE X(L9+T8) = FILEVAL
1220               PRINT X(L9+T8),:PRINT #1,X(L9+T8);
1230           NEXT L9
1240           T8 = T8 + SEQLEN
1250       NEXT K9
1260     PRINT
1270 RETURN
2000 REM ================================================= CTB6.22
2010 REM *******************>> SEQXTRCT <<*********************
2020 REM =======================================================
2030 REM                 Sequence-Group Retrieval Subroutine
2040 REM =======================================================
2050 REM                     Variable Descriptions
2060 REM     Entering -
2070 REM       X(): array containing sequence & keys
2080 REM     Exiting -
2090 REM       none (subroutine is procedural)
2100 REM     Local -
2110 REM       S8: sequence counter
2120 REM       K9: loop index, pointer to array X()
2130 REM =======================================================
2140     S8 = 0
2150       FOR K9= 1 TO 10000
2160           IF EOF(1) THEN 2190 ELSE INPUT #1,X(K9)
2170           IF X(K9) < 1000 THEN PRINT X(K9), ELSE PRINT : S8 =
S8 + 1 : PRINT "SEQUENCE";S8 : PRINT INT(X(K9)/1000),
2180       NEXT K9
2190 RETURN
```

RUN (Seqfile)

```
FILE LOOKS LIKE THIS ---
  1008            2               3               4               5
  6               7               8               2008            4
  6               8               10              12              14
  16              3015            6               9               12
  15              18              21              24              27
  30              33              36              39              42
  45              4013            8               12              16
  20              24              28              32              36
  40              44              48              52              5008
  10              15              20              25              30
  35              40
EXTRACTED SEQUENCES LOOK LIKE THIS --

SEQUENCE 1
  1               2               3               4               5
  6               7               8
SEQUENCE 2
  2               4               6               8               10
  12              14              16
SEQUENCE 3
  3               6               9               12              15
  18              21              24              27              30
  33              36              39              42              45

SEQUENCE 4
  4               8               12              16              20
  24              28              32              36              40
  44              48              52
```

SUBROUTINE: Scorform

Purpose

Merge separate files containing musical parameter data for one instrumental voice into a single notelist file.

Notes

To test Scorform, the DRIVER PROGRAM generates random-order data (range 1 to 50) for placement in four preliminary files: P1.DAT, R1.DAT, A1.DAT, and V1.DAT. Each file receives 50 integers for assignment to Pitch, Rhythm, Articulation, and Volume parameters.

The task of Subroutine Scorform is to bring together the individual parameter data files and place them in a comprehensive notelist containing all musical attributes of a melodic sequence for a single instrumental part. The filed data may be actual parameter values or groups of pointers to parameter element tables.

The output score is read left to right, top to bottom, four rows at a time. Simple modification of the main routine will allow filing of multiple parts within a single program run. Check your BASIC manual for any variations in filing procedures which may be necessary.

Programming Ideas

Write an interactive program that:

- Generates parameter data for four musical note attributes.
- Places data for each parameter in separate files using Subroutine Group SEQFILE.
- Returns a full notelist score when processing is completed.

Program Listing

```
100 REM =============================================================
110 REM                       DRIVER PROGRAM
120 REM                        (Scorform)
130 REM =============================================================
140    PRINT "FIFTY RANDOM VALUES FROM 1-50 ARE BEING PUT IN"
150    PRINT "PITCH, RHYTHM, ARTICULATION, AND VOLUME FILES"
160    PRINT "NAMED 'P1.DAT','R1.DAT','A1.DAT','V1.DAT' -----"
170    FOR J1 = 1 TO 4
180       IF J1 = 1 THEN OPEN "O",#1,"P1.DAT" ELSE IF J1 = 2 THEN
OPEN "O",#2,"R1.DAT" ELSE IF J1 = 3 THEN OPEN "O",#3,"A1.DAT"
ELSE OPEN "O",#4,"V1.DAT"
190       FOR J2 = 1 TO 50
200          NUM = INT(RND * 50)+1
210          PRINT #J1,NUM;          '<< put 50 values in each file
220          IF J2 MOD 15 = 0 THEN PRINT #J1,      '<< 15 per line
230       NEXT J2
240    CLOSE #J1
```

```
250    NEXT J1
270    PRINT:PRINT "NOW THE 4 SEPARATE PARAMETER FILES ARE BEING"
280    PRINT "PLACED IN FINAL SCORE FILE NAMED 'SCORE.DAT' ---"
300    PRINT : GOSUB 1000              '<< call score formatting
310 END
1000 REM ================================================= CTB6.23
1010 REM ******************>> SCORFORM <<***********************
1020 REM =====================================================
1030 REM              Formatted-Score-Filing Subroutine
1040 REM =====================================================
1050    X$ = "+" : Z$ = "SCORE.DAT"
1070    OPEN "I",#1,"P1.DAT"
1080    OPEN "I",#2,"R1.DAT"
1090    OPEN "I",#3,"A1.DAT"
1100    OPEN "I",#4,"V1.DAT"
1110    OPEN "O",#5,Z$
1120    PRINT #5,"NOTELIST:"
1130       WHILE NOT EOF(1)
1140          LINE INPUT #1,A$
1150          PRINT #5,"P ";A$
1160          LINE INPUT #2,B$
1170          PRINT #5,"R ";B$
1180          LINE INPUT #3,C$
1190          PRINT #5,"A ";C$
1200          LINE INPUT #4,D$
1210          PRINT #5,"V ";D$
1220          PRINT #5,"/*";STRING$(55,X$);"*/"
1230       WEND
1240    CLOSE #1,#2,#3,#4,#5
1250    PRINT "HERE IS FINAL SCORE --"
1260    OPEN "I",#5,Z$
1270       WHILE NOT EOF(5)
1280          LINE INPUT #5,A$
1290          PRINT A$
1300       WEND
1310    CLOSE #5
1320 RETURN
```

RUN (Scorform)

```
FIFTY RANDOM VALUES FROM 1-50 ARE BEING PUT IN
PITCH, RHYTHM, ARTICULATION, AND VOLUME FILES
NAMED 'P1.DAT','R1.DAT','A1.DAT','V1.DAT' -----

NOW THE 4 SEPARATE PARAMETER FILES ARE BEING
PLACED IN FINAL SCORE FILE NAMED 'SCORE.DAT' ---

HERE IS FINAL SCORE --
NOTELIST:
P  9   9  28  23  10  16  42  41  33  24   2  23  19  34  21
R 35  34  24  28  45  14  17  19  28  13  39   3  32  38  14
A 22  28  11  17  11  22   6  16  24  15  45  11  18  12  27
V 32  18  15  38  25   8  47   6  46  32  29   7  12  36  17
/*+++++++++++++++++++++++++++++++++++++++++++++++++++++++*/
P 29  22  20  45  25  40  11  49  42  20  44  40   6  22  20
R 40  49  17  47  41   8  18  26  21  31  27  35   6   3  37
A  6  18  20  48  19  13  45   6   6  25   1  24   5  31  35
V  4  50  48  17   7  47   8  50  30  22   9  28  18  11   2
/*+++++++++++++++++++++++++++++++++++++++++++++++++++++++*/
```

```
P   33    32    42    27    26    27    2    27    48    4    50    3    17    15    25
R   29    8     8     9     24    7     16   29    47    4    45    44   48   24    33
A   29    39    3     9     45    33    8    2     6     41   21    16   21   40    1
V   40    27    6     8     7     27    16   6     40    9    36    14   22   6     28
/*+++++++++++++++++++++++++++++++++++++++++++++++++++++++++++++*/
P   19    8     38    31    42
R   2     26    44    12    2
A   50    7     34    31    37
V   1     40    33    15    47
/*+++++++++++++++++++++++++++++++++++++++++++++++++++++++++++++*/
```

Subroutine Index

Index

Other Bestsellers of Related Interest

EXCEL MACROS FOR THE IBM® PC—Shelley Satonin

Here is the most comprehensive manual available for writing macros for the IBM PC using Microsoft Excel. Using plenty of examples and illustrations, Satonin covers everything from the basics of macro writing to recipes for building advanced customized macros of your own. Also included: a complete directory of Excel macros that you'll find an invaluable programming reference. 265 pages, 156 illustrations. Book No. 3293, $19.95 paperback only

Microsoft Macro Assembler 5.1: Programming in the 80386 Environment—John Mueller and Wallace Wang

This book provides comprehensive instructions for using the most popular assembler for the IBM PC with the most powerful microprocessor available for personal computers. You'll find full details on the unique features of Microsoft's Macro Assembler as well as techniques for taking advantage of of these features when programming the 80386 processor. 752 pages, 270 illustrations. Book No. 3179, $19.95 paperback only

LOTUS® 1-2-3® SIMPLIFIED, RELEASE 3—David Bolocan

"This book . . . (is) absolutely invaluable."

—THE IBM PC User Group CONNECTIVITY

All of the features of Release 3 are carefully examined: three-dimensional spreadsheets, new print options, sophisticated graphics capabilities, as well as information on using the more than 30 new commands and functions. Over 25 sample spreadsheet applications; clear explanations of functions, commands, and macros; and an abundance of diagrams and illustrations are included. 376 pages, 235 illustrations. Book No. 3088, $28.95 hardcover, $19.95 paperback

From the Stephen Cobb Series . . .

THE STEPHEN COBB USER'S HANDBOOK TO EXCEL FOR THE IBM® PC—Stephen Cobb

Take advantage of EXCEL's power potential! From fundamental concepts to advanced functions and procedures, from managing information to organizing complex business tasks to handling the relationship between EXCEL and other programs, this excellent handbook shows how you can increase your efficiency and productivity. 704 pages, 594 illustrations, two color throughout. Book No. 3170, $31.95 hardcover, $22.95 paperback

LOTUS® 1-2-3® SIMPLIFIED, RELEASE 2.2—David Bolocan

". . . an honest warts-and-all view of Lotus 1-2-3 . . . a helpful and valuable aid to any Lotus user."

Personal Computer World

David Bolocan gives you hands-on experience with all of 2.2 popular new features, including: single-cell information linking, on-spreadsheet searches, a macro library manager for sharing macros among spreadsheets, an optional add-in manager, print-setting sheets for simpler printer configuration, natural language interfacing, and improved graphing and charting. 272 pages, illustrated. Book No. 3440, $28.95 hardcover, $19.95 paperback

NORTON UTILITIES 4.5: An Illustrated Tutorial—Richard Evans

This completely revised edition of Richard Evans' bestselling guidebook demonstrates the vast capabilities of the Norton Utilities package, and features the exciting new additions to release 4.5. You'll find straightforward, step-by-step instruction on using every program in the Norton Utilities, for every version from 3.0 to the current 4.5. All the details of the command structure and common applications are presented. 224 pages, 98 illustrations. Book No. 3359, $19.95 paperback only

ADVANCED MS-DOS BATCH FILE PROGRAMMING—Dan Gookin

Batch file programming is a way of communicating with your computer . . . a way of transforming DOS into a system that works the way you want it to. In this book, Dan Gookin explains unique methods of using batch files to create a work environment that will improve your efficiency, productivity, and overall relationship with your computer. All the necessary tools, batch file structures, commands, and helpful techniques can be found here. 400 pages, 733 illustrations. Book No. 3197, $34.95 hardcover, $24.95 paperback

LOTUS® COMPANION: Added Software Resources—Ronny Richardson

Now you have somewhere to turn for help in the search for Lotus® add-on software! Searching out software packages for Lotus can often be a confusing, expensive, and discouraging proposition. Now there is a book that ends the guesswork. *Lotus Companion: Added Software Resources* takes a close look at over 100 Lotus add-ons, and gives you a clear description of the results. The claims have all been tested and the comparisons made. 480 pages, 290 illustrations. Book No. 3128, $18.95 paperback, $22.95 hardcover

LOTUS® AGENDA®: Information Management Applications—Jeff Guenther and Anne Wayman

Put your thoughts into action—with Lotus Agenda! Here's your opportunity to learn how to use Lotus Agenda to your advantage. Authors Guenther and Wayman illustrate a wide range of applications—from simple everyday tasks to scientific research—that are particularly suited to the capabilities of this versatile software. Their idea-generating approach is designed to help you get the most out of Agenda, by showing you practical uses for a relational database. 272 pages, Illustrated. Book No. 3169, $17.95 paperback only

---

Look for These and Other TAB Books at Your Local Bookstore

To Order Call Toll Free 1-800-822-8158
(in PA and AK call 717-794-2191)

or write to TAB BOOKS Inc., Blue Ridge Summit, PA 17294-0840.

Title	Product No.	Quantity	Price

Subtotal $ _____

☐ Check or money order made payable to TAB BOOKS Inc.

Charge my ☐ VISA   ☐ MasterCard   ☐ American Express

Postage and Handling ($3.00 in U.S., $5.00 outside U.S.) $ _____

In PA, NY, & ME add applicable sales tax $ _____

TOTAL $ _____

Acct. No. _____ Exp. _____

Signature: _____

Name: _____

City: _____

State: _____ Zip: _____

TAB BOOKS catalog free with purchase; otherwise send $1.00 in check or money order and receive $1.00 credit on your next purchase.

Orders outside U.S. must pay with international money order in U.S. dollars.

TAB Guarantee: If for any reason you are not satisfied with the book(s) you order, simply return it (them) within 15 days and receive a full refund.
BC

Computer Composer's Toolbox

If you are intrigued with the possibilities of the programs included in *Computer Composer's Toolbox* (TAB Book No. 3384), you should definitely consider having the ready-to-run disk containing the software applications. This software is guaranteed free of manufacturer's defects. (If you have any problems, return the disk within 30 days, and we'll send you a new one.) Not only will you save the time and effort of typing the programs, the disk eliminates the possibility of errors that can prevent the programs from functioning. Interested?

Available on either 5¹/₄" or 3¹/₂" disk requiring 360K at $24.95, plus $2.50 shipping and handling. You need an IBM PC or compatible and DOS version 2.0 or newer.